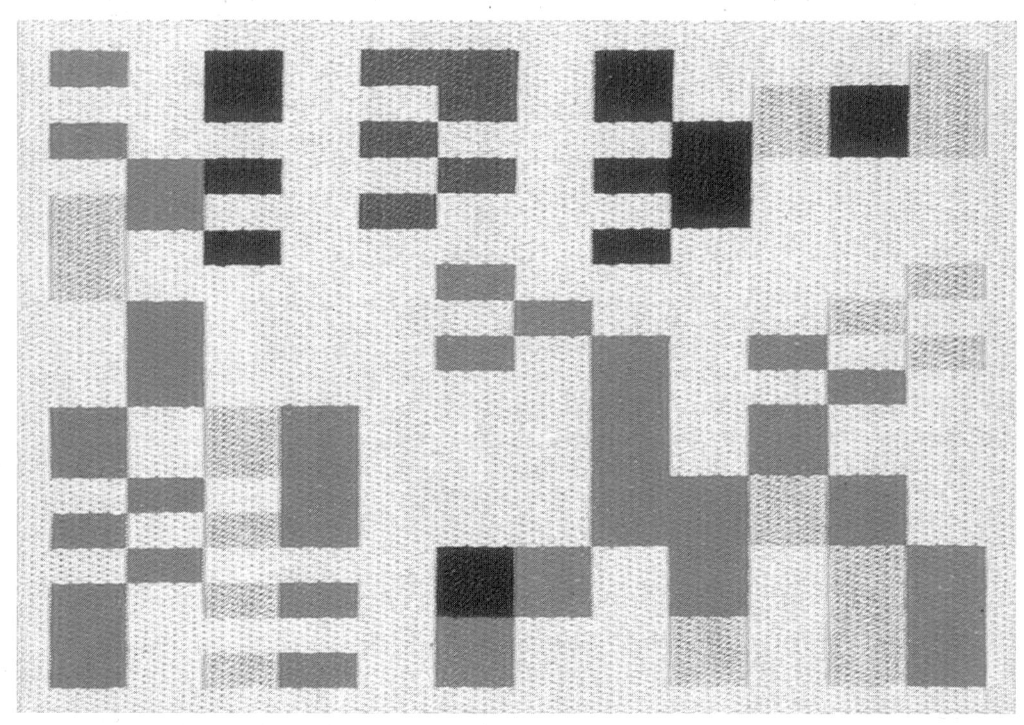

Sophie Taeuber-Harp, *Composition*, 1916
Color silkscreen, 25.5 × 20 cm

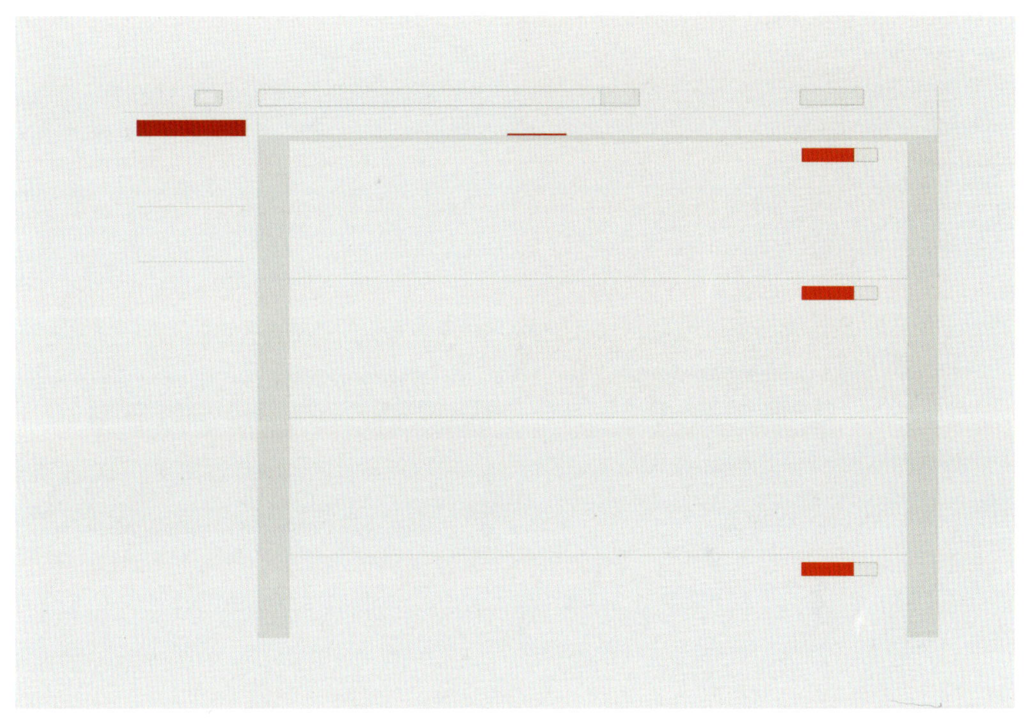

Wired magazine was the first to spot the Webdriver Torso phenomenon in 2014, as part of a feature on bizarre YouTube clips. Each of the almost 80,000 clips—uploaded over a seven-month period—followed the same pattern—10 slides, each with a red rectangle, a blue rectangle and a computer-generated tone. The Webdriver Torso mystery was finally solved by website *Engadget* following revelations that Webdriver was part of a network called ytuploadtestpartner_torso, which in turn was associated with social media accounts that name-dropped several Google employees based at its Zürich office.

YouTube, *Webdriver Torso*, (video still), 2014

Dadabot
—An Introduction to Machinic Creolization

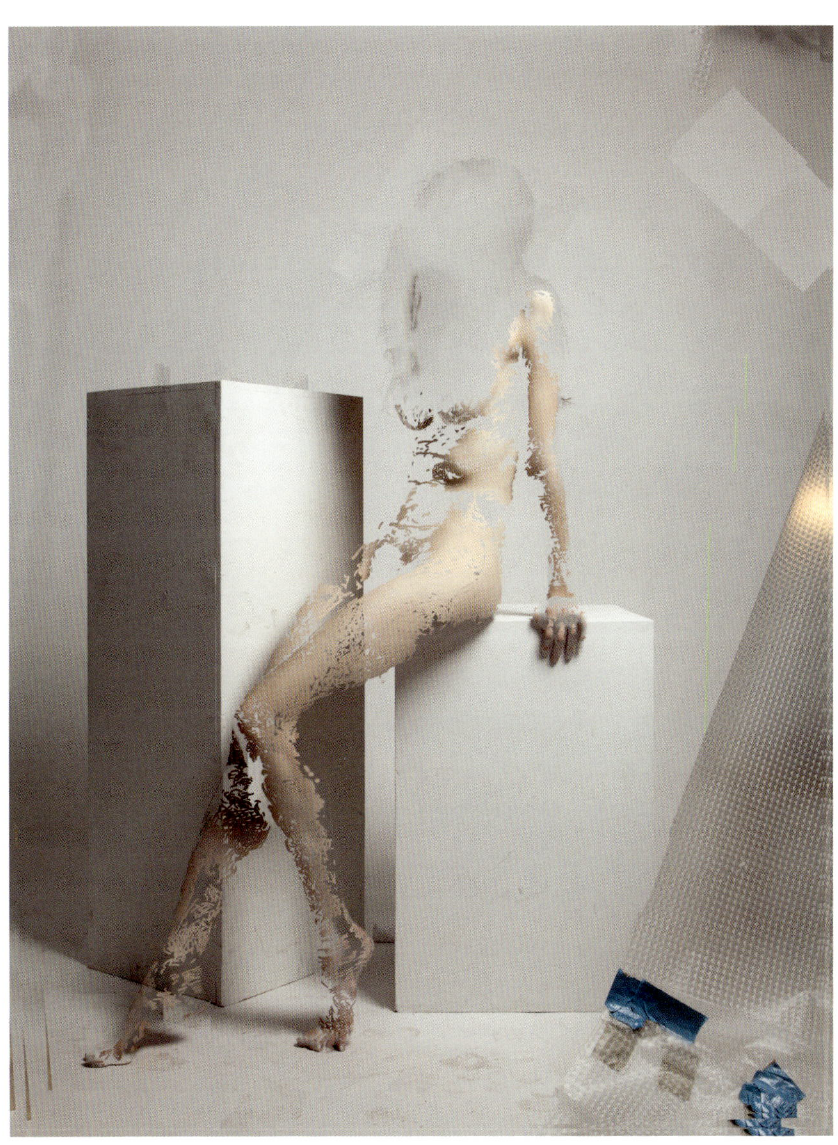

 Joshua Citarella, *Study in Contemporary Gesture II*, 2012

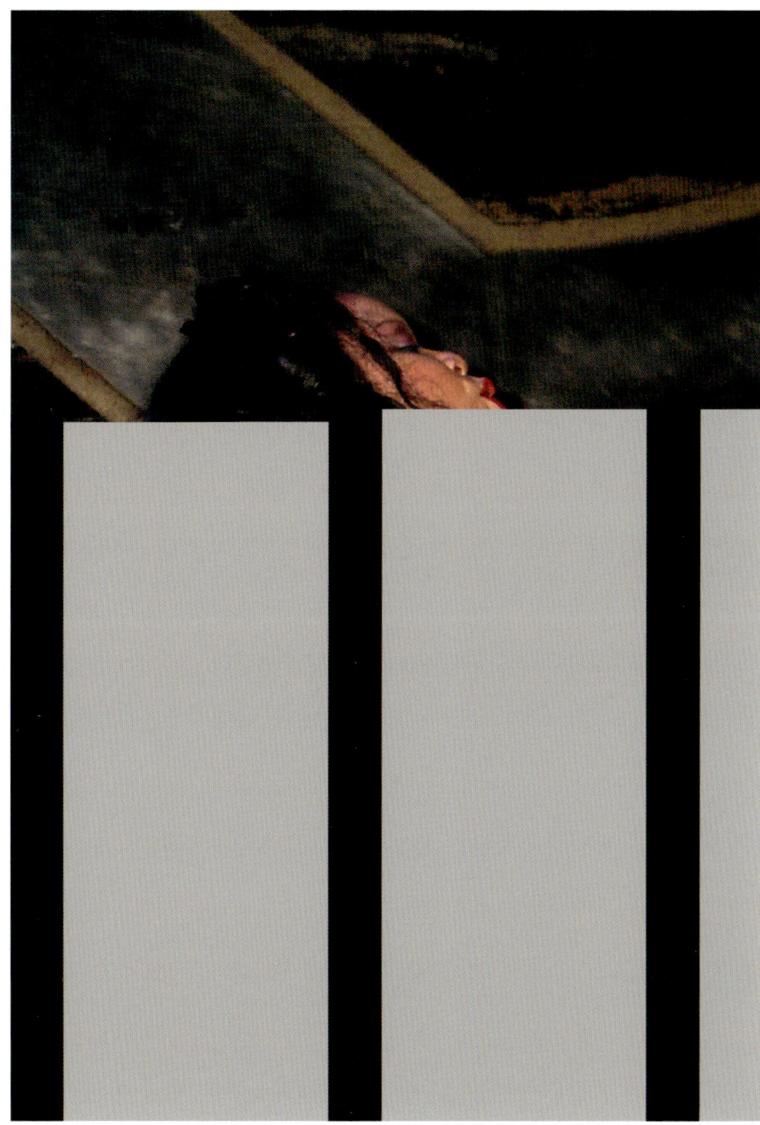

 Diego Collado, *Data Recovery*, 2010–2014

July 1916: one year after creating the Cabaret Voltaire with his partner Emmy Hennings, Hugo Ball delivers the first public reading of his Dada Manifesto. He begins with an excursus on the "international" nature of the term,[1] and ends by describing the power of words to define the world around us: "The word, gentlemen, is a public concern of the first importance." Through their consummate art of provocation, the adherents of Dadaism intended to subvert the norms of their epoch by liberating words and languages from their arbitrary assignations.

Sparta My Have

June 2012: the security team at the electronic commerce company Amazon.com discovers a type of unauthorized publication. It is neither a manipulation of user comments, nor is it promotional spam. The "problem" concerns a massive influx of books of an unfamiliar nature, absurd works written by digital programs. For four years, the software is flooded with such evocatively titled books as *Sparta My Have* by Loafrz Ipalizi, *Weird Song You Cute* by Timsest Pitigam, or *Alot Was Been Hard* by Janetlw Bauie. Each opus consists of short texts signed by a pseudonym. The statements read like transcripts from delirious conversations between adolescents sitting in front of TVs rather than novels situated within a prizewinning literary canon.

As it turns out, they have been compiled from accumulated Youtube comments. Extracted by a software program, they are then reassembled into book form before being published—and sold—on Amazon. Some weeks later, the books were removed from the site, and the guilty parties were revealed to be the Austrian art collective Traumawien and the German Bernhard Bauch. The authors of this intricate performance—called *Ghost Writers*—describe the result as

→ p.21

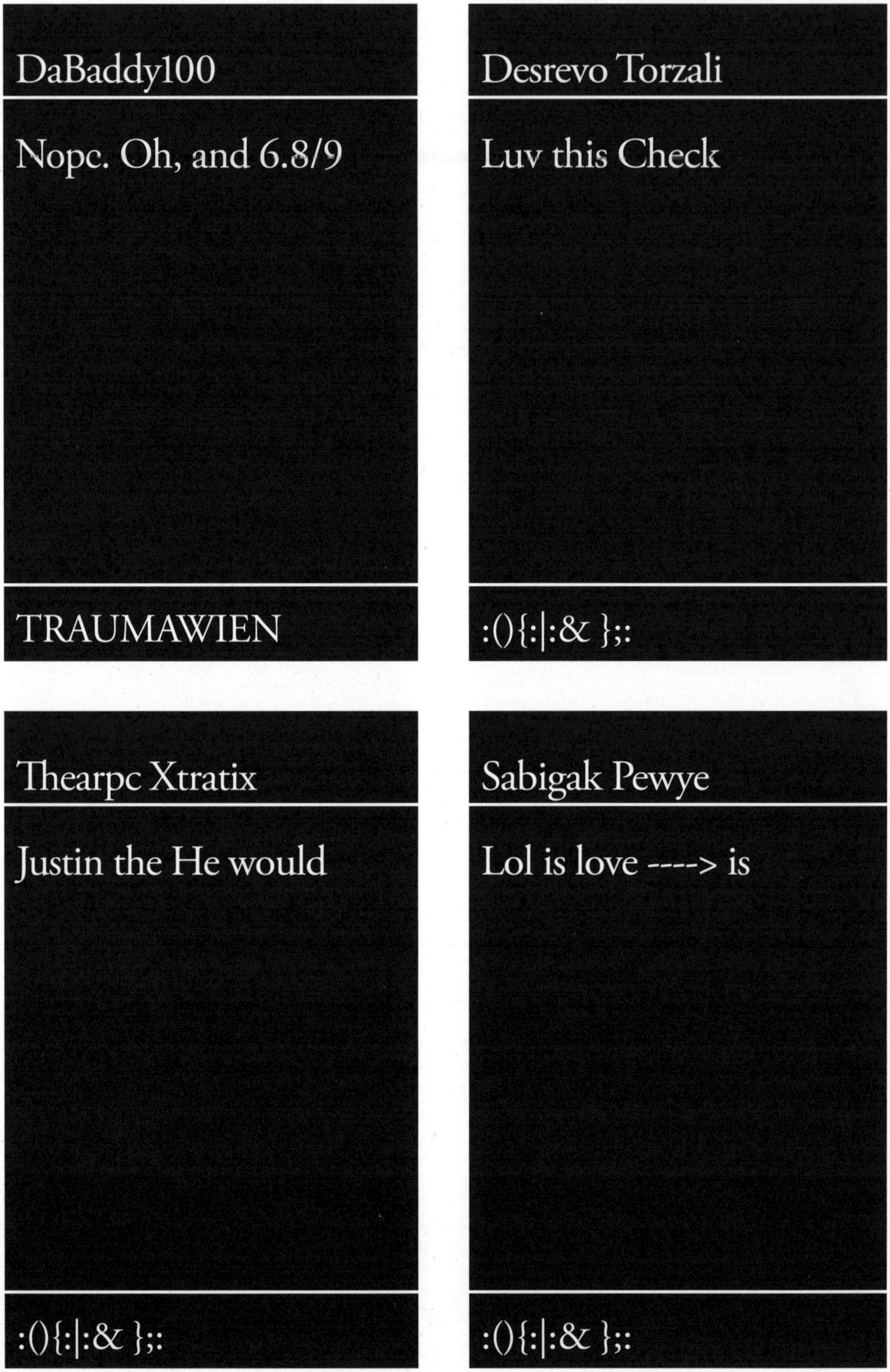

DaBaddy100

Nopc. Oh, and 6.8/9

TRAUMAWIEN

Desrevo Torzali

Luv this Check

:(){:|:& };:

Thearpc Xtratix

Justin the He would

:(){:|:& };:

Sabigak Pewye

Lol is love ----> is

:(){:|:& };:

Traumawien and Bernhard Bauch, *Ghost Writers*, 2012

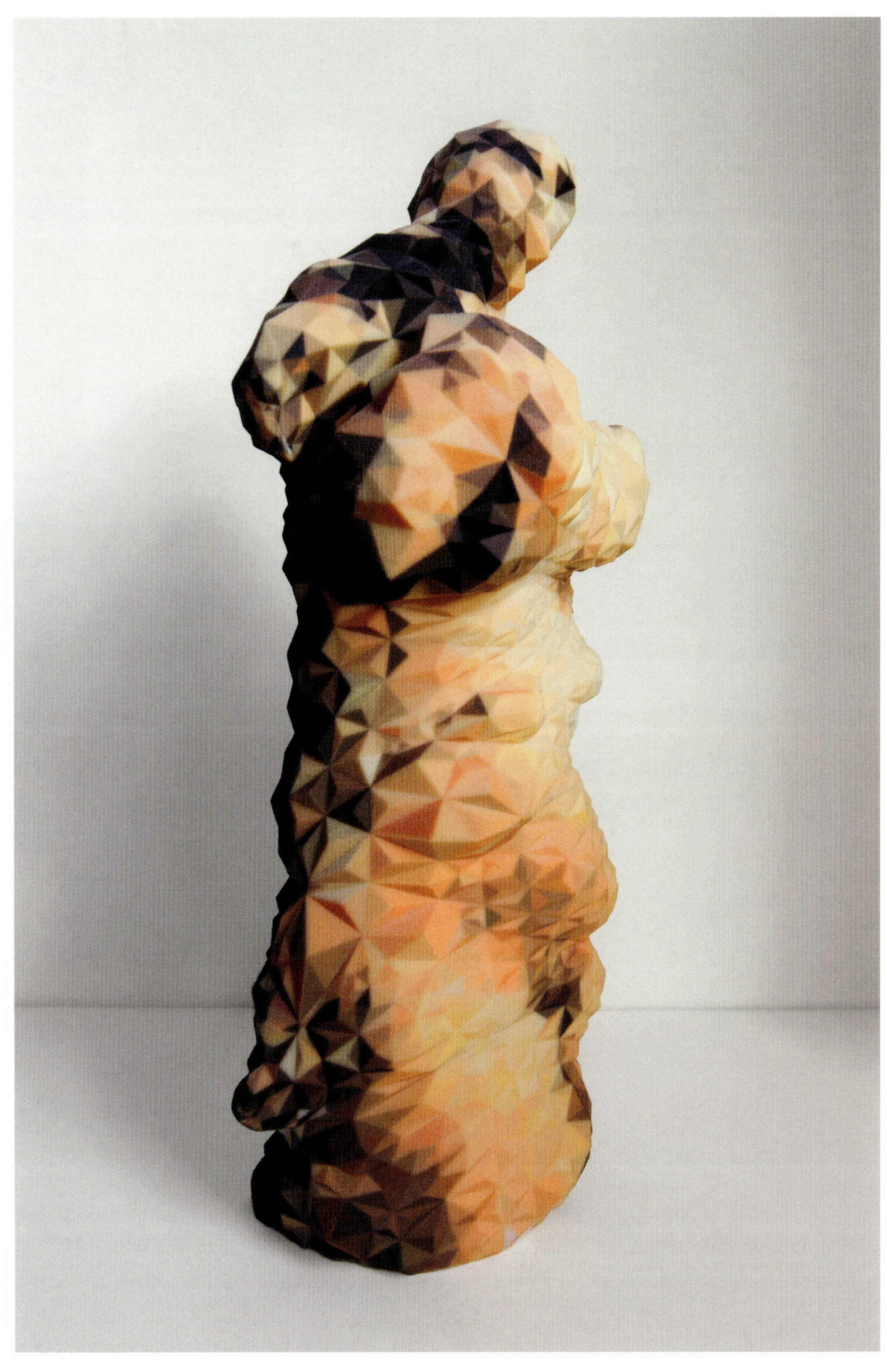

  Matthew Plummer-Fernandez, *Venus of Google*, 2013
3D printed (17 × 9 × 30)

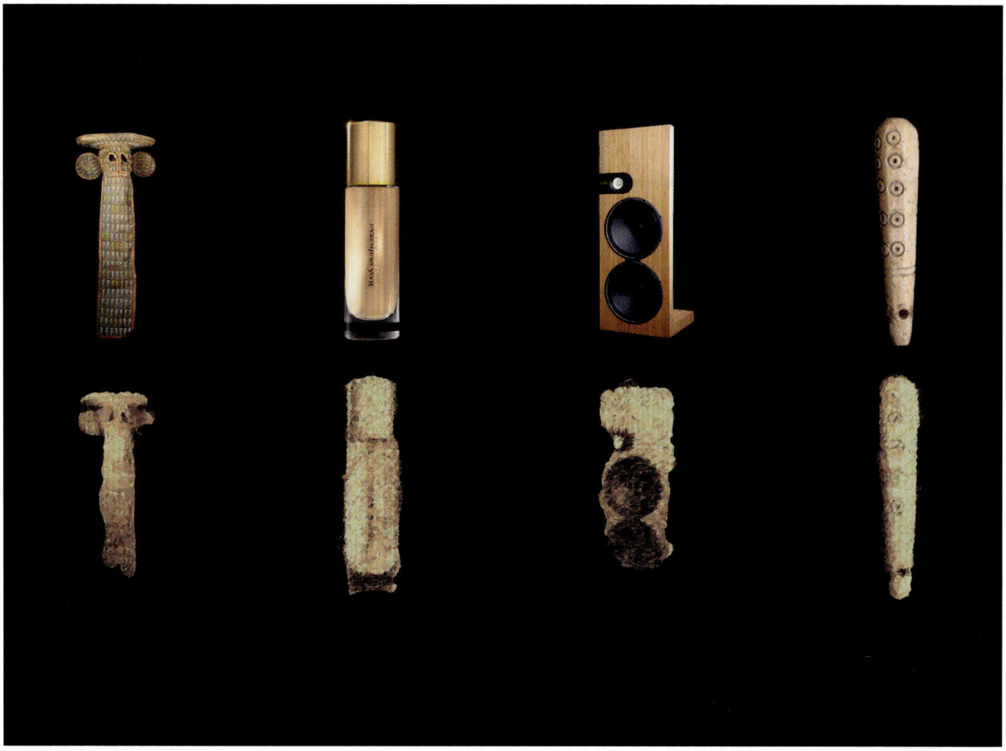

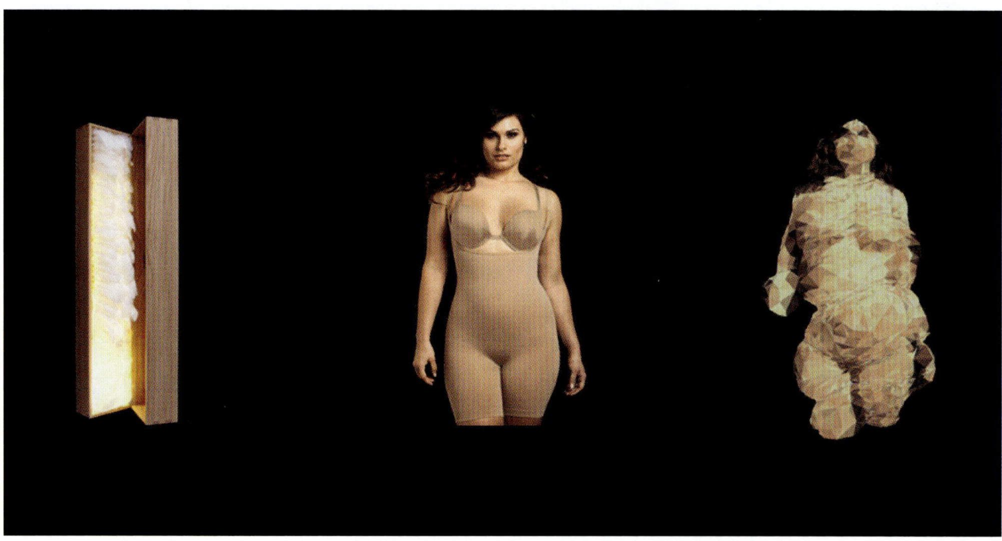

The *Venus of Google* was found via a Google search-by-image, googling a photograph taken of an object Matthew Plummer-Fernandez had been handed over in a game of "exquisite corpse." The Google search returned visually similar results, one of these being an image of a woman modelling a body-wrap garment. He then used a similar algorithmic image-comparison technique to drive the automated design of a 3D printable object. The "Hill-Climbing" algorithm starts with a plain box shape and tries thousands of random transformations and comparisons between the shape and the image, eventually mutating towards a form resembling the found image in both shape and colour. The artist is interested in this early era of artificial intelligence, computer vision and algorithmic artefacts, exemplifying the paradox of technology being both advanced and primitive at the same time. This piece investigates the potential use of algorithms to create virtually infinite cultural artefacts, inspired by stories of algorithmic books and t-shirts.

Interview with Matthew Plummer-Fernandez

Q1: Can you start with a short description about who you are and how you became interested in algorithms?
A: I'm a designer and a computer/mechanical engineer by training, but now a practitioner in art and research. I draw upon my background to inform and supplement both my independent arts practice and my research at Goldsmiths, University of London where I am a PhD candidate. My interest in algorithms began by using them to make things as they are the backbone of computer programming which I do a lot. I took a more formal interest in algorithms a year and a half ago when I started *algopop*. I wouldn't call myself a blogger; *algopop* is more like an archive than an opinion column and I'm its archivist.

Q2: What's the motivation behind *algopop*?
A: I started reading claims that algorithms were taking over the world, from commerce to finance, as both academics and journalists were started to pen their concerns. I then realized there was a disparity between such critical reflections on algorithms and the use of them in practice, so I wanted a blog that reported anecdotes about the rising notoriety of algorithms alongside documentation of any artist, designer or coder that may be using that as a context to their work, and not just utilizing algorithms for technical goals. Such a blog did not exist so I started one.

Q3: With the *algopop* tumblr you accumulated a lot of material about algorithms and their influence. In general, when one does this, a sort of typology slowly emerges out of the case. Is that the case in *algopop*? What kinds of categories do you see happening?
A: Yes, having done this long enough I have noticed patterns emerge. One category would be the research and start-up press releases that claim that their new algorithm automates

or powers so and so idea. For instance one start-up made extra-comfortable socks thanks to algorithms. I report these cautiously as an alternative to how the press often get carried away and misinform the latest tech advances. A category in itself would be the countless Google and Facebook interaction anecdotes, for instance how Grandmas struggle to use Facebook because the service autocompletes their sign off to say "love from Grandpa and Grandmaster Flash." I report a lot of algorithmic services going wrong, such as recommendation systems making inappropriate suggestions, or computer vision looking at the wrong thing. I wouldn't call these glitches, the code is not "buggy," usually it's an anomaly caused by the complexity of the system. Another category would be systems that you would not even suspect to be powered by algorithms such as Tesco's shelf layout or the production of fresh orange juice.

The category I'm most proud of documenting are the practitioners that make interesting uses of algorithms or intervene in algorithmic systems in some way through their work. I guess you could split that into two categories. On one hand you have an activist or subversive approach to using Google, Facebook, Spotify, Amazon, etc. One person made fanbots to constantly listen to his (also bot-made) music on Spotify to exploit the royalty payment system. The other type of practitioner uses algorithms to produce things of artistic merit, however I'm reluctant to report on simple technical achievements, for me this art is successful when it invigorates a meaningful discussion about the work. There is no recipe for that, I currently use my instinct to pick up on it, but I'm trying to formulate a better understanding of what makes some generative/bot art interesting and others simply an algorithm with a pretty output. Usually it's because the artist touches another nerve, demonstrating a commitment to something else like social issues, playfulness and humour, data privacy, and so on.

Q: Overall, what does it say about our culture/society? What kind of trends do you see happening based on these cases?

A: I'm finding that *algopop* is becoming a silent, open conversation about these topics, with artists perpetually making more interesting work in this field. From my biased perspective it feels like a micro-trend that I am helping advance and document. But it is hard to make grand claims about culture and society as I'm quite aware that an interest in algorithms and bots is mainly seen in small, fringe communities of coders, designers and artists. Most people don't talk of such things even though they interact with them constantly. Paradoxically that's the grandness of it; its ubiquity as a technology and trend in global computational infrastructure. The world algorithmically powered by Google, Facebook, Microsoft, Apple and Amazon, as well as the Ubers and the Netflixs. The critical arts/design response however is fairly low profile, but very timely.

Q4: Besides *algopop* you have your personal practice, I'm curious about how the material you uncover and present on the tumblr influence your work. Can you tell us a bit about your projects about this topic?

A: Well *algopop* really started out as a means to inform my practice, like an online sketchbook, but with over 12,000 followers it doesn't feel so private anymore! I've been slow to respond to my own research as it has become an output in its own right. There is a before and after *algopop* split in my work; just before I made a collection of algorithmically deformed objects called *Digital Natives*. Very pretty and technically accomplished for its time, but not much else. To elevate that I started a line of work that included themes of copyright and file-sharing with pieces such as *sekuMoi Mecy*. Then after *algopop* my first piece was also an algorithmically deformed object but this time using Google Image Search results as a muse for the process. That piece is *Venus of Google*. I've also used Google Image Search in a triptych of images titled

The Codification of Leadership as a response to how Bush was painting world leaders identical to how they appear at the top of Google Image search results.

So I'm starting to include those algopop topics in my work but I have been also quietly on a learning curve to get the hang of using APIs, web servers, and so on. I'm finally getting to grips with *Computer Vision* and have a line of work developing around it. My latest piece is *All Eyes* which is a bot that can detect eyes in images and scrapes Flickr for images tagged with terms like "face" or "selfie" to "steal" eyes, creating an archive of cropped eye images. This hopefully is more than a technical feat and stirs thoughts on automated gazing and online surveillance through computer vision.

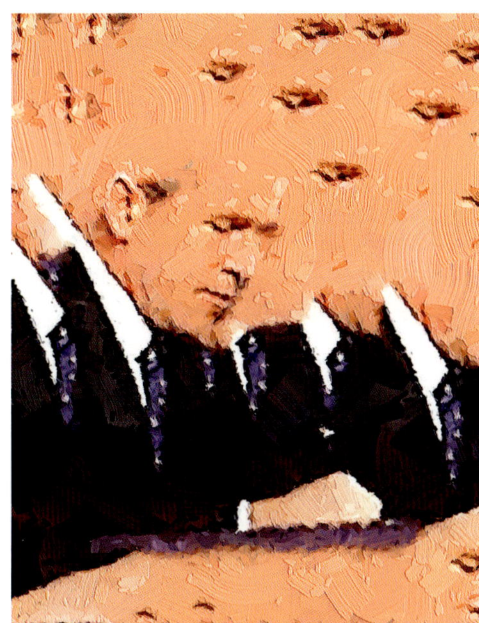

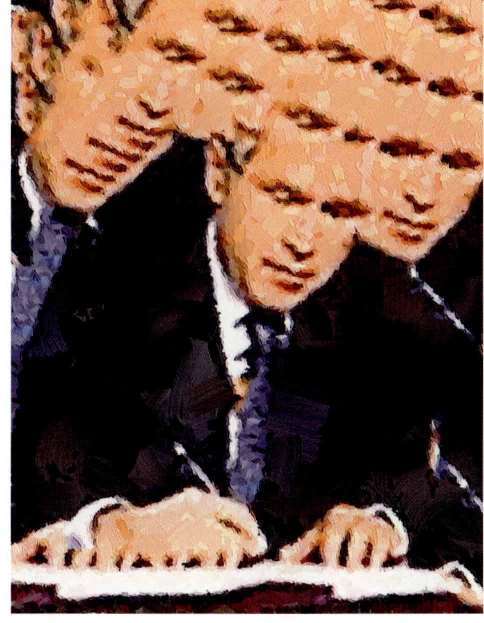

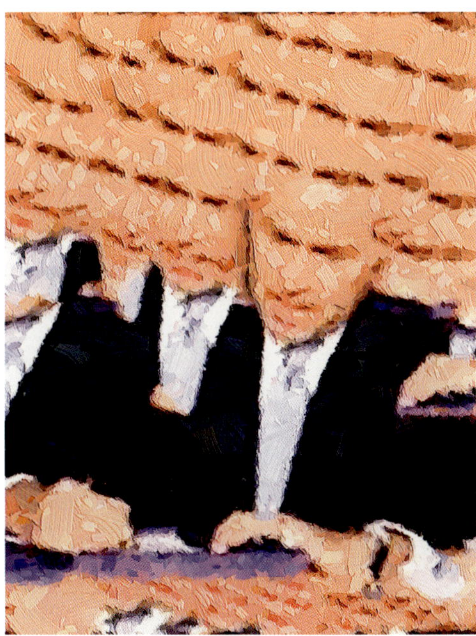

The first image results from Google searches for G.W. Bush signing into law the Patriot Act, the Homeland Security Act and the Intelligence Reform Act are distorted with Photoshop's "Content-Aware" Fill algorithm and then recreated as synthetic paintings by an autonomous painting script. The fully code-driven image-making aims to mirror current problematic systems of counter-terrorism, security and surveillance that were codified into law by the Bush administration. The magnitude and complexity of these covert operations are increasingly resolved through the use of databases and algorithmic procedures, indefinitely activating the code of law.

 Matthew Plummer-Fernandez,
The Codification of Leadership (Triptych), 2014

a collection of e-books portraying the contemporary micro-dramas at play on community websites. For them, what is at issue is a new form of emergent literature produced by the users of the online video host. Halfway between literary experimentation and robot, these quasi-random modes of expression comprise the first characteristic of the "Dadabot."[2]

July 2014: the Associated Press announces that its quarterly earnings articles will henceforth be handled automatically by a software written by the firm Automated Insights. By analyzing the economic datasets of Zacks Investment Research, the program instantly produces dispatches of between 150 and 300 words that are then circulated on nearly 150 Anglophone economic press websites. In an interview on the subject, Lou Ferrara explained that by allowing journalists to spend less time crunching financial numbers, the software frees them up to produce more penetrating coverage of social issues.[3] The same strategy was used by Narrative Science, a start-up that automatically compiles the outcomes of football and baseball games based on statistical data.[4] Seen in the light of this automatic writing of the present, the "ghost writers" of Traumawien figure within an evolution of editorial practices that goes beyond mere schoolboy pranks. The principal literary trait of these books lies in the algorithmic procedures that determine their agencement. What do these automated combinations of heterogeneous content disclose? What is the aesthetic status of such productions? Who is the author?

These different examples demonstrate that a single logic is at work in the creation of this editorial material, in the online works as well as their print counterparts. Their production is "algorithmic," i.e. software instructions automate the research, assembly, and creation of content. Over the past few decades this functional model has surfaced in obvious and not so obvious ways within various sectors of cultural life. → p.27

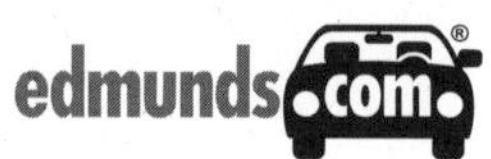

The Times beats Street 4Q forecasts
New York Times Co. tops 4Q net income and revenue expectations
February 3, 2015 8:48 AM

Forbes

NEW YORK (AP) _ The New York Times Co. (NYT) on Tuesday reported fourth-quarter net income of $34.9 million.
The New York-based company said it had profit of 22 cents per share. Earnings, adjusted for one-time gains and costs, came to 26 cents per share.
The results exceeded Wall Street expectations. The average estimate of analysts surveyed by Zacks Investment Research was for earnings of 23 cents per share.
The newspaper publisher posted revenue of $444.7 million in the period, also topping Street forecasts. Analysts expected $437.2 million, according to Zacks.
For the year, the company reported profit of $33.3 million, or 20 cents per share. Revenue was reported as $1.59 billion.
The Times shares have dropped 3.5 percent since the beginning of the year. The stock has declined roughly 10 percent in the last 12 months.

This story was generated by Automated Insights (http://automatedinsights.com/ap) using data from Zacks Investment Research. Access a Zacks stock report on NYT at http://www.zacks.com/ap/NYT

Keywords: New York Times Co., Earnings Report

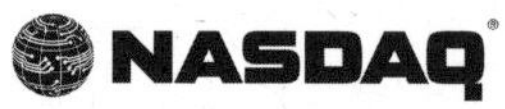

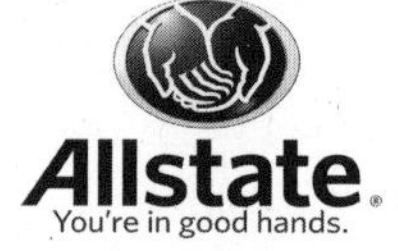

Default Systemz is a research project conduct-
ed by Pablo Berger, David Stadel, Thomas Walsh
(Berger+Stadel+Walsh), framed around a series
of workshops initiated to discover the different
graphic solutions within the Apple Macintosh
computer using only the stock standard programs
that come with a newly purchased system (iLife,
Core Image Fun House, etc).

This includes all applications, utilities and content which are provided on the basic system where
no external content is allowed. Hacking standard
operating system functions is paramount for
Default Systemz. The main aim is to create an in-
tuitive relationship with the computer by understanding its inner and outer working methodolo-
gies, inevitably bettering our experience as users
and tailoring its use as a tool in graphic design
and other daily activities.

 Berger+Stadel+Walsh, *Default Systemz*, 2014

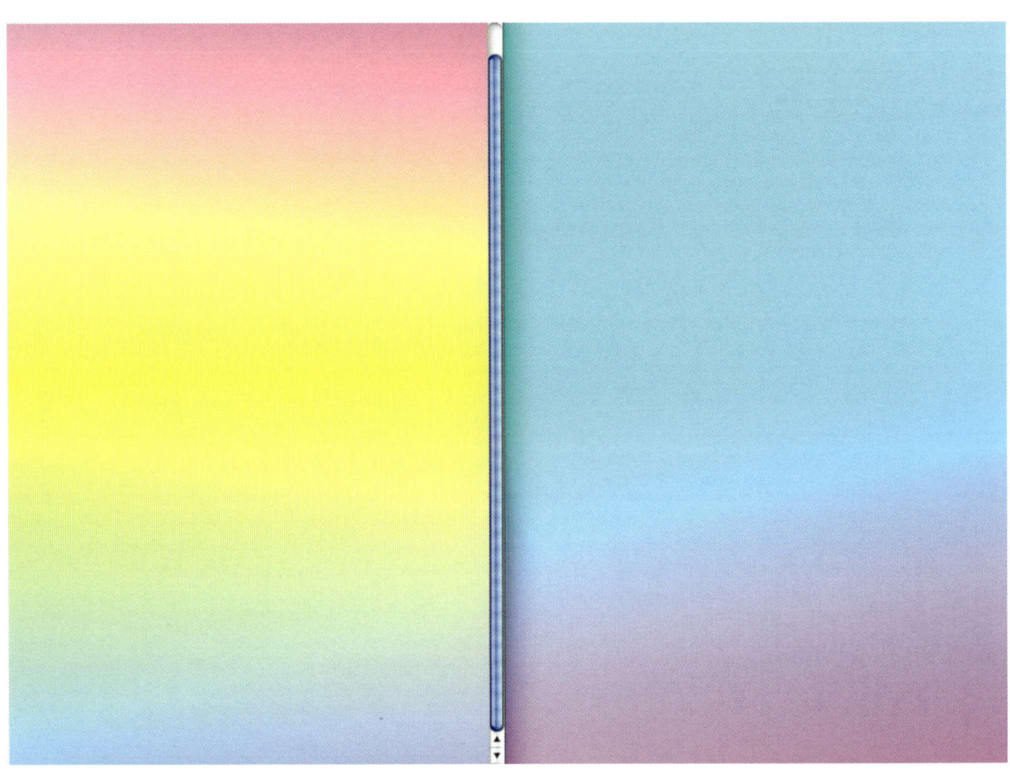

Berger+Stadel+Walsh, *Default Systemz*, 2014

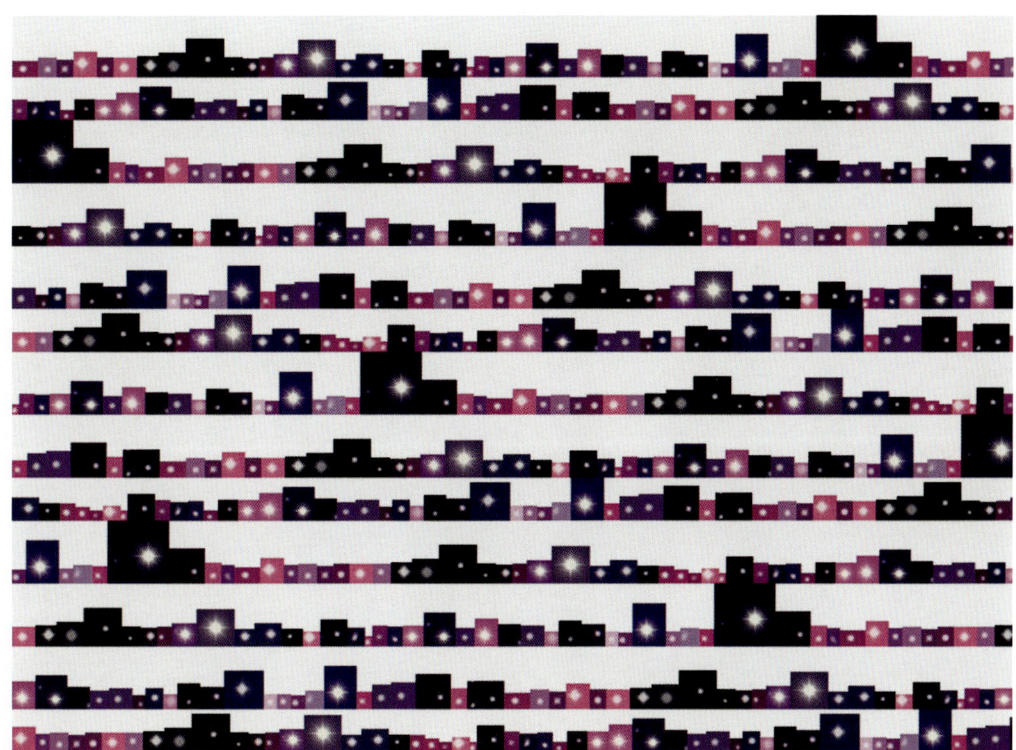

 Berger+Stadel+Walsh, *Default Systemz*, 2014

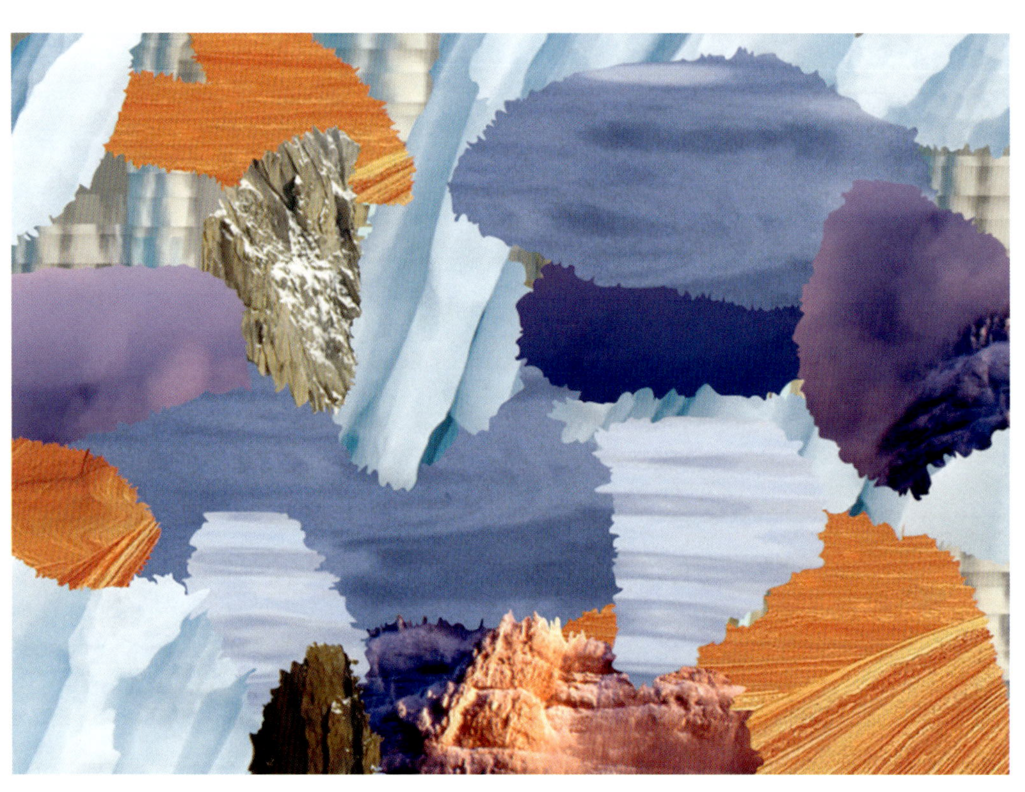

Berger+Stadel+Walsh, *Default Systemz*, 2014

In the domain of radio, the automated management of content sent over antennae is a well-known practice. The personae of Max Headroom certainly contributed more than any other to the popularization in media of "bots," officiating over British Channel 4's *The Max Headroom Show* from 1984 onward. Since the technology at the time did not allow the creation of an entirely virtual personae, a human host still had to assume the appearance of a humanoid.

Taste Disorders

Algorithmic logics are not always so spectacular. A program such as *DAD*, designed to manage radio content, can vary playlists so as to avoid artists from the same decade, or play only English rock or Eurodance according to selected settings or the type of station. Pandora, Spotify and Netflix all utilize algorithms select suggested viewing and listening choices, as does Amazon with its recommendations. These services rely to an enormous extent on the role of "suggestions" to direct users towards automated choices of cultural products.

In addition to such mechanisms of suggestion, the contents themselves may come to be influenced by the very digital programs that give birth to them. In the early 90s, the group Oval explored the aesthetic potential of noises and other cracks, notably in their repurposed use of CDs. By simple gestures such as using CD readers as instruments, they contributed to laying the sonic foundations that would give rise to glitch. From noise to musique concrète, contemporary variants of such initiated music have rendered the border between musical production and sonic nuisance ever more porous. With their flat bass and their metallic high notes, the little samples of sound made by smartphones these days unmistakably indicate their MP3 compression and the presence of

→ p.31

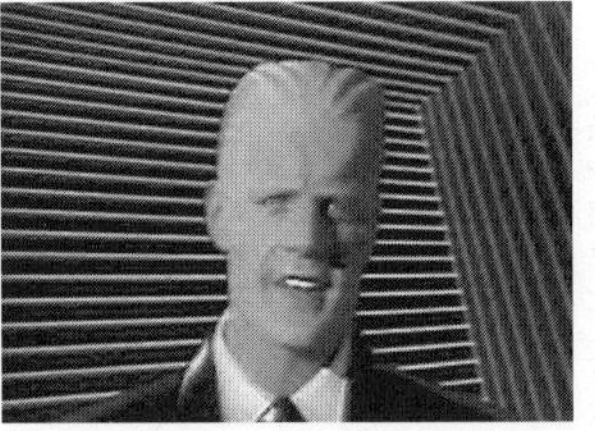

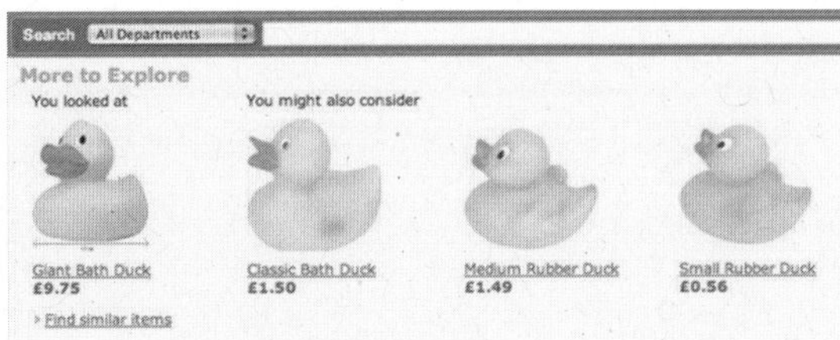

Left: Chrysalis, *Max Headroom: 20 Minutes in the Future*, 1986
Right: Amazon recommandation engine, c. 2010

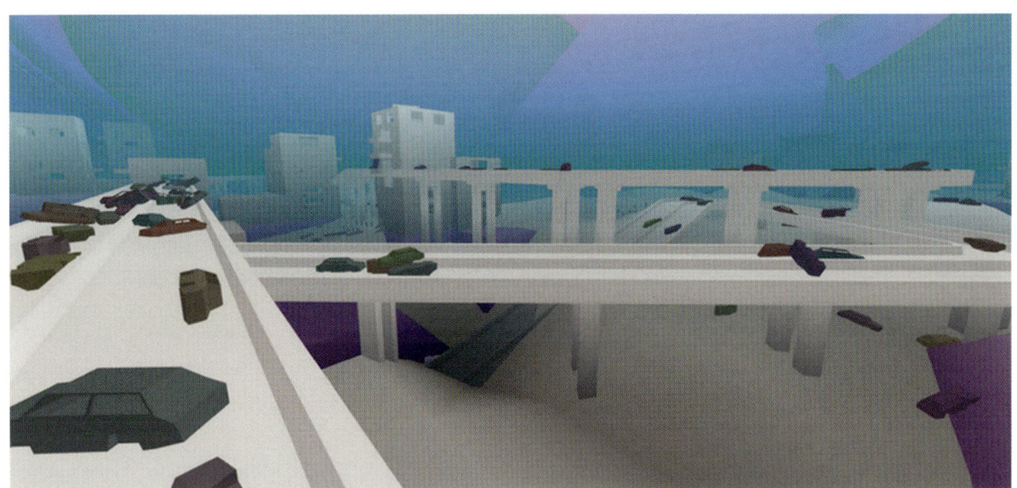

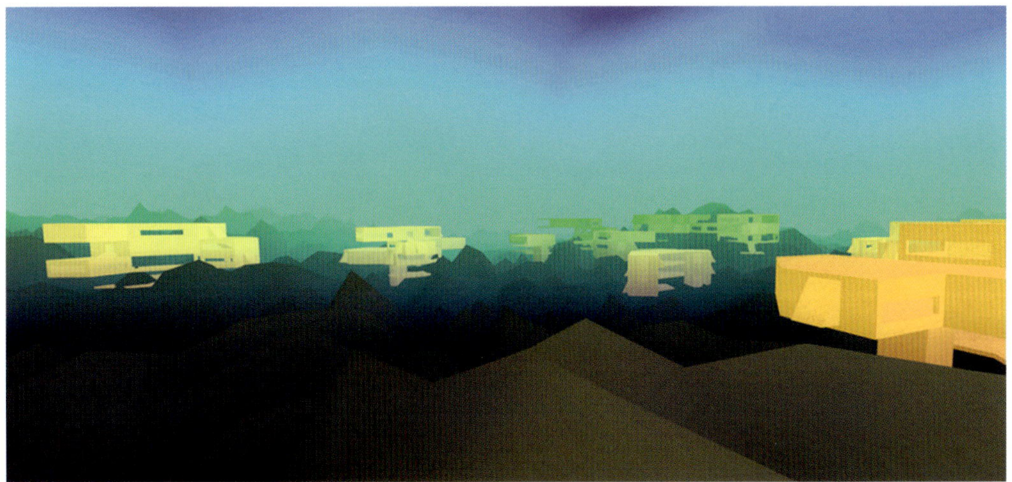

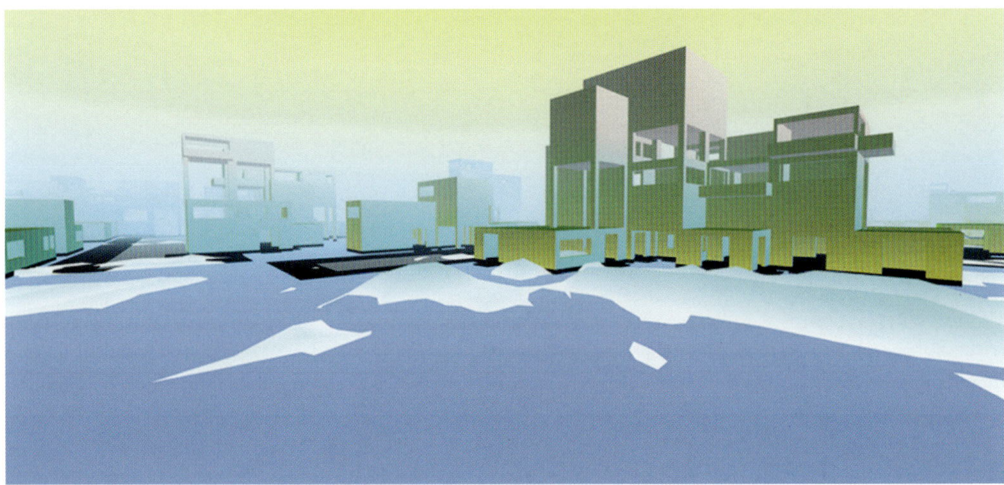

 Strangethink, *Procedural Worlds*, 2014

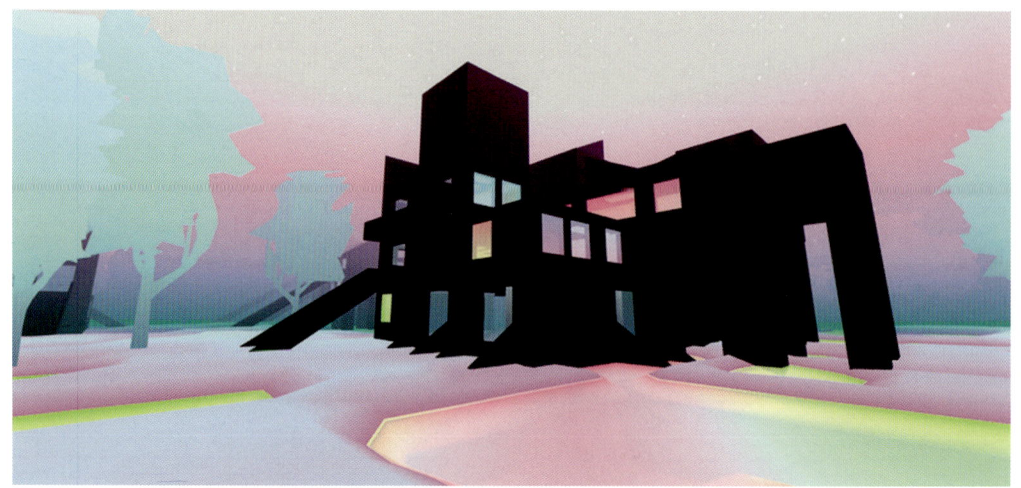

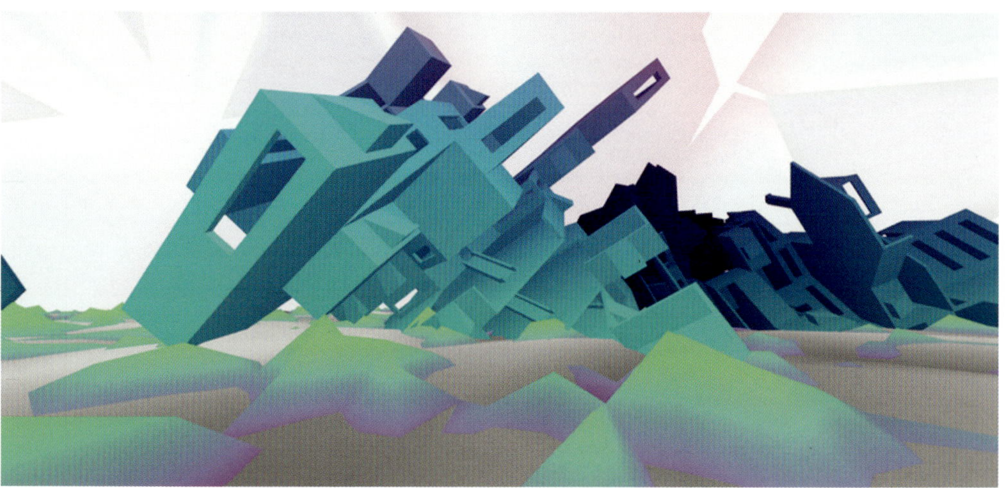

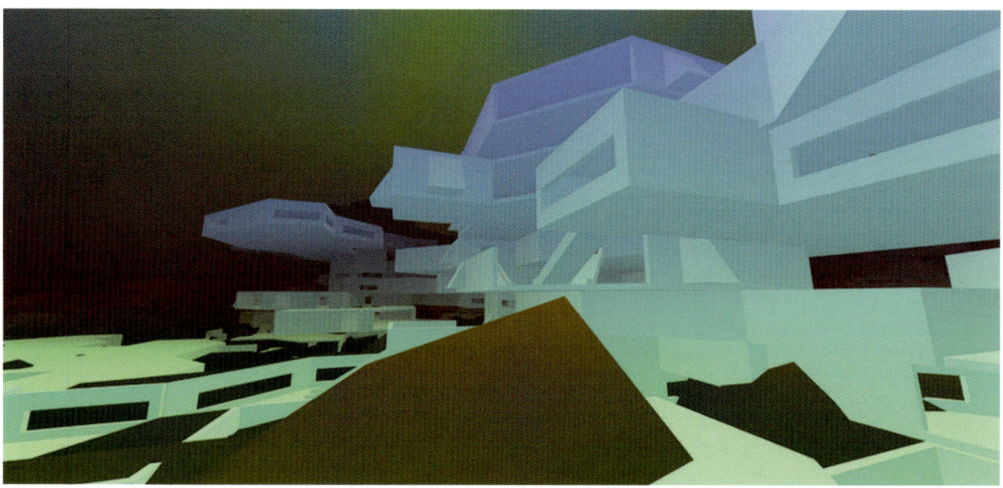

Strangethink, *Procedural Worlds*, 2014
Independent games developerm Strangethink uses procedural/generative methods to create "strange computer worlds" and it's alien architecture. Some of the themes of the work include dystopia, colour gradients and exploration.

autotuning. As for the written word, the consultation of
e-books is accompanied by a series of innovations as discreet
as they are determinant for our way of accessing information.
It is today possible to synchronize the viewing of a single document across multiple reading apparatuses, to annotate the
text, underline contents, or export the data to your profile. Yet
the strangest novelty comes from the possibility of viewing
things underlined by others, and of seeing how many of these
others have done the same.

Algorithmic Culture

Such examples testify to the increasing impact of software
functions in the diffusion and production of new cultural content. In other words, we are witnessing the appearance of an
"algorithmic culture,"[5] one reflecting the increasing influence of the digital and of computer programming in the production and diffusion of cultural products. By "culture," we
understand the ensemble of practices affecting domains as
diverse as music, literature, cinema, sculpture, journalism,
photography, gastronomy, fashion, etc. The term "algorithmic," used here as an adjective, points to the motor of com-
puting, that is, to the use of coded processes in programs that
make possible the organization, compression, assembly, sift-
ing, comparing, and classifying of information, on the basis
of preexisting coordinates. The software used in our day-to-
day management of information is composed of a multitude
of algorithms permitting the execution of tasks for which
they have been designed. This can mean, on the one hand, fur-
nishing productive tools to users, for example the possibility
of creating a virtual world in 3D with a program called Unity.
On the other hand, enabling one to access and modify preexisting content in a more or less exhaustive manner.

→ p.49

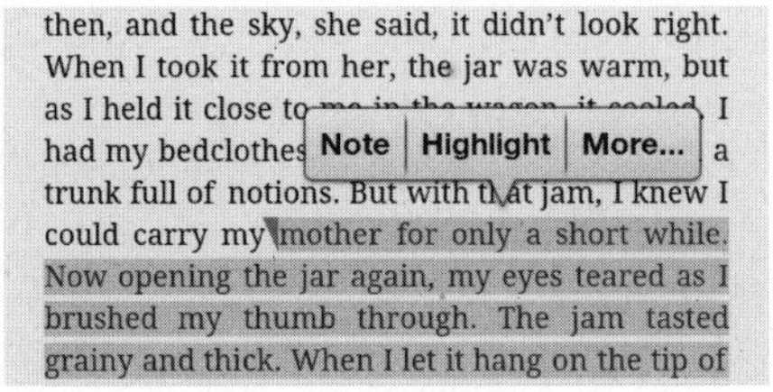

then, and the sky, she said, it didn't look right.
When I took it from her, the jar was warm, but
as I held it close to me in the wagon, it cooled. I
had my bedclothes Note | Highlight | More... a
trunk full of notions. But with that jam, I knew I
could carry my mother for only a short while.
Now opening the jar again, my eyes teared as I
brushed my thumb through. The jam tasted
grainy and thick. When I let it hang on the tip of

Amazon Kindle's highlights and notes, 2010

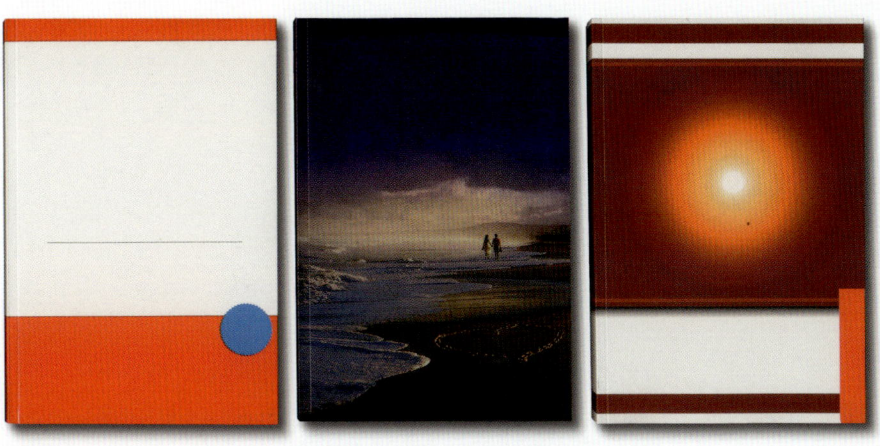

Networked Optimization is a series of three crowdsourced versions of popular self-help books. Each book contains the full text, which is however invisible because it is set in white on a white background. The only text that remains readable consists of the so-called "popular highlights" – the passages that were underlined by many Kindle users – together with the amount of highlighters. Each time a passage is underlined, it is automatically stored in Amazon's data centers.

 Silvio Lorusso, Sebastian Schmieg and Amazon Kindle users, *Networked Optimization*, 2013

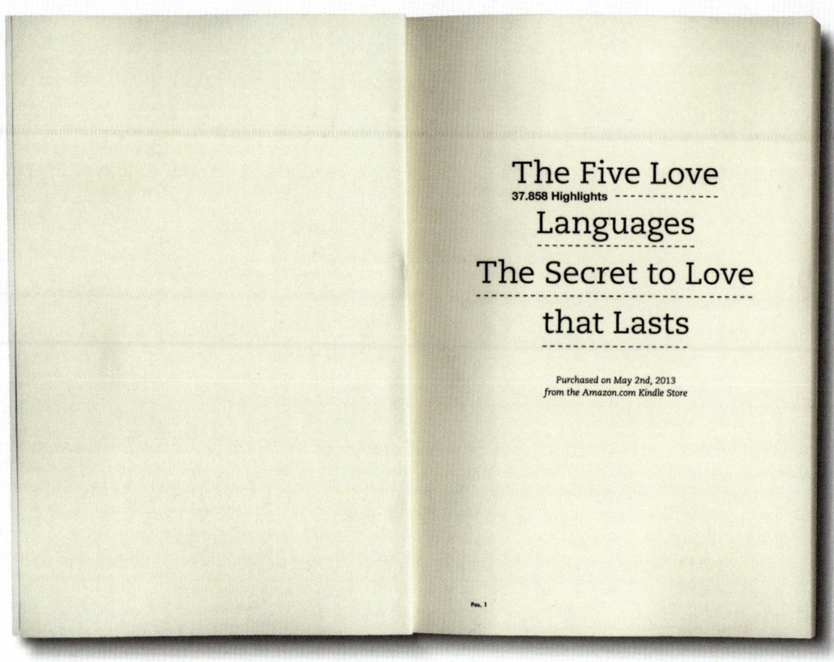

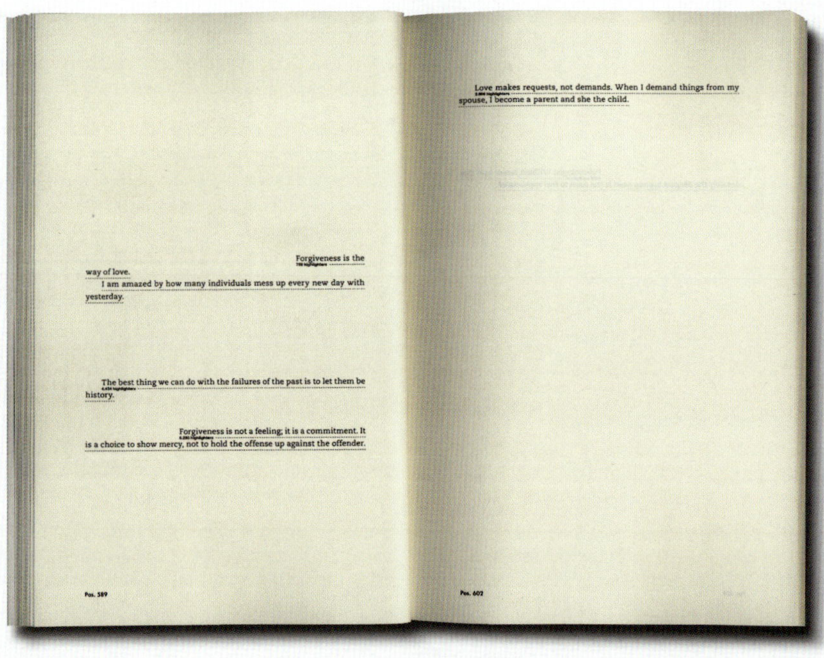

Among the books with the most popular highlights, there is a striking number of self-help books. This points to a multi-layered, algorithmic optimization: from readers and authors to Amazon itself. Harvesting its customers micro-labour, the act of reading becomes a data-mining process.

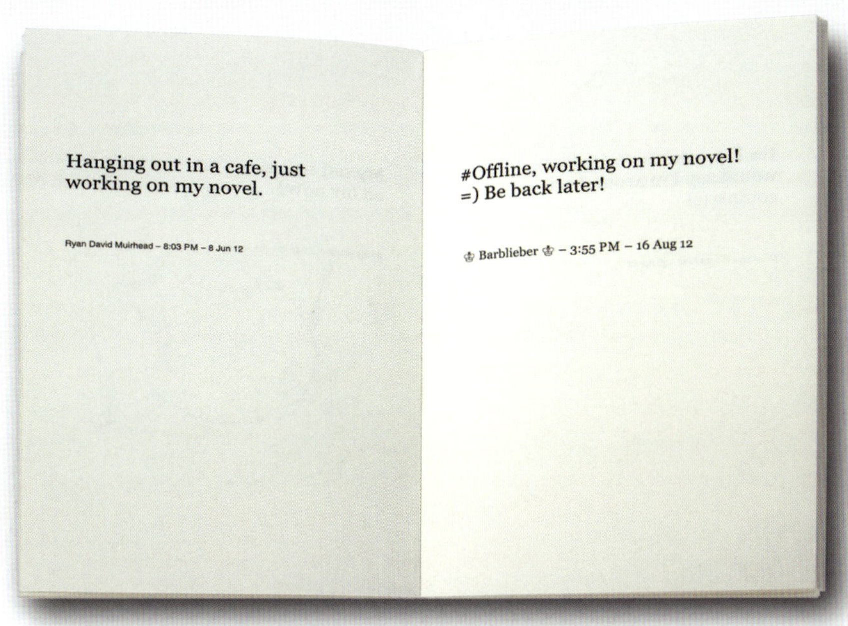

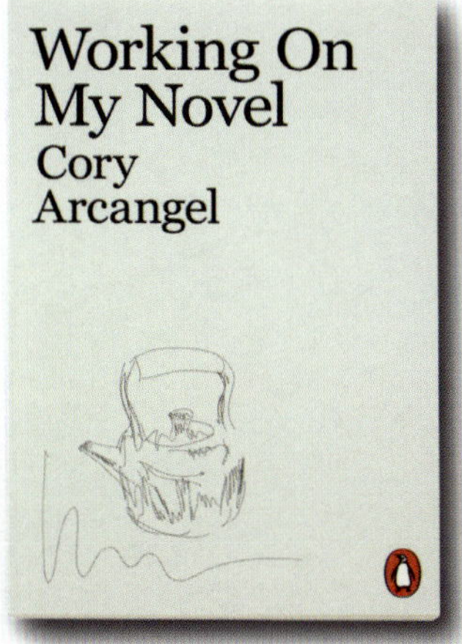

Working On My Novel is a book which is based on a twitter feed that re-tweets the best posts featuring the phrase "working on my novel." How is it possible to find a space for the demands of writing a novel in a world of instant communication? *Working On My Novel* is about the act of creation and the gap between the different ways we express ourselves today. Exploring the extremes of making art, from satisfaction and even euphoria to those days or nights when nothing will come, it's the story of what it means to be a creative person.

Cory Arcangel, Penguin Books Ltd.,
Working On My Novel, 2014

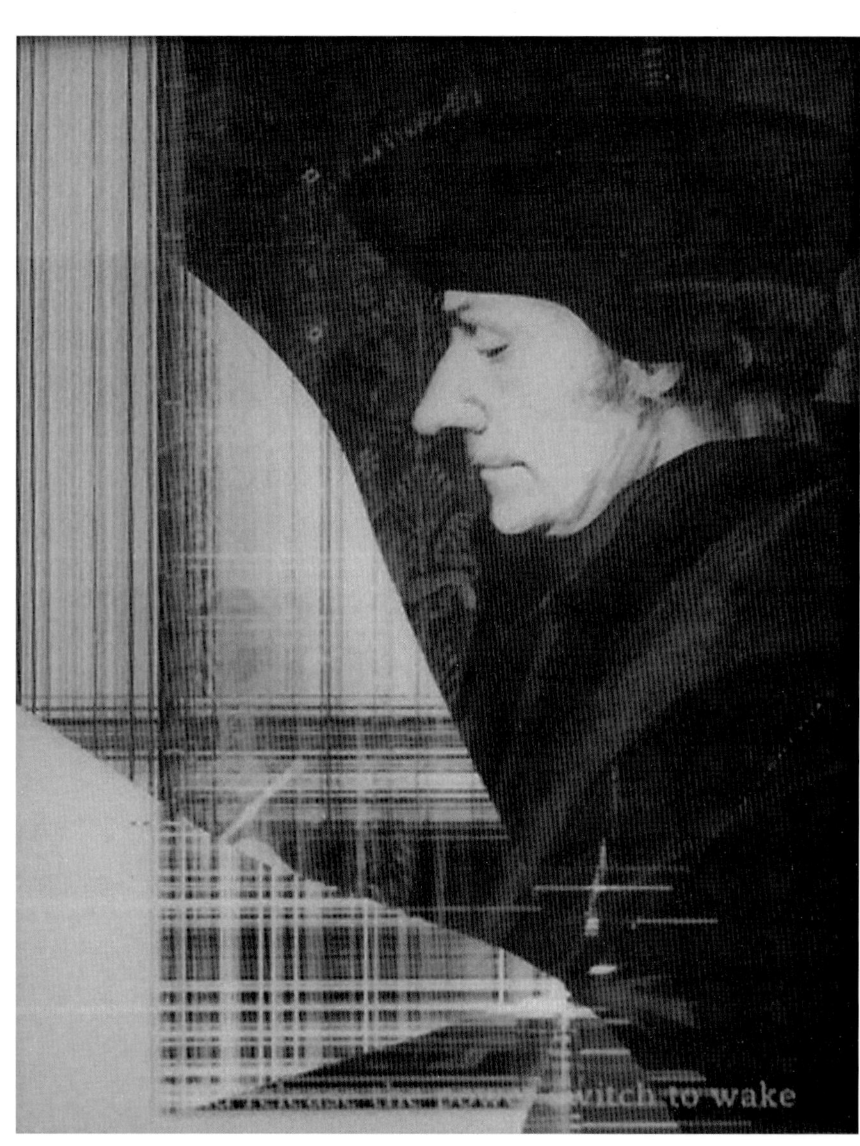

 Silvio Lorusso and Sebastian Schmieg,
56 Broken Kindle Screens, 2012

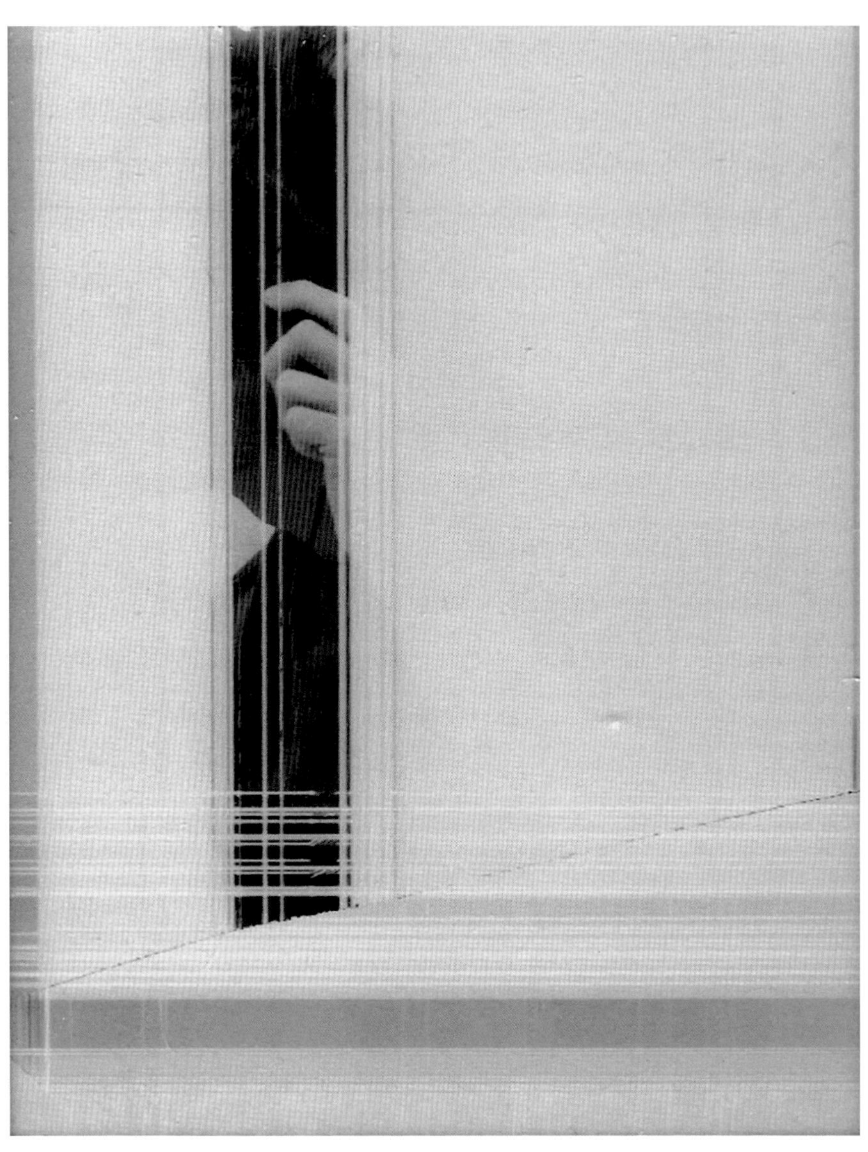

Silvio Lorusso and Sebastian Schmieg,
56 Broken Kindle Screens, 2012

Interview with Silvio Lorusso

Q1: Can you start with a short description about who you are and how you became interested in new forms of publications?
A: I'm an artist and designer currently based in Milan, Italy. My ongoing PhD research in Design Sciences at Iuav University of Venice is focused on experimental publishing which is informed, directly and indirectly, by digital technology.
I became interested in new forms of publications while I was doing an internship at the Institute of Network Cultures, an Amsterdam based research center founded and directed by media theorist Geert Lovink. I was asked to investigate different publishing channels and formats, such as Print On Demand and EPUB. I also interviewed several Dutch art and design publishers in order to understand the way in which they approached these emerging possibilities. Back then, I perceived a mix of curiosity and anxiety.
At the beginning, my experiments were quite frustrating, as EPUB seemed to me pretty limited from a design perspective. Similarly, POD's quality was—and often still is—quite poor in terms of book's materiality. It took me some time to develop a specific focus on what can be loosely defined "post-digital publishing;" such focus is highly influenced by the work of, among others, Alessandro Ludovico and Florian Cramer.

Q2: More specifically, a big chunk of your work is devoted to algorithmic production of content. What's exciting here? What are the best examples you saw recently? Why?
A: I can identify three aspects that are relevant to me, each of which is "human-centred," so to speak. The first one has to do with the relationship between algorithms and human labor. In many of the softwares we use on a daily basis, the machine part is only the tip of the iceberg. Consider Google Translate: it works only because it can harvest a huge quantity of documents produced by human beings. Human labor is increasingly hidden and presented as pure AI: the motto of

Mechanical Turk, Amazon's cheap labor platform, is "artificial artificial intelligence." I think it's important to develop strategies that highlight the human role. A good example in this sense is *reCAPCHAT*, a web-based piece by Jimpunk, in which users are asked to fill in a CAPTCHA, which is in turn anonymously tweeted by a dedicated account.

The second aspect can be summed up by saying that "reading is writing." It has to do with the new forms of writing that are made explicit by computers' tracking systems. Aside from generating novel textual material, these systems deeply affect the way in which content is produced. This is already happening in platforms such as *Oyster and Scribd*, where reading habits might soon determine the value of texts. We need to look at the feedback loops between reading and writing in order to have a broad understanding of the life cycle of content. In relation to this, I think of Evan Roth's *Internet Cache Self Portrait* series: big prints made out of the images automatically stored in the artist's browser cache. "The new memoir is our browser history" according to uncreative writing guru Kenneth Goldsmith.

Finally, I think it's fascinating to look at the human reaction to algorithmic reading and writing processes. Nowadays, it's not uncommon to stumble upon bots talking to each other on Twitter, sometimes without even noticing. SEO has a profound impact on contemporary writing practices. The question is: to what extent do we adapt to these systems? According to Jaron Lanier, the renowned Turing test, more than showing whether a machine is able to think like a human being, manifests how humans lower themselves to a level that is accepted by machines. In her *Spam Bibliography*, writer Angela Genusa reorganizes the spam she received via email in the form of an academic bibliography, somehow validating automatically generated texts that are commonly considered garbage.

Q3: Can you describe two of your recent projects?
A: I'd like to mention two projects that are connected to the

points made above. The first one is a collaboration with German artist Sebastian Schmieg and Amazon Kindle users. *Networked Optimization* is a series of three crowdsourced versions of popular self-help books. Each book contains the full text, which is however invisible because it is set in white on a white background. The only text that remains readable consists of the so-called "popular highlights"—the passages that were underlined by many Kindle users—together with the amount of highlighters. Each time a passage is underlined, it is automatically stored in Amazon's data centers. The project puts in place a process of recursive optimisation, in which self-help books, which are generally meant to "optimise" certain aspects of behavior, are in turn optimized by the readers themselves. While the coincidence of reading and writing is shown in its "natural" context of literature, the quantification characterizing popular highlights affects the value that readers attribute to a certain passage.

The second project is entitled *Douglas Rushkoff's New Book*. Douglas Rushkoff, author of *Program or Be Programmed*, quit Facebook in 2013 because "it does things on our behalf when we're not even there. It actively misrepresents us to our friends, and worse misrepresents those who have befriended us to still others." Using MySocialBook—an online platform that allows to print books from personal Facebook profiles, the ones of friends, and pages—I made a book out of the fan page that Rushkoff abandoned in 2013, selecting the period of time in which he was actively using it. The book's layout is automatically determined by Facebook's metadata; for instance the most popular photo—paradoxically the one in which Rushkoff announces that he's leaving the social network—occupies the first page, together with the amount of likes it received.

Q4: Most of the projects you conduct/you're interested in via P–DPA are quite experimental. I'm definitely fascinated by them and I found them utterly intriguing. However, when working with friends and clients on the future of publishing, I find it hard for them to understand what it means and how they anticipate the evolution of publications. What's your take on this? How do you think examples such as the one discussed in Q2 pave the way for the future of publishing?

A: I think that the reason why it's difficult to relate these experimental works to the publishing industry is exactly because they push the boundaries of what we generally mean by "publishing." The examples discussed in Q2 provide a radically inclusive, holistic notion of publishing, not easy to adopt for commercial purposes, but nonetheless part of our networked lives. The projects I conduct and the ones I'm interested in show at least that digital publishing is not just about rich media, slick interfaces and smooth gestures. Hoping not to sound reactionary, I believe that traditional formats like the printed book can be the appropriate output for genuinely digital practices. After all, Print On Demand could not exist without Web 2.0, PDF, etc.

That said, some connections between experimental practices and publishing as an industry do exist. Uncreative writing is going mainstream: a few months ago a book by artist Cory Arcangel, including a curated collection of tweets containing the phrase "working on my novel." was published by Penguin. The field of spam books is growing day by day: these algorithmic assemblages of open access materials, such as Wikipedia articles, are generated in bulk and actually sold by *ad hoc* publishing houses. Economist Phillip M. Parker, who in 2008 had already published more than 200,000 books, even patented a way to produce them.

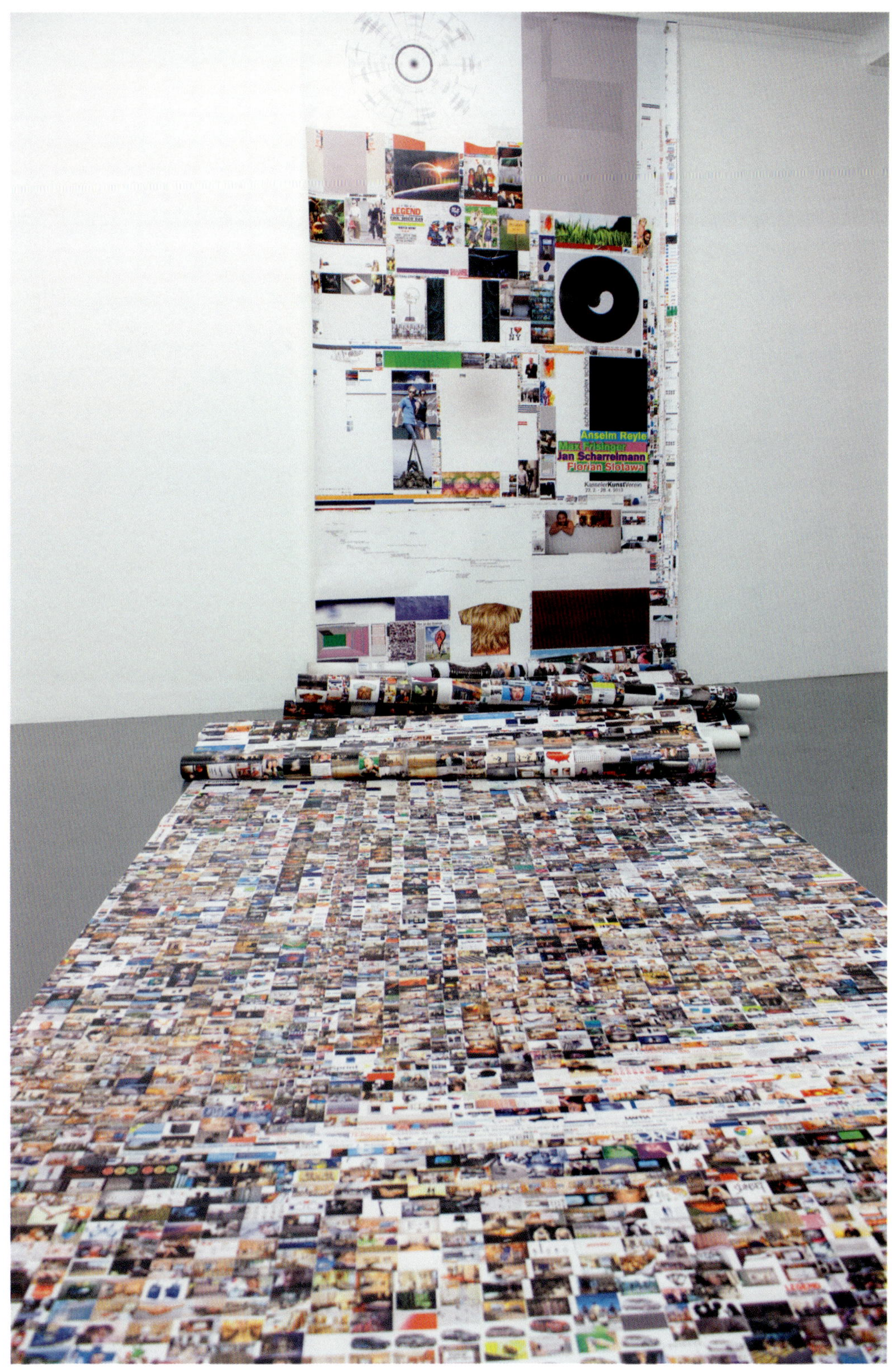

43 Evan Roth, *Internet Cache Portrait series*, 2014
Vinyl print, 150 × 1560 cm

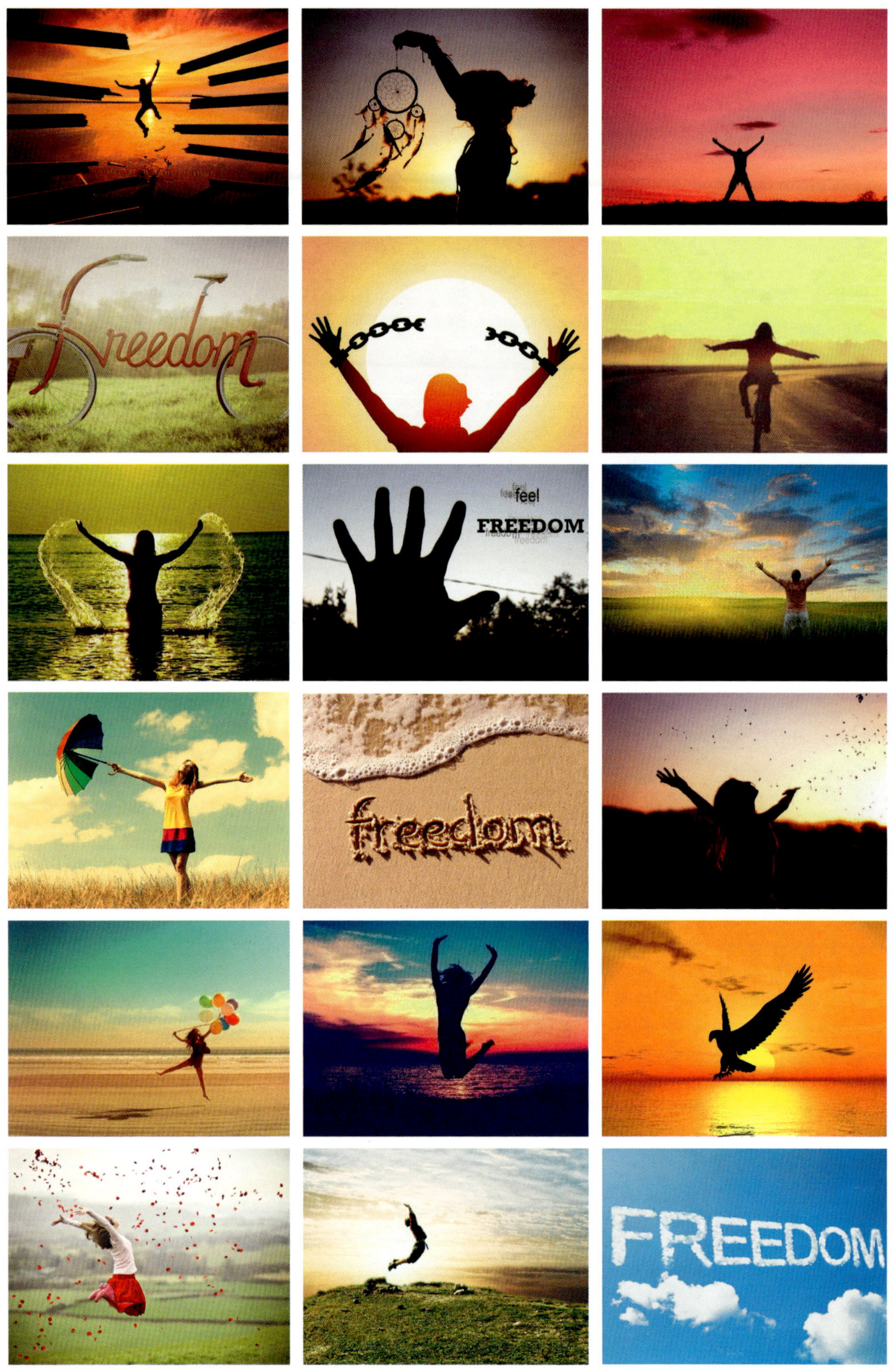

"Freedom," Google Search, 13.05.2015
English

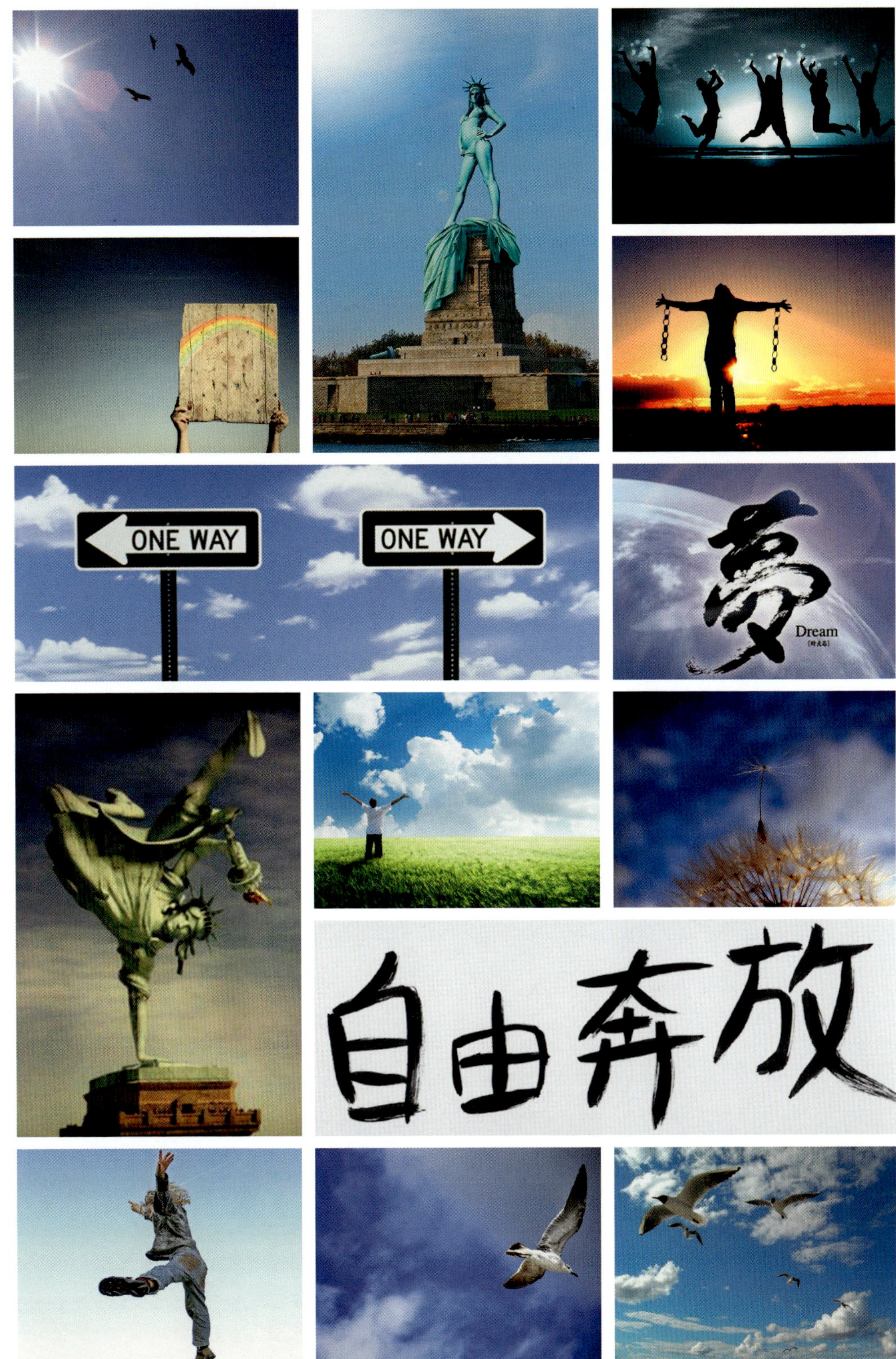

"Freedom," Google Search, 13.05.2015
Japanese

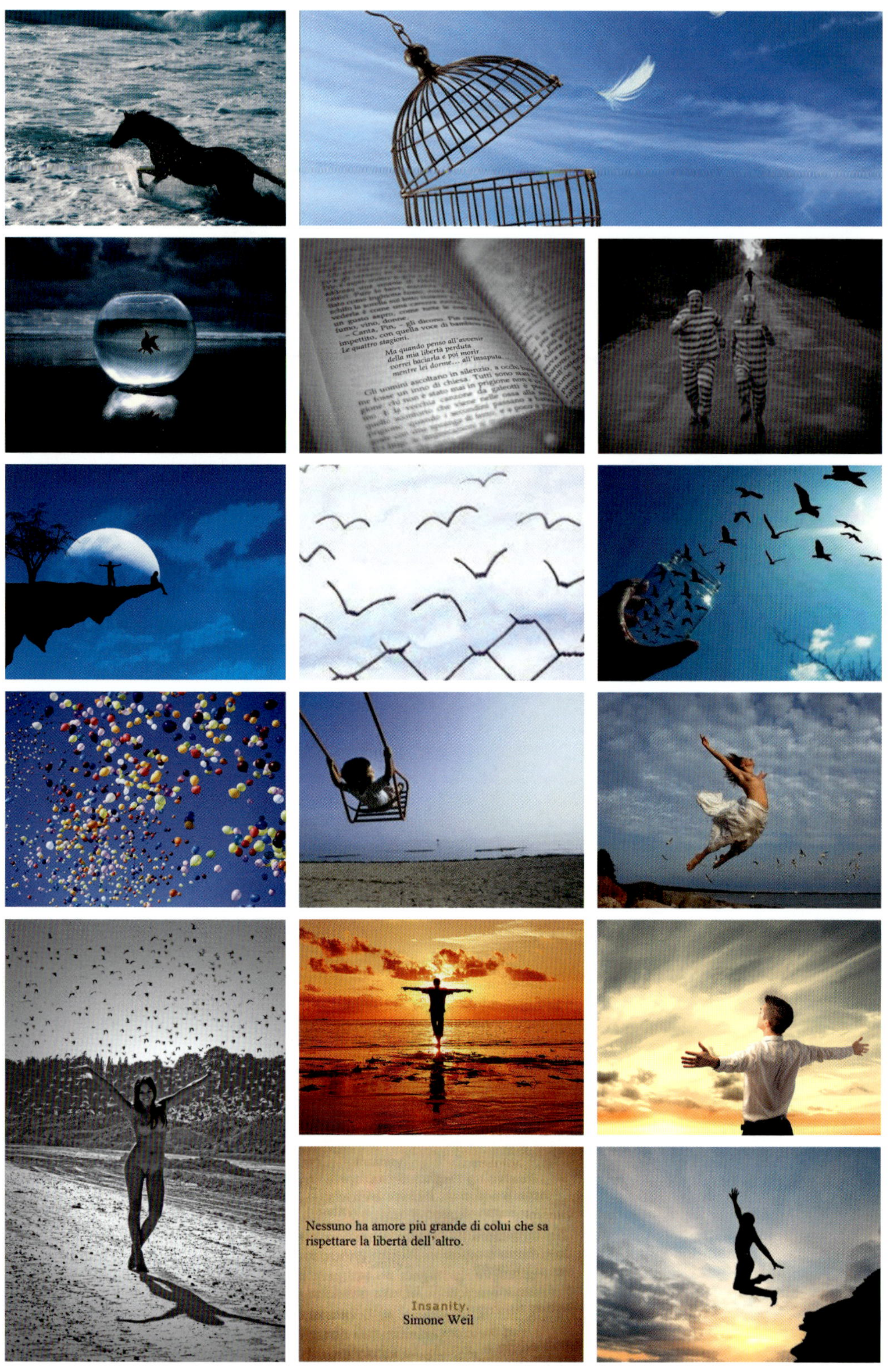

"Freedom," Google Search, 13.05.2015
Italian

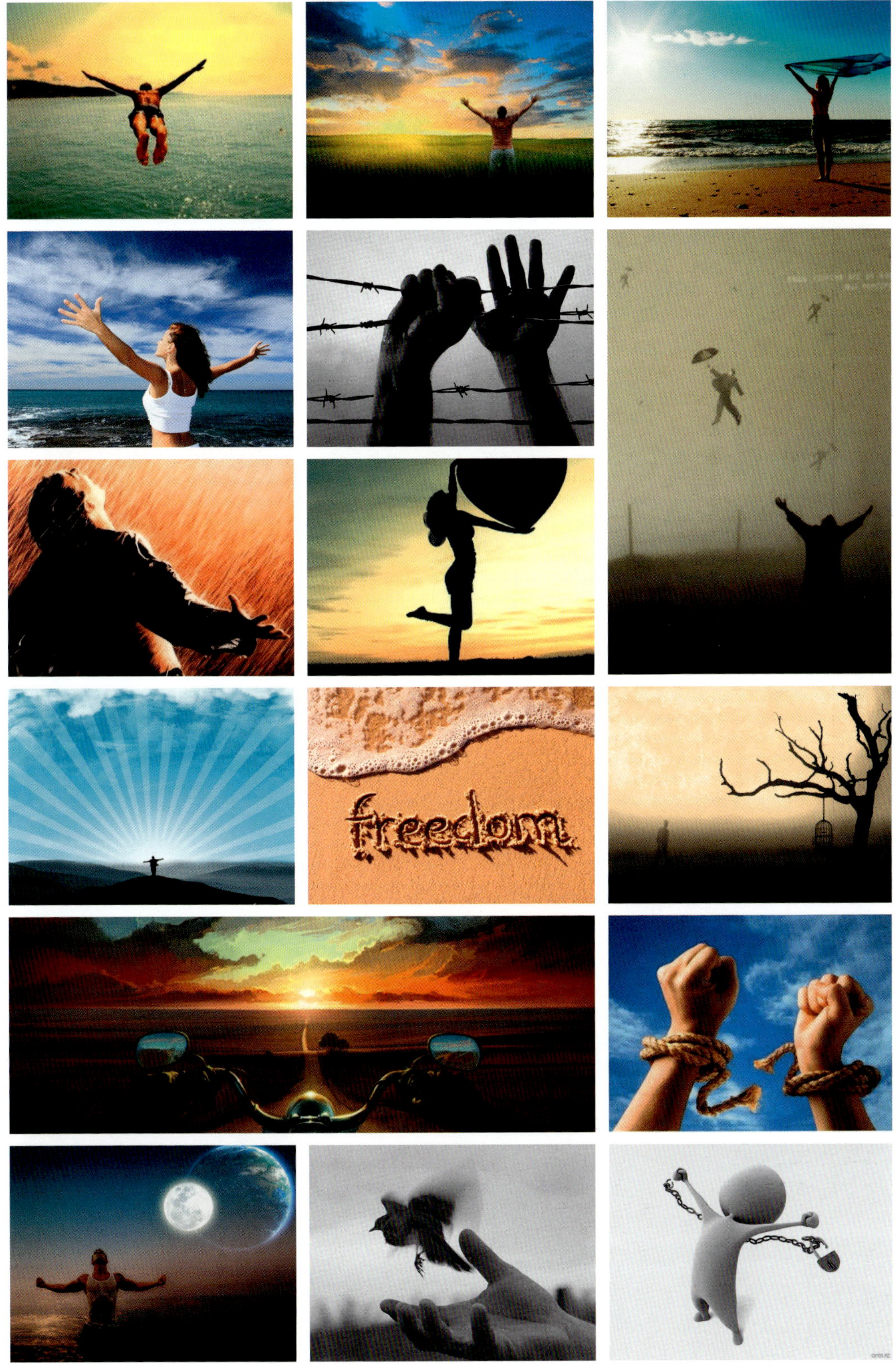

  "Freedom," Google Search, 13.05.2015
Russian

At the same time, the use of bots has been generalized. This shortening of the word "robot" refers to an automatic or semi-automatic program capable of interacting with computer servers. These programs are typically employed at the point where the rapidity of the action becomes a prevalent criteria. In the world of finance it is the case everywhere, and above all in high frequency trading, where bots buy, sell, and negotiate market exchanges in microseconds. Likewise, sites like eBay make use of bidding robots named Auction Sniper or eSniper that enable automated bidding during the last seconds of an online auction.

The exploration of this "algorithmic culture" reveals the determining influence of computation on cultural content itself. In certain cases, this can give rise to its own specific aesthetic, as in the case of chiptune[6] music or the glitch[7] current. In other cases, it can give rise to "augmented" practices or experiences of reality. Video games present a type of content intrinsically related to algorithms implemented within digital technologies, and which enable the creation of virtual universes in which users can carry out actions whose effects are visually registered on a screen. Lastly, the notion of algorithmic culture can just as easily produce an effect of hierarchization in the selection and suggestion of certain content rather than others, the most familiar of which are the product suggestions displayed on Amazon.com following the selection of any object.

In this respect we may distinguish between algorithms whose purpose is to aid in the selection/diffusion of cultural goods and algorithms of production. It is their productive function that interests us here. In an epoch in which computer programs take charge more and more of what previously figured as properly human activities, the increasing automation of creative processes constitutes a pertinent point of reference → p.53

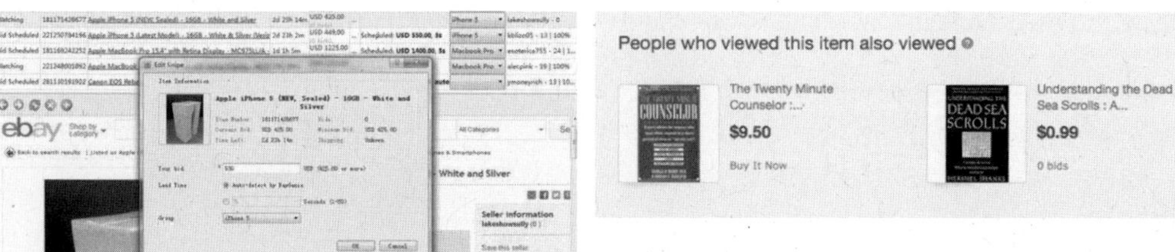

Left: eBay, Auction Sniper, c. 2010
Right: Amazon recommendation engine, 2015

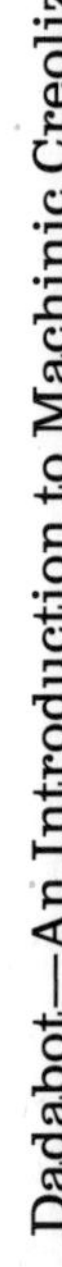

my cat

my cat **from hell**
my cat **likes to hide in boxes**
my cat **saved my son**
my cat **is yellow**

it is bad if

it is bad if **i have a crush on my sister**
it is bad if **your poop floats**
it is bad if **you swallow gum**
it is bad if **you pee alot**

america is the

america is the **the only country that went from barbarism to decadence without civilization in between**
america is the **beast**

from which to grasp the automation of algorithmic processes in our society. It is not a question here of restoring the primacy of the author in the creative process. It is a matter rather of putting into perspective the specter of productions and human-machine collaborations engendered by these sorts of hybridizations. The aesthetics and the coherence that spring from these productions can never be fully foreseen, for they are always the fruit of a generative process that is never completely random.

The Language of New Media

In his book *The Language of New Media*, Lev Manovich introduces the notion of new media objects[8] to describe the content produced by digital technologies. What interests him are the principles governing their functioning. The first such principle concerns the presence of a digital representation. A photograph taken on Instagram, a piece of music on Soundcloud, a GIF found on Tumblr, a tweet, etc.—all of these cultural elements are encoded in a numeric format. A second important characteristic lies in the modularity of digital objects, the way in which they tend to be imbricated in one another. Whether it be a piece of music, a YouTube video, a PDF text, etc., every "media object" consists of an assemblage of blocks that can take various forms. These different blocks can be combined among themselves and this is the exact logic at work in the books produced by the *Ghost Writers* bots. They function as aleatory media objects, of textual commentaries and visuals extracted from YouTube, the outcome of which can then be considered independently. The selection criteria and agencement of this heterogeneous content is accessible and "readable" only by means of the potentialities defined within the program in question.

→ p.59

Left: Lev Manovich, *The Language of New Media*, 2002
Right: Fragment of a PNG image code, 2014

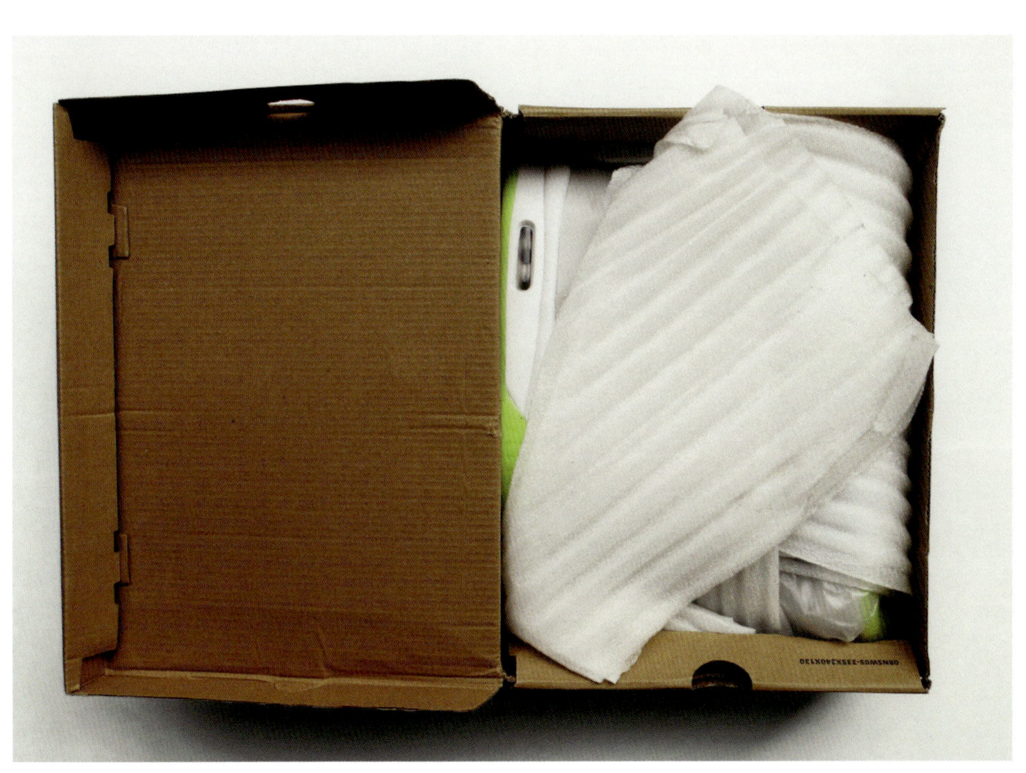

The Random Darknet Shopper is an automated online shopping bot which, once a week, went on shopping spree in the deep web where it randomly choses and purchases one item for a value of USD 100. The items were shown in the exhibition *The Darknet. From Memes to Onionland* at Kunst Halle St. Gallen. Each new object ads to a landscape of traded goods from the Darknet.

 !Mediengruppe bitnik, *The Random Darknet Shopper*, 2014

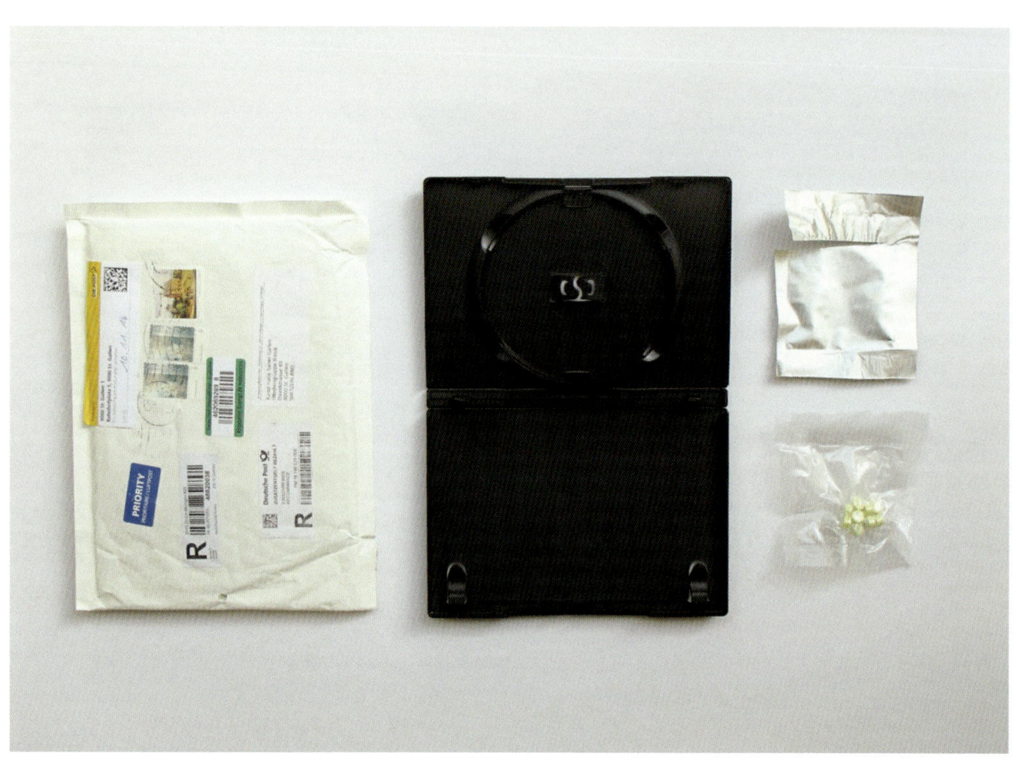

!Mediengruppe bitnik, *The Random Darknet Shopper*, 2014

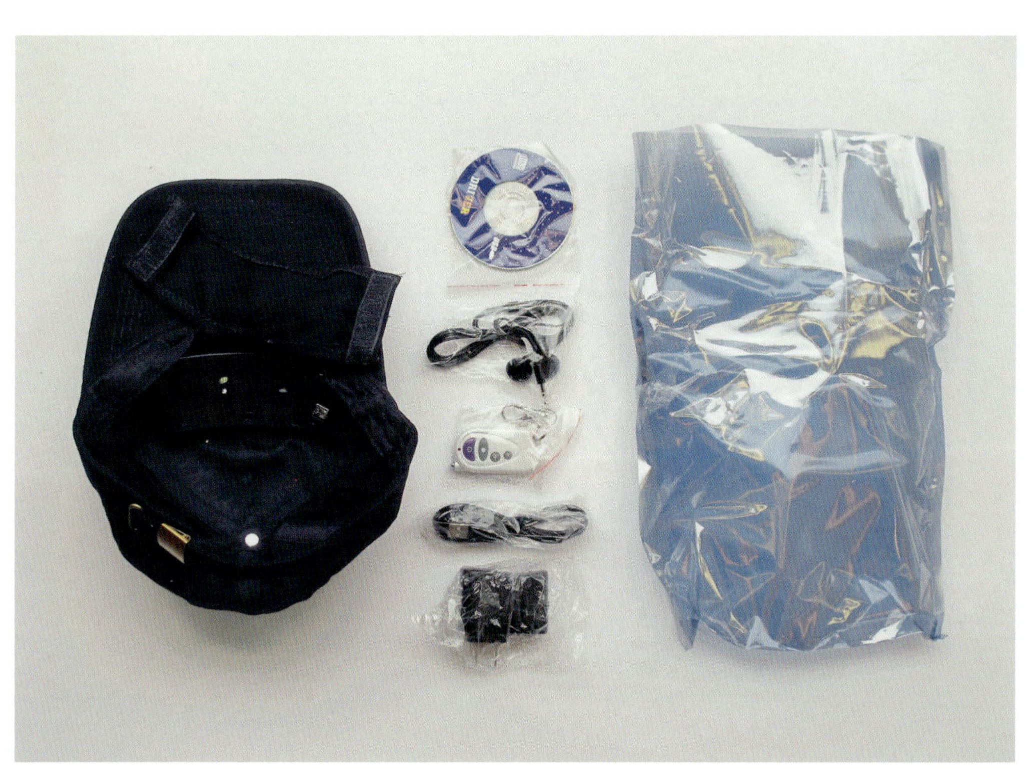

57 !Mediengruppe bitnik, *The Random Darknet Shopper*, 2014

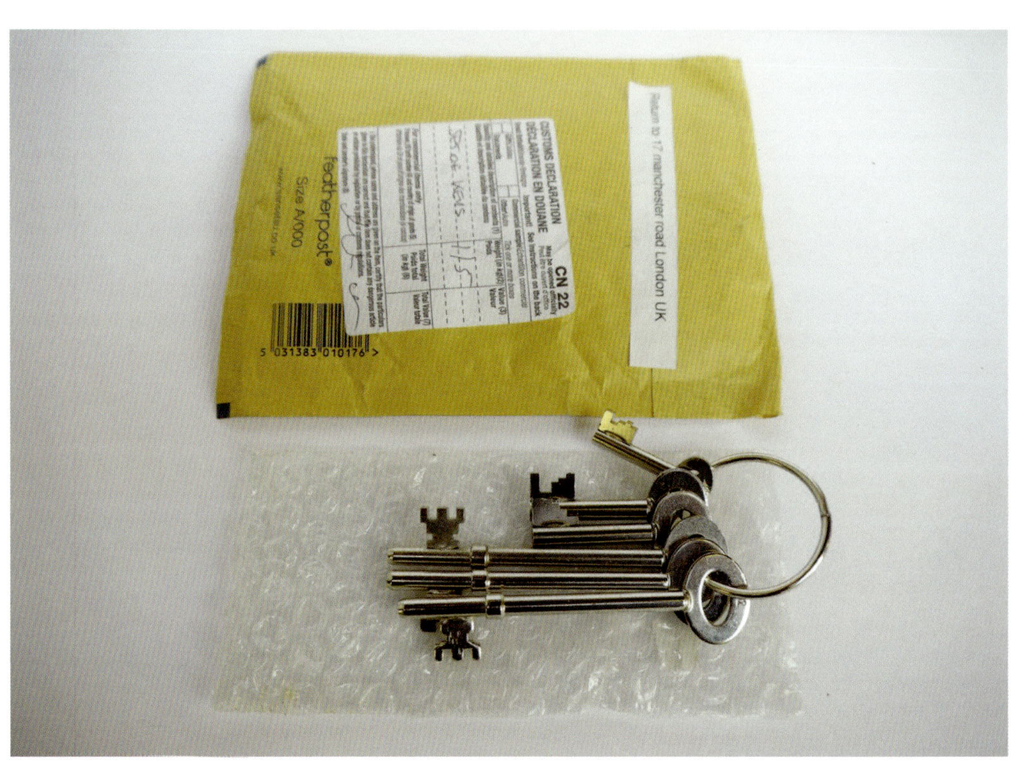

!Mediengruppe bitnik, *The Random Darknet Shopper*, 2014

However, despite their smooth and integral character, not all digital objects are composed of bricks of the same nature. For example, Google Earth is composed of photographs, satellite imagery, and 3D models or navigation tools. This type of "media hybrid"[9] is common among the online and mobile services that we use everyday, such as the most basic sites compiling text articles, videos, weather maps and a search function accessing a database. In each case, we encounter digital objects of distinct natures, combined with the aim of creating a coherent experience.

More and more designers and artists are taking advantage of this hybrid rhetoric, developing increasingly advanced projects. Consider James Bridle's *A Ship Adrift* (2013). Using a website updated on a daily basic, Bridle reconstructs the journey of a navigator adrift. The virtual movement of the boat follows the speed and force of winds detected by sensors situated in the statue of a boat placed on the roof of the Southbank Centre in London. In parallel, a program tracking geolocated content such as Tweets, Wikipedia entries, or ads posted online on bulletin boards are linked to places and events situated in the vicinity of the supposed position of the boat. Each day, data is selected and posted to the site. This project reveals another characteristic of digital objects: photos, videos, sound extracts and texts are accompanied by "metadata."[10] Photographs carry with them the date, time, camera model and settings, as well as the geolocation at which they were taken. James Bridle's project functions specifically through the usage of geographical metadata which serve as a point of reference in relation to which diverse and daily cultural elements can be reassembled.

Various sociological theories allow us to account for such phenomena. Owing to its decentering of Western themes, Basil Zimmermann's work[11] on the role of technical objects

→ p.75

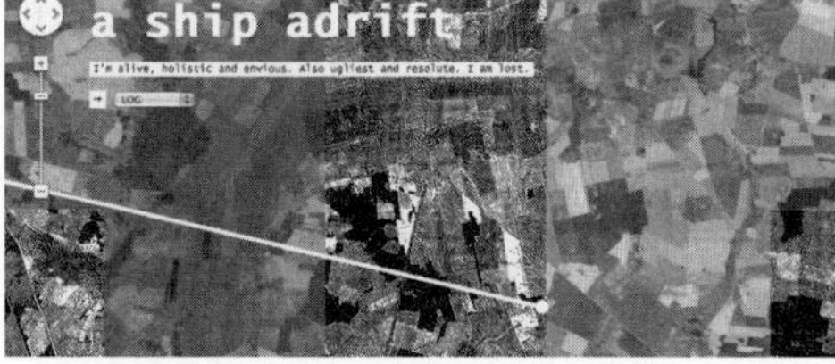

James Bridle (in association with Artangel), *A ship adrift*, 2012

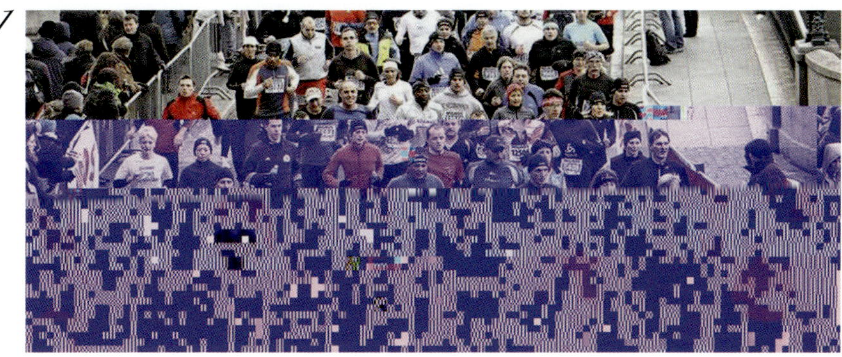

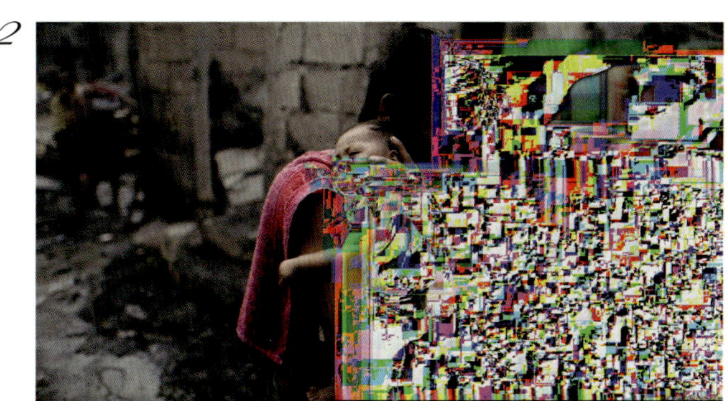

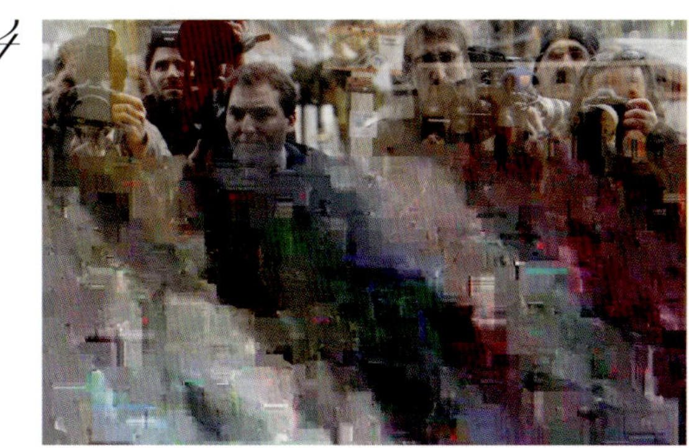

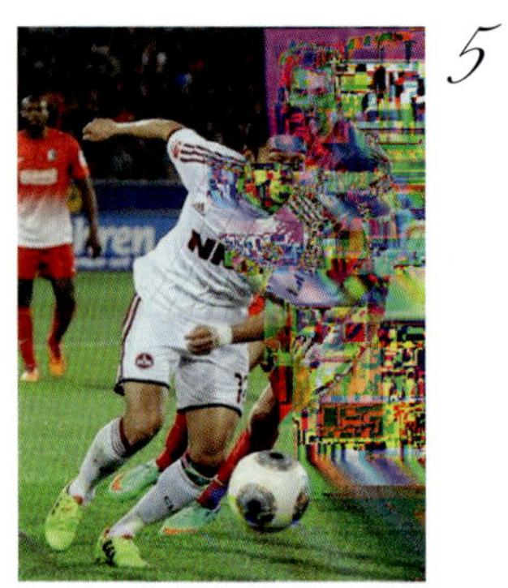

5

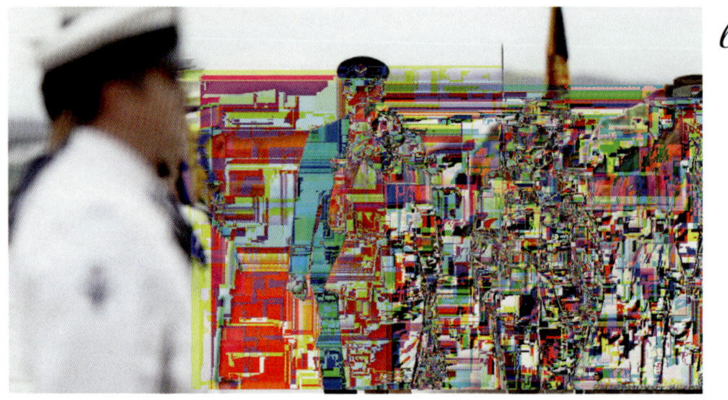

6

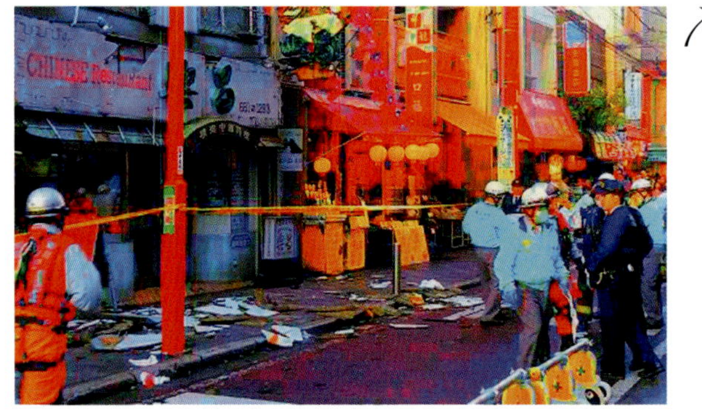

7

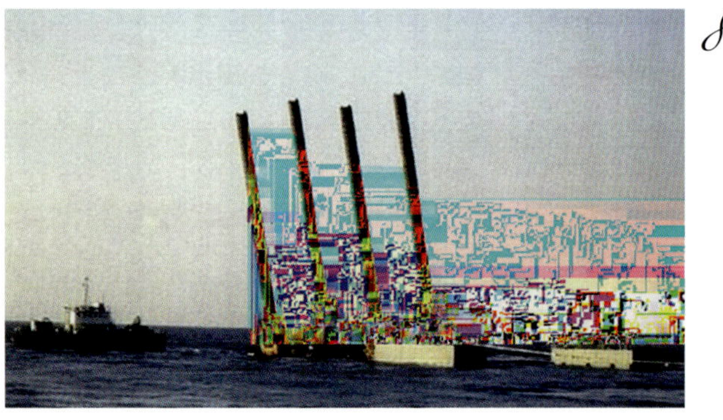

8

Assignment proposed on rapidworkers.com:
Please write a short description of what you see in this image.
The photography is corrupted and we want you to help us
covering what you see in there.

Total length: 400–500 characters
Deadline: 2 hours

1. It's a kind of a marathon where p[...]
all walks of life can join for a good ca[...]
It must have been organised for a good cause,
such as London Marathon in UK, Mumbai
Marathon in India, etc. One shouldn't be a
professional marathon runner to be a part of this
novel deed, indeed. In my opinion, It represents
the commitment of people for any good cause
which represents the humanity and leaves
behind any notion of inequality in terms of race/
ethnicity, class, nationality, origin, etc. I've
been getting involved in such occasions time and
again as such events are organised frequently in
my country for the sake of betterment of human
race as a whole. We should push ourselves
 forward for such novel causes in the days to
come as well for a better world to live in.
(Author TaskID-28646)

2. In the Image the one man and small child.
The man is out side her home. The man is not
wearing a shirt only Pent. The towel is one
shoulder of the man. In the behind of the man

three people watching the man where to doing.
I think the very poor people and In the picture the
house is net well. The picture show them one man
and her child with them and walking to home
I think the man is very poor because not weaning
a good dress. (Author TaskID-286975)

3. The picture is not clear but I understand
them the two man in the train and good bye the
that person who taking a picture. The train
color is yellow and blue and I thing train is on
the platform. When the train is read to going
the two man in train giving a good bye to the
person who know them. The man is also give the
smail and shake the hand to show them good bye.
The Train is two window and two man is good
bye and smail the. (Author TaskID-286977)

4. In the image show that a six to seven peoples
with a camera taking a picture. I think this
picture is taking them when a press conference a
political person. The photographer taking a
picture of the person who press conference them.
and also write the speech of the person what
is they speaking. The photographer are taking a
picture for news paper and magazine. The
photographer are record the video for news
channels. The picture clear show the peoples and
taking a picture. (Author TaskID-286988)

*5. The Picture show the football match the two
players are play the football and run to goal net.
The One Player run to other team goal*
and one player want to get football,
player behind the seen watching th
to pass the football and run and d
The one player dodging other play
the football. The football is running a
*player hit the football and pass to other player
of the her team. (Author TaskID-286968)*

*6. It represents what we can call the "Sprint of
the Life."
More preciseley, it is our eternal and everlasting
attempt to reach nearly impossible goals, or
goals that are impossible to reach in the time we
would like to. By attempting to run to fast,
we often delay ourselves and slow down. Often,
we finish by completely stop and burn ourselves
totally discouraged.
We should rather starting a little more slower, but
far more securely. Then, we wouldn't burning
ourselves, and finish literally booth mentally
and, even sometimes, physically sick.
Sportsmen and sportswomen that run marathon
never rush at the beginning of the competition,
but, on the contrary search to keep the same
regular peace all the 40 kilometers that they know
they had to run entirely.*

Contrary to what people generally think, life resemble far more to a marathon than to a 100 meters sprint. Sometimes, there are 100 meters sprint during the daily life, but it is only short moments. (Author TaskID-286966)

7. In the image clearly show that a bazaar and there are many restaurant side by side. In the image show that a accident out side the restaurant. The police and rescue them in the image show them. I think the restaurant are chines and chines country. I think the small blast out side the restaurant. After the incident the police and rescue team take them in incident place and cordon off the area and rescue them and collect the evidence in the restaurant. (Author TaskID-286986)

8. The corrupted image show that a very huge sea and four big tower in the image. One Ship in the image. The corrupted image show that the Machines and equipment for sea oil production. In the image show that a big machines are found a oil in the sea. I think oil found in the near sea point because the two concrete block are in the image. The bridge also show in the corrupted image. (Author TaskID-286991)

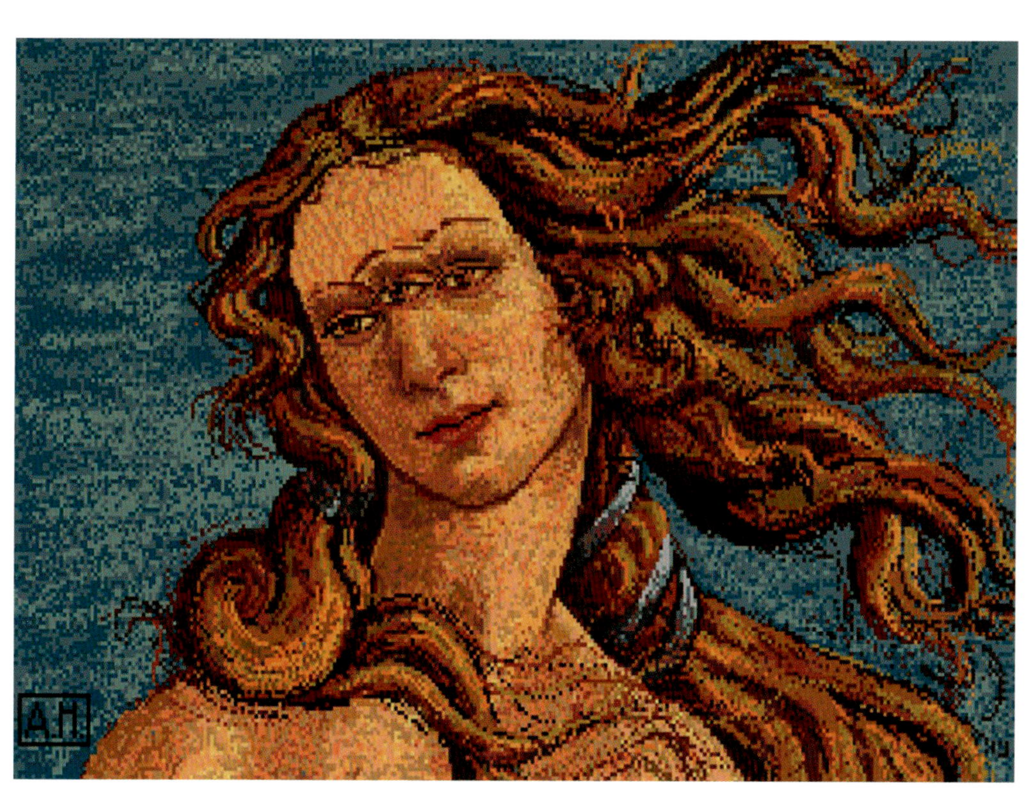

In 1985, computer and electronics manufacturer Commodore International commissioned Andy Warhol to create art using the company's Amiga 1000 computer. Warhol saved many of his experimental images to Amiga floppy disks which were turned into physical prints only 30 years later.

   Andy Warhol, *Venus (made with computer Amiga)*, 1985

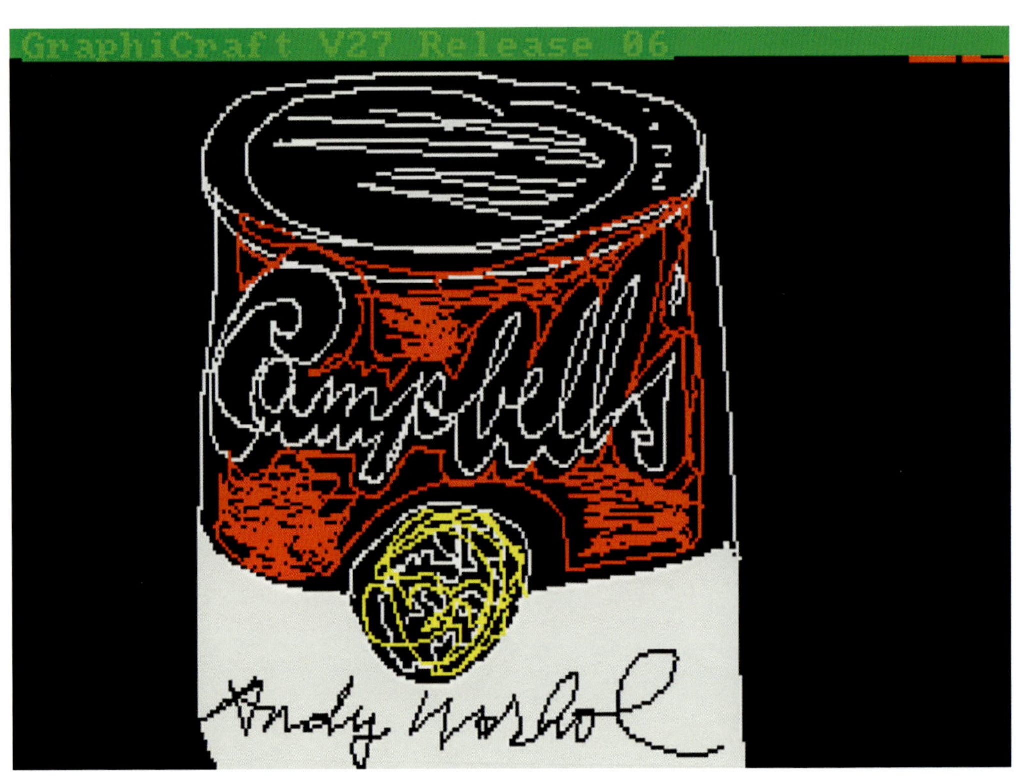

Andy Warhol, *Campbell's (made with computer Amiga)*, 1985

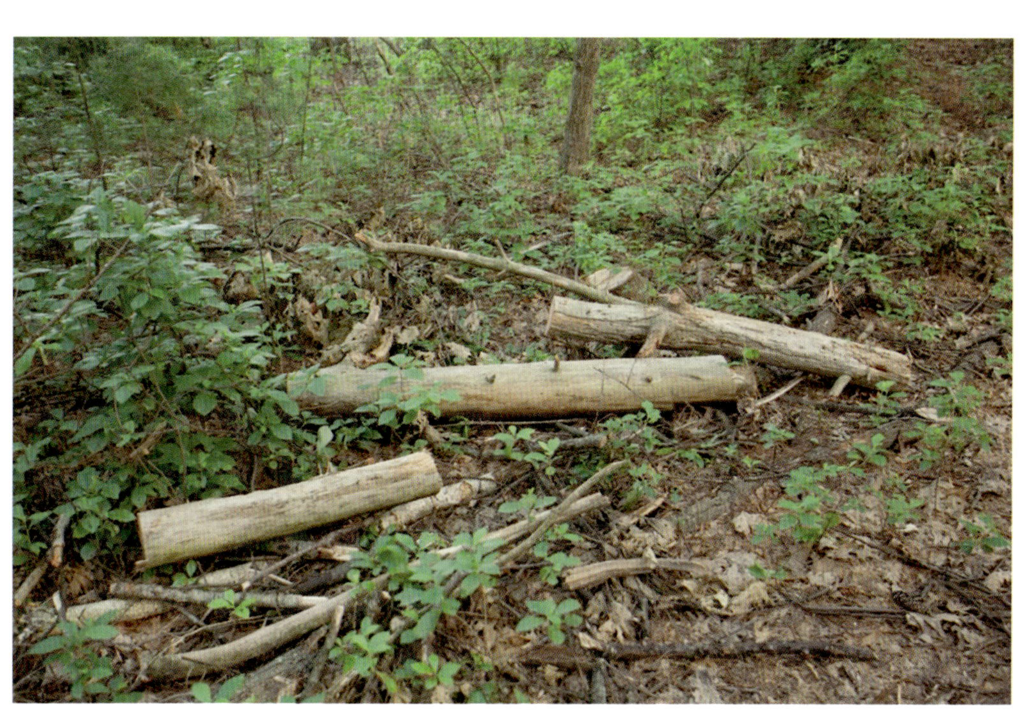

"We address the problem of camouflaging a 3D object from the many viewpoints that one might see it from. Given photographs of an object's surroundings, we produce a surface texture that will make the object difficult for a human to detect. To do this, we introduce several background matching algorithms that attempt to make the object look like whatever is behind it. [...] Our models are forced to make trade-offs between different perceptual factors, such as the conspicuousness of the occlusion boundaries and the amount of texture distortion. We use experiments with human subjects to evaluate the effectiveness of these models for the task of camouflaging a cube [...]."

 Andrew Owens et al., *Camouflaging an Object from Many Viewpoints*, 2014
See p.208

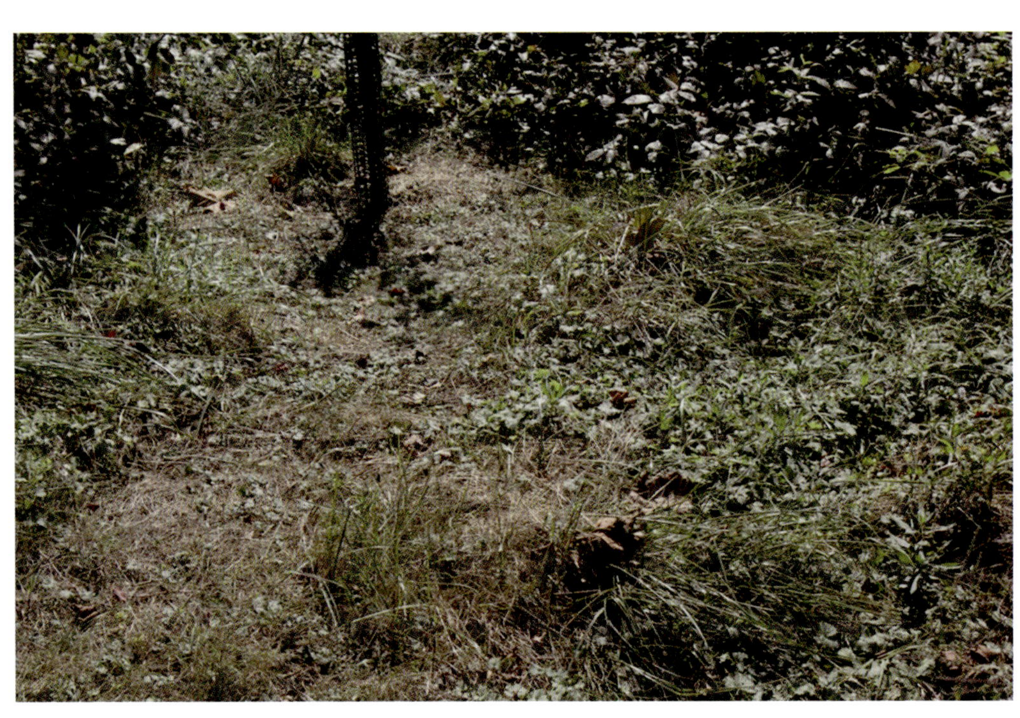

Andrew Owens et al., *Camouflaging an Object from Many Viewpoints*, 2014
See more p.208

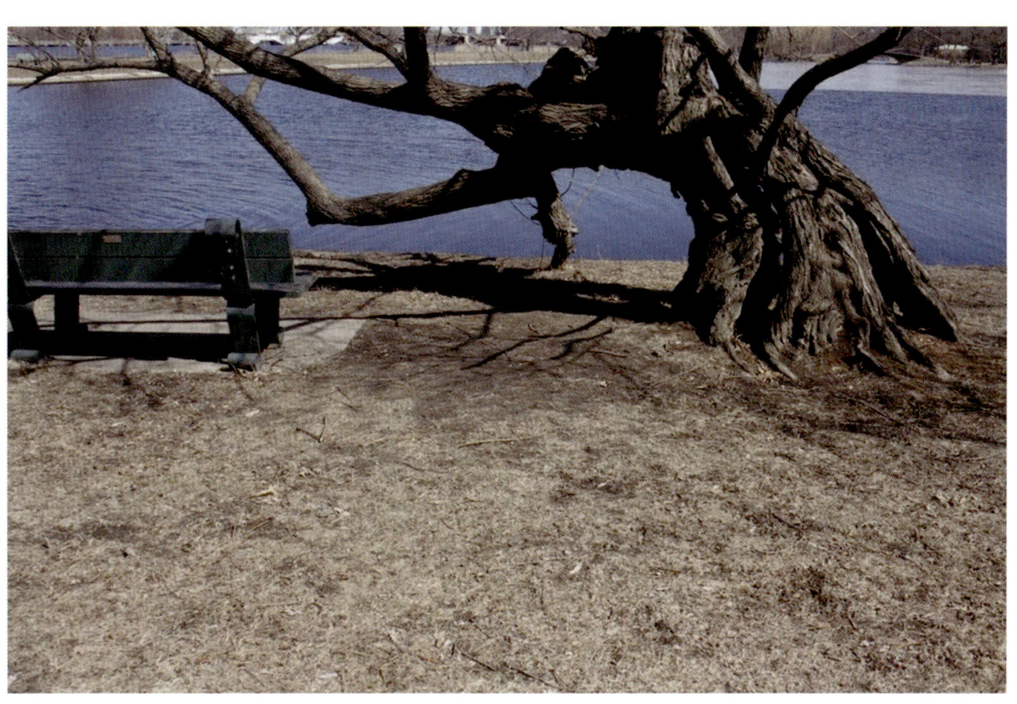

73 Andrew Owens et al., *Camouflaging an Object from Many Viewpoints*, 2014
See more p.208

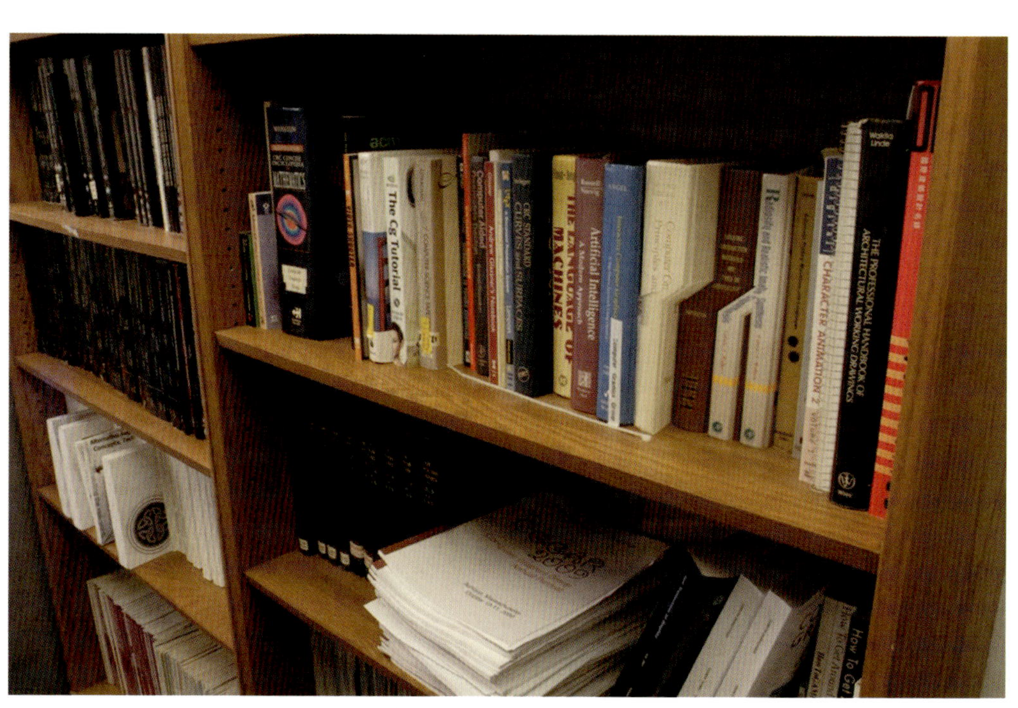

Andrew Owens et al., *Camouflaging an Object from Many Viewpoints*, 2014
See more p.208

in the creation of electronic music in China opens particularly fruitful paths for such purposes. In his research on
memes,[10] Zimmermann outlines an atomic approach to "culture." Observing how "Western" content can circulate inside
China by means of electronic music samples, he proposes the
notion of a "cultural element." The latter refers to the way in
which every content or cultural object—including Manovich's
new media objects—can be composed of subordinate uni-
ties.[13] For example, we could say that the *Ghost Writers* of
Traumawien or James Bridle's *A Ship Adrift* combine diverse
cultural elements in order to produce a new artistic work. As
we have seen, by encoding content of distinct natures in a
common fashion, new media objects are intrinsically hybrid.

From Remix to Hauntology

February 24, 2004 was a watershed moment in this history:
the day Danger Mouse's *Grey Album* was circulated online by
fans across the world after being banned by EMI. Bridging
Jay Z's rhythms with the Beatles, Danger Mouse showed the
public a new form of telescoping made possible by digital
music production. When the affiliated record labels largely
decided to drop their charges, this contributed to the recognition of a practice that was already widespread in dance music
circles in the form of remixes and club versions. Certain other
artists pushed this logic of multiple and automatic reference
to its extreme limits. Girl Talk is the most emblematic of this
tendency. Definitively turning his back on a certain artistic ideal of authenticity and uniqueness, each of his albums
or live performances is awash in reams of samples, *All Day*
using 373 in total, stitched together with a frenetic energy.[14]
This inclination toward impromptu associations is found no
less in the visuals accompanying these productions. The latter often contain willfully coarse cut-ups combining extremes
or *détourning* symbols, composing accidental aesthetics.

→ p.79

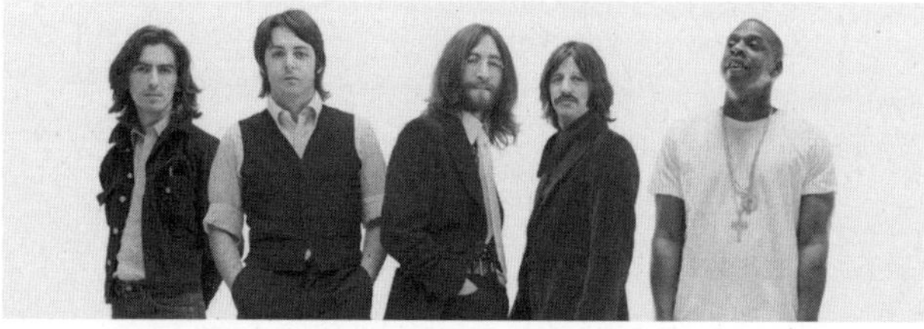

Unknown, *The Beatles and Jay-Z*, 2014
Bridging Jay Z's rhythms with the Beatles (Danger Mouse, *The Grey Album*, 2004), Danger Mouse showed the public a new form of telescoping made possible by digital music production.

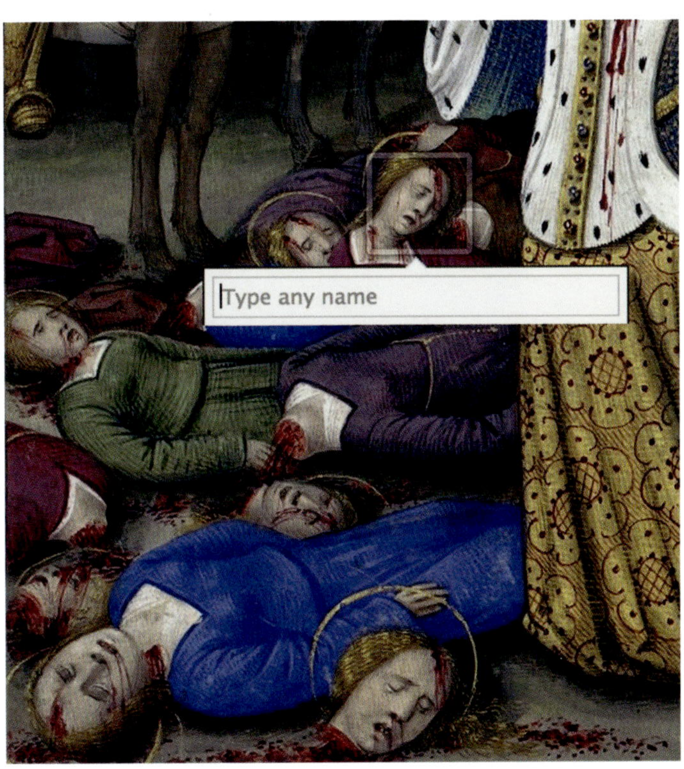

We currently use facial recognition software that uses an algorithm to calculate a unique number ("template") based on someone's facial features, like the distance between the eyes, nose and ears. This template is based on your profile pictures and photos you've been tagged in on Facebook. We use these templates to help you tag photos by suggesting tags of your friends. If you remove a tag from a photo, that photo is not used to create the template for person whose tag was removed. We also couldn't use a template to recreate an image of you.

  Facebook, Tagging Photos, c. 2013

The principle of hybridization comes out of a long tradition in musical, audiovisual, and literary fields. The tendency underwent a popular explosion in the 2000s due to the newfound usage of digital mixing software as well as the unprecedented availability of material provided by the internet, and in particular of specialized blogs. Old and new samples, serious and kitsch versions, hard rock, disco, folk, hip-hop, house, or pop music offer infinite repositories of *genres* on the basis of which new aesthetic directions can be redefined. This tendency for "remixing" can be traced back to Jamaican sound systems[15] and, at the turn of the century, has been particularly significant with the production of bootlegs, also known as mashups. A mashup consists of two or more samples which are combined to form a new sample. Regardless of period or *genre* —the old and the new, the kitsch and the serious, the riffs and the kicks, folk, hip-hop, house, etc.—everything can potentially be combined and generate a new aesthetic direction.

The term mashup has progressively migrated from the musical to the field of Web design, notably with the Web 2.0 culture emerging in the mid 2000s,[16] the accumulation and resurgence within the creative process of fantasmatic traces from the past. Said differently, a "virtual presence"[17] characterizes those "'absent' actors with whom users collaborate through the mediation of technology."[18] For example, a recognizable guitar sample captured in a digital content can give the impression that the musician in fact participated in its creation.[19] The cultural element of a "guitar sample" circulates thus from piece to piece through the mediation of machines. Internet memes and musical mashups constitute interesting examples of processes of hybridization at work in contemporary creation. However, things are advancing further still, since it often happens that these recombinatory operations take place as an effect of the digital programs themselves, without even being consciously intended by their authors. → p.97

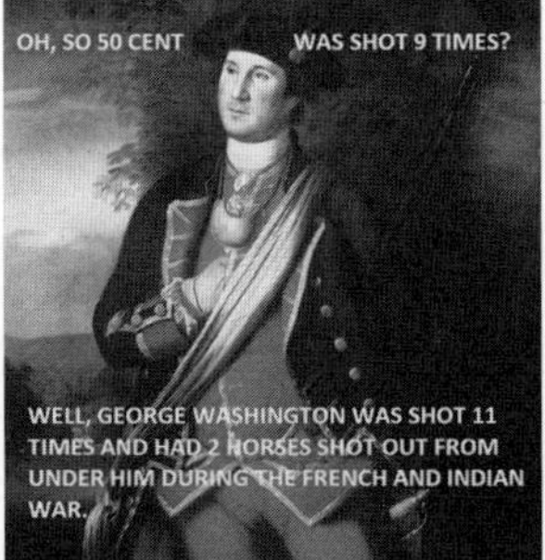

50 cent and George Washington, c. 2010

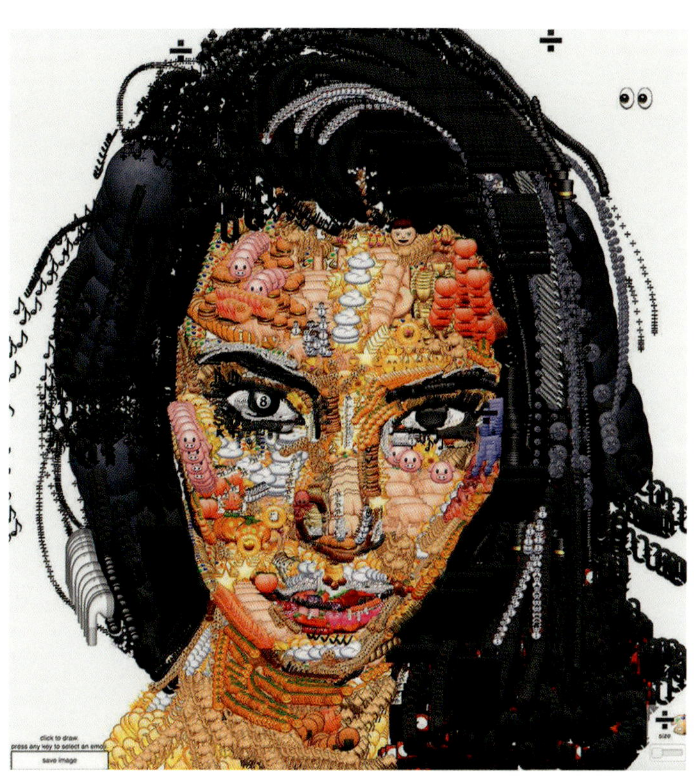

1   Yung Jake, *Emoji Kim Kardashian*, 2015

Emoji Ink is an interactive site by Vince Mckelvie that allows users to use emojis as stamps to draw pictures.

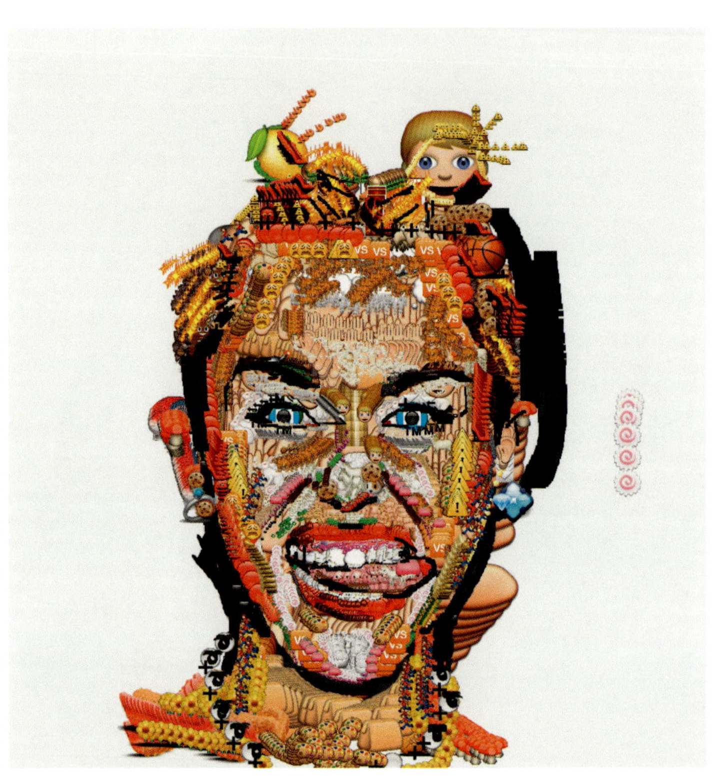

Yung Jake, *Emoji Miley Cyrus*, 2015

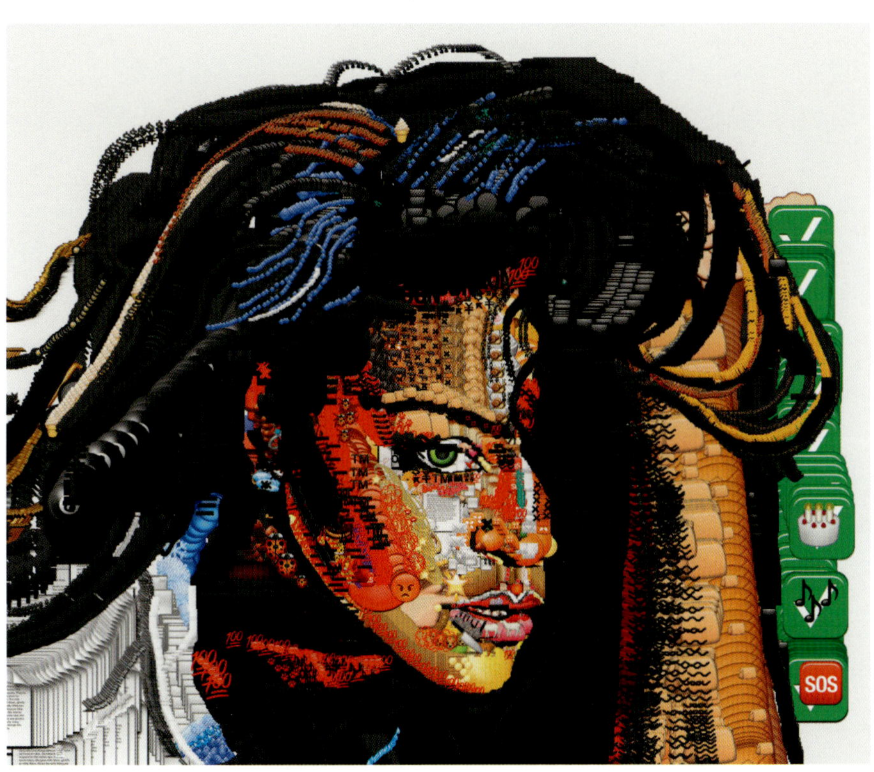

83   Yung Jake, *Emoji Rihanna*, 2015

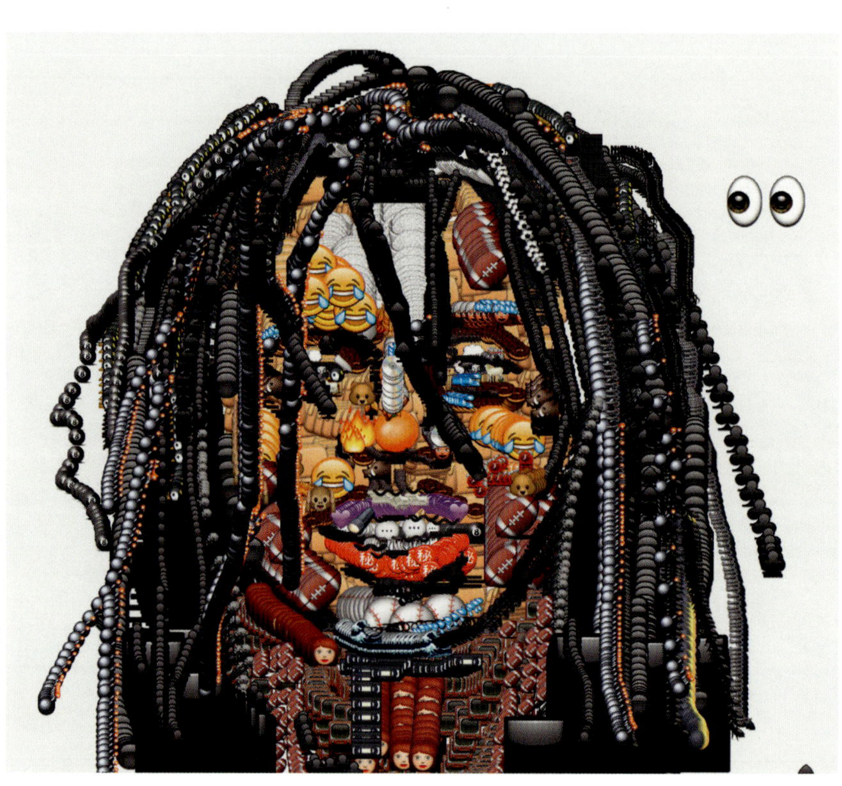

Yung Jake, *Emoji Chief Keef*, 2015

Lexicon

Algorave

"Algoraves focus on humans making and dancing to music. Algorave musicians don't pretend their software is being creative, they take responsibility for the music they make, shaping it using whatever means they have. More importantly the focus is not on what the musician is doing, but on the music, and people dancing to it. Algoraves embrace the alien sounds of raves from the past, and introduce alien, futuristic rhythms and beats made through strange, algorithm-aided processes. It's up to the good people on the dancefloor to help the musicians make sense of this and do the real creative work in making a great party."[1]

Aphex Face

In 1999, Aphex Twin released a 12' called *Windowlicker* on Warp Records. The title track and one songs from the other side called $\Delta Mi{-}1 = -\alpha\Sigma n{=}1NDi[n][\Sigma j{\in}C[i]Fji[n - 1] + Fexti[n{-}1]$, known as *[Equation]* or *[Formula]*, reveals hidden images when they are seen through a spectograph program. The sound spectrum shows a spiral and the second a devilish face that is commonly called *Aphex Face*.

Amen Break

The *Amen Break* is a six-seconds sample that became one of the most iconic examples of the cross-polination in musical productions. It originally appeared in the track *Amen, Brother* (1969) by The Winstons. But the fame started only in 1986, after it was featured in the first *Ultimate Break* compilation and became instantly a key segment in hip-hop and, above all, in breakbeat and drum'n'bass scenes.

Arabix

A term coined by Fatima Al Qadiri to refer to the "large-scale mutation [that] appeared in the 1990s with the advent of text messaging, when people started using the Latin alphabet in conjunction with a set of numbers, to represent consonants that exist in Arabic. For instance, my name is spelled 'Fa6ma,' in Arabix. The '6' represents a consonant that does not exist in English, hence the need to transliterate it via a numerical symbol. I adopted the Catholic 'Fatima' as a Latinate spelling to accommodate the disorientation of non-Arabic speakers."[1]

Balconisation "We are all outside on teh [sic] balcony now. Standing on a platform made out of a tweet into corporate versions of public space. We are not stored in a cloud, opaque or translucent to whomever. We publish, we get read. Ok. Private publishing does not exist, we now know we always get read (hi)." (Constant Dullaart)

Bot A software application that runs automated tasks over the Internet. Typically, bots perform tasks that are both simple and structurally repetitive, at a much higher rate than would be possible for a human alone. Common use of bots range from web spidering (an automated program collect and analyses information from web servers), twitter usage (the program produce tweets based on textual reconfigurations), or Wikipedia editing.

Black MIDI A type of music using the Musical Instrument Digital Interface (MIDI) technical standard to create compositions with a very large numbers of notes only machines could play; which basically means that if you look at the music in the form of standard notation, it looks like almost solid black. Those who compose black MIDI tracks are referred to as "blackers."[3]

Crack "The 'crack' is a point of rupture or a place of chance occurrence, where unique events take place that are ripe for exploitation toward new creative possibilities." (Caleb Kelly)

Creolization The linguistic, and cultural, process that takes place between different cultural elements when they interact and then creatively merge with pre-existing traditions to create totally new and unexpected forms.

Dadabot
A computer program that create the hybridization of various cultural elements, leading to a form of "machinic" creolization. This term also corresponds to a project that explores *Socially Automated Dadaist Music Remix Bots* by CJ Carr.[4]

Database Aesthetics
The role of data, and databases, in creating a new way of experiencing and making art and cultural content

Data Bending
The process by which a digital format is manipulated with tools designed for other formats (e.g. images hacked in a text editor, images edited with audio processors).

Data Moshing
The exploitation of video compression techniques to create visual distortion of movement in digital images and videos.

Entropy Coding
A type of lossless encoding to compress digital data by representing frequently occurring patterns with few bits and rarely occurring patterns with many bits.

Frankenstein mash-up/Frankendesigns
"The 'Frankenstein mashup' is to just take elements of past, present, and future and just collide'em together, in sort of a collage. More or less semi-randomly, like a Surrealist "exquisite corpse'" (Bruce Sterling).

Ghosting
From cathode-ray screen to LCD screen, displays have always present a similar phenomenon called image persistence, image rentention or more comonly ghosting. It happens when the residues of an image (typically a bright image on a black back-

ground) are still visible when a new image replaces it (typically an image with a dark background).

Glitch Art
In a technical sense a glitch is the unexpected result of a malfunction and the designation glitch art may apply to diverse modes of creation, whether in audible or visible forms, that explore the aesthetic potentialities of the irregular fluctuations that happen during the transmission of datas. For Michael Betancourt, "the glitch may serve as an interruption of the aura of the digital's illusion of perfection."

Infomorph
A virtual body of information that can possess emergent features such as personality (Charles Platt).

Interlacing
(Bitmap). Interlacing (also known as interleaving) is a method of encoding a bitmap image such that a person who has partially received it sees a degraded copy of the entire image. When communicating over a slow communications link, this is often preferable to seeing a perfectly clear copy of one part of the image, as it helps the viewer decide more quickly whether to abort or continue the transmission.[7]

Machinic creolization
The process by which machines, among other digital technologies, foster creolization.

Machine humor
A style of humor based on machine-like idioms, machine-generated formulations and syntaxic mistakes. See also "Weird Twitter."

Mimemorph
Twitter bots that learn vocabulary from a specific user (or group of users) and generate new utterances every so often (Henry Cooke).

New Aesthetic

A term, coined by British technologist and artist James Bridle, that refers to the increasing manifestation of computational aspects in everyday life. For instance, in the increasing appearance of the visual language of digital technology and the Internet in the physical world.

Procedural rhetorics

"A type of rhetoric tied to the core affordances of computers: running processes and executing rule-based symbolic manipulation" (Ian Bogost). It refers to the practice of using processes persuasively, for example in video games that rhetorically make arguments through their interactivity.

Transcoding

The conversion for an encoding format to another. This term is also used by new media theorist Lev Manovich to describe how the computer logic has a significant influence on media content: "Since new media is created on computers, distributed via computers, stored and archived on computers, the logic of a computer can be expected to have a significant influence on the traditional cultural logic of media… The result of this composite is the new computer culture: blend of human and computer meanings…" (Lev Manovich).

Robocopyright

The machine-enabled enforcement of copyright on Internet platforms, e.g. Content ID, which is YouTube's system for scanning videos for copyrighted content and giving content owners choices on what they want us to do with them.

Virtual presence

A notion theorized by Basile Zimmermann that refers to the persistence of "absent" actors through the mediation of technology: "People's decisions, choices, mistakes, whatever we choose to call them, are stored within the technology. In turn, users, among them artists, are collaborating with the virtual presence of the (often many) people whose actions have been embodied, temporarily or permanently, inside the tools." (Baslie Zimmerman)

Weird Twitter

"A loosely connected group of Twitter users who are known to experiment with spelling, punctuation and format for humor or poetry. The style of writing can be considered surrealist by participants in the group, with subject matter ranging from creating absurd scenarios to attempting to describe abstract feelings by choosing words for their 'verbal aesthetic appeal.'"[8]

01   algorave.com/about
02   frieze.com/issue/article/future-fictions
03   rhizome.org/editorial/2013/sep/23/impossible-music-black-midi
04   dadabots.tumblr.com
05   wired.com/2010/02/atemporality-for-the-creative-artist
06   *Critical Glitches and Glitch Art*
07   wikipedia.com
08   knowyourmeme.com

A+
A#
Abap
Abc
Action!
ActionScript
Actor
Ada
Afnix
Agena
Aldor
Aleph
Algae
Algo
Algol
Alma-0
Alphard
Altran
AmigaE
Ampl
Ani
Anubis
ApeScript
Apl
AppleScript
APT
Arduino
ARS
Asm.js
AspectJ
ATLAS
Autocode
AutoIt
Averest
Awk
Axiom
Bash
Basic
BAL
BCPL BeanShell
Beta
Bigwig
Bistro
Bliss
Blocky
BODOL
Boo
Bourne shell
Bpel
C--

C++
C#
C Shell
Caché ObjectScript
Caml
Cayenne
Cecil
CeeBot
Ceylon
CFScript
Cg
Charity
CHILL
CHR
Chrome
ChucK.m Cilk
Clarion
Clay
Clean
Clipper
Clojure
Clu
Cobol
CobolScript
Code
CoffeeScript
ColdFusion
Comal
Component Pascal
Comit
Cool
Coral66
Corn
Cowsel
Crack
Csh
See C Shell
Curl
Curry
Cyclone
Databus
Dart
DCL
Delphi
Dibol
Disco
DRAKON
Dylan
ECMAScript
Edinburgh IMP

Eiffel
Elan
elastiC
Elixir
Elm
EGL
Epigram
Erlang
Esterel
Euclid
Euphoria
Euler
Exec
F#
Fabric
Factor
Fantom
Felix
Ferite
FL
Flow-Matic
Focal
Focus
Foil
Forth
Fortran
Fortress
FP
Frink
Gams
Gml
Go
Godiva
Goedel
Gosu
GPSS
Groovy
Hack
Halide
Hal/S
HaScript
Haskell
Heron
HLA
Hugo
HyperTalk
H2o.IALICI
Icon
IDL
IMP

Inform
IPL
Intercal
IO
IswimJ
Java
JavaFX Script
JavaScript
JCL
Jif
Joss
Joule
Jovial
Joy
JSP
JScript
Julia
Jython
Kid
Kiev
Kogut
Kotlin
L.LabView
Lagoona
Lava
Leda
Lexico
Lfyre
Limbo
Linc
LinearML
Lingo
Lingo
Lisaac
Lisp
LISt Processing
LLJS
LLVM
Logo
Lua
Lucid
Lush
Lustre
LYaPAS.M
M#
M4
MAD
Magma
Maple
Mary

Mathematica
Matlab
Mercury
Mesa
Metal
Metro
MicroScript
Mimic
Miranda
Miva
Mixal
ML
Moby
Modula-2
Modula-3
Mondrian
Mortran
Moto
MSIL
Mumps
Napier 88
Nemerle
Nesl
NetRexx
Newspeak
Newsqueak
Ngl
Nial
Nice
Nickle
Nimrod
Noop
Nu
Nosica
O.o:Xml
Oberon
Objective-C
Objective Caml
Objective J
Objective Modula 2
Obliq
OCaml
Occam
Occam-Pi
occam-π
Octave
OOC
Opal
OPL
Ops5
Orc
Oz
Pascal
PBasic
Perl
PHP

Pico
Pike
Pilot
Pizza
PL 11
PL/0
PL/B
PL/C
PL/I
PL/M
Planner
Plankalkül
Pliant
Pop-11
Poplog
Portran
Pov-Ray
Processing
Profan
Prograph
Prolog
P-Tac
Pure
Purescript
Python
QuakeC
QML
QPL
Quorum
R++
Rascal
Ratfiv
Ratfor
RC
Realbasic
Rebol
Red
Refal
Revolution
RPG
RPL
Rexx
Rigal
Rlab
RSL
Ruby
Rust
S2
Sail
SAM76
SAS
Sather
Scala
Scheme
Scratch
Scriptol

Sed
Stream EDitor
Seed7
Self
SETL
Short Code
SimsScript
Simmunity
Simula
SISAL
Slate
Slip
Smalltalk
Snobol
SOAP
Spitbol
SPARK
SP/k
SPL
Squeak
Squirrel
SR
SSL
Standard ML
Subtext
SuperCollider
SuperX++
Swift
SyncCharts
Synergy/DE
TACL
Tacpol
TADS
TAL
Transcript
Tcl
Telcomp
Tempo
Tinn-r
Titanium
TI-Basic
Tom
Tpu
Trac
TTCN-3
Turing
Tutor
TypeScript
TXL
Ubercode
Uncol
Unicon
UnrealScript
UrbiScript
UML
Verilog HDL

VHDL
VDS
Virt
Visual Basic
Visual Basic
VBScript
Water
Whitespace
Winbatch
Wiring
Wolfram
XOTcl
XPL
XL
Xtend
YAFL
Yorick
Z notation
ZPL

Ook. Ook? Ook. Ook. Ook. Ook. Ook. Ook. Ook. Ook. Ook. Ook. Ook. Ook. Ook. Ook. Ook.
Ook. Ook. Ook. Ook! Ook? Ook? Ook. Ook. Ook. Ook. Ook. Ook. Ook. Ook. Ook. Ook. Ook.
Ook. Ook. Ook. Ook. Ook. Ook. Ook. Ook? Ook! Ook! Ook? Ook! Ook? Ook. Ook! Ook. Ook.
Ook? Ook. Ook. Ook. Ook. Ook. Ook. Ook. Ook. Ook. Ook. Ook. Ook. Ook. Ook. Ook! Ook?
Ook? Ook. Ook. Ook. Ook. Ook. Ook. Ook. Ook. Ook. Ook. Ook? Ook! Ook! Ook? Ook! Ook?
Ook. Ook. Ook. Ook! Ook. Ook. Ook. Ook. Ook. Ook. Ook. Ook. Ook. Ook. Ook. Ook. Ook.
Ook. Ook. Ook! Ook. Ook! Ook. Ook. Ook. Ook. Ook. Ook. Ook. Ook! Ook. Ook. Ook? Ook.
Ook? Ook. Ook? Ook. Ook. Ook. Ook. Ook. Ook. Ook. Ook. Ook. Ook. Ook. Ook. Ook. Ook.
Ook. Ook. Ook! Ook? Ook? Ook. Ook. Ook. Ook. Ook. Ook. Ook. Ook. Ook. Ook. Ook? Ook!
Ook! Ook? Ook! Ook? Ook. Ook! Ook. Ook. Ook? Ook. Ook? Ook. Ook? Ook. Ook. Ook.
Ook. Ook. Ook. Ook. Ook. Ook. Ook. Ook. Ook. Ook. Ook. Ook. Ook. Ook. Ook. Ook. Ook.
Ook! Ook? Ook? Ook. Ook. Ook. Ook. Ook. Ook. Ook. Ook. Ook. Ook. Ook. Ook. Ook. Ook.
Ook. Ook. Ook. Ook. Ook. Ook. Ook? Ook! Ook! Ook? Ook! Ook? Ook. Ook! Ook! Ook! Ook!
Ook! Ook! Ook! Ook. Ook? Ook. Ook? Ook. Ook? Ook. Ook? Ook. Ook! Ook. Ook. Ook. Ook.
Ook. Ook. Ook. Ook! Ook. Ook! Ook! Ook! Ook! Ook! Ook! Ook! Ook! Ook! Ook! Ook! Ook!
Ook! Ook. Ook! Ook! Ook! Ook! Ook! Ook! Ook! Ook! Ook! Ook! Ook! Ook! Ook! Ook! Ook!
Ook! Ook! Ook. Ook. Ook? Ook. Ook? Ook. Ook. Ook! Ook.

An esoteric programming language (sometimes shortened to esolang) is a programming language designed to test the boundaries of computer programming language design, as a proof of concept, as software art, or as a joke. The use of esoteric distinguishes these languages from programming languages that working developers use to write software. Usually, an esolang's creators do not intend the language to be used for mainstream programming, although some esoteric features, such as visuospatial syntax, have inspired practical applications in the arts.

 "Hello World" in *Ook!*, c. 2015

Ook! is an esoteric programming language designed to be understood by Orangutans. It is derived from Brainfuck with a reduced syntax.

The Advent of the Bots

We are all used to modifying photographs, or adding a sound-track to a video with digital programs. These are fairly straight-forward cases of hybridization. However, it is increasingly common for these processes to be automated. For example, we use software whose algorithms gather and optimize the contrasts and contours of faces in photographs that we take on our smartphones. Once launched by their users, such software automatically calculates the optimal levels according to preset parameters put in place by their programmers.

In the field of culture, "software automation" is used more and more to carry out repetitive tasks, which can thus be accelerated. Sometimes, they operate in a highly discreet manner, as in the case of Wikipedia, where they carry out an increasingly variegated set of typographical, syntactical and semantic modifications. Hence the updates and links between articles that continually augment the collaborative encyclopedia.[20] Even if these sorts of interventions into contents may appear elementary, the progress made in the automatic generation of text is palpable. Reports prepared by the bots are longer and more precise all the time. Their applications extend far beyond financial statistics, and we are presently witnessing the appearance of more in-depth analysis, particularly in the domain of sports. This integral automation of content production constitutes the second defining mechanism of dadabots.

Bot progamming language

Twitterbots, the conversational agents[21] used in the social networking site, offer yet another even more current example. Numerous accounts on the social network generate absurd, comedic, or poetic messages. The term "Weird Twitter" is generally used to refer to the vast ensemble of accounts

→ p.101

Zoey @zoey_l4d • 8 janv. 2009
Too right, @bill_l4d. That was fun. We should do that again sometime.

Bill @bill_l4d • 8 janv. 2009
Damnit @francis_l4d, you should be more gragteful – at least we're being regularly maintainted.

Francis @francis_l4d • 8 janv. 2009
Thanks, @zoey_l4d
Voir la traduction
11:50 - 13 déc. 2008 • Détails

Zoey @zoey_l4d • 8 janv. 2009
In memory of @louis_l4d. and @francis_l4d.

Zoey @zoey_l4d • 8 janv. 2009
Get your ass into the house @bill_l4d.

Louis @louis_l4d • 13 déc. 2008
I've got you, @francis_l4d.

Tom Armitage, *Twit 4 dead*, 2008

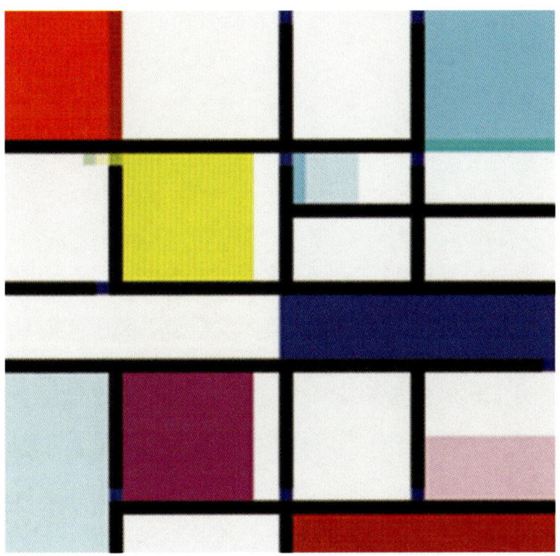

An esoteric programming language is a programming language designed to test the boundaries of computer programming language design, as a proof of concept, as software art, or as a joke. Such languages are often popular among hackers and hobbyists. Usability is rarely a goal for esoteric programming language designers—often it is quite the opposite. Their usual aim is to remove or replace conventional language features while still maintaining a language that is Turing-complete, or even one for which the computational class is unknown.

 David Morgan-Mar, *Piet,* 1990–ongoing

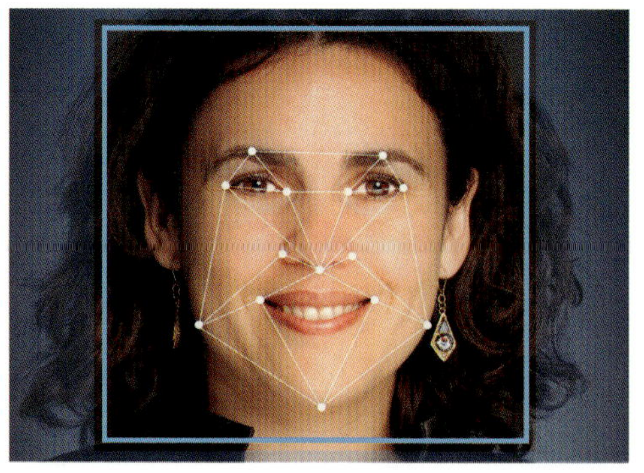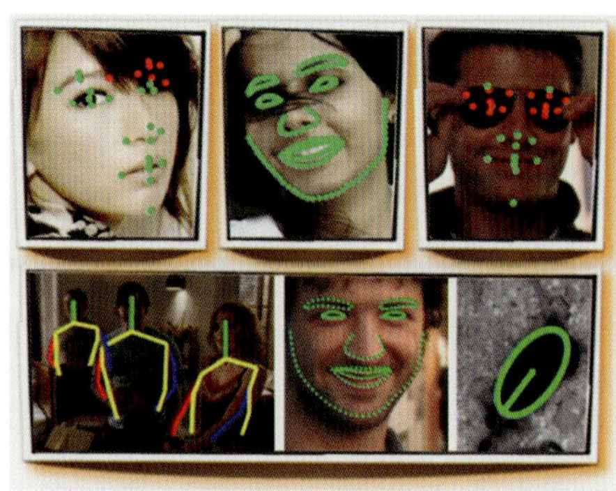

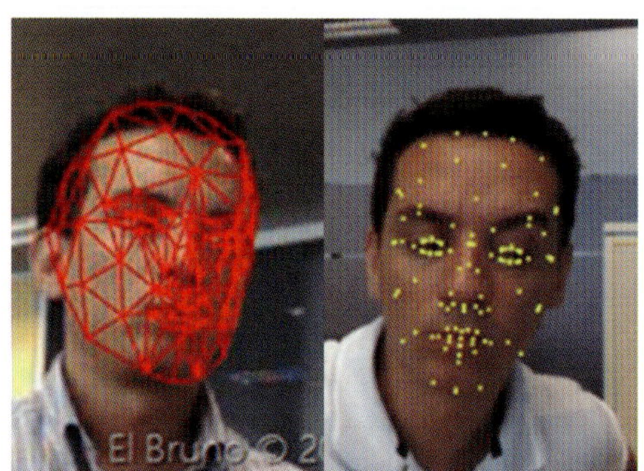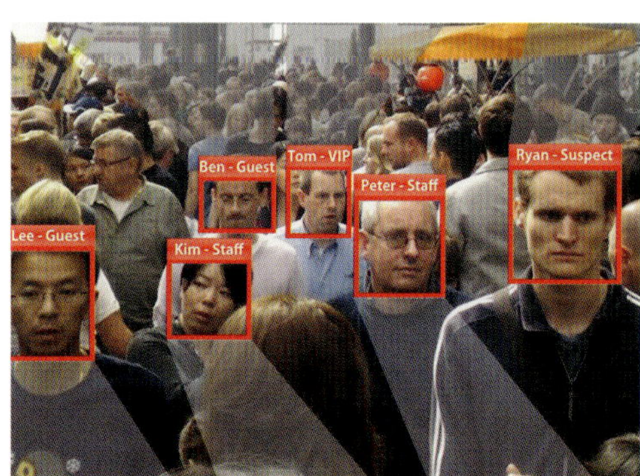

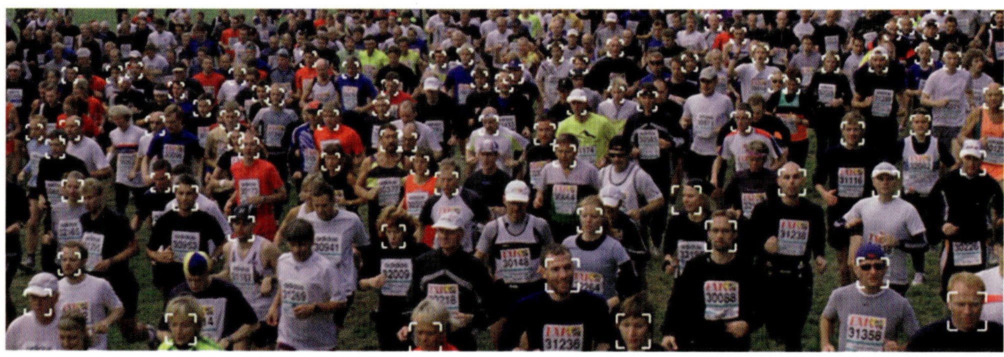

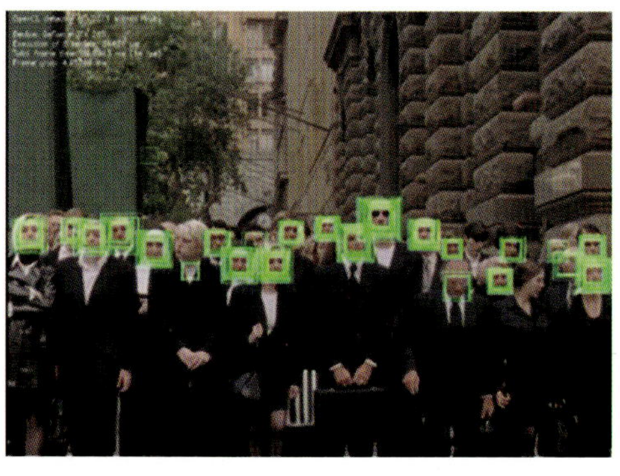

A number of innovations in facial recognition continue to get large press coverage in the prevailing securitarian milieus. The discourse asserting the necessity of such apparatuses has consolidated itself in the wake of the Boston Marathon attacks. One of the noteworthy features of the latter investigation was the extremely poor quality of the visual traits, which made the suspect illegible by the conventional recognition apparatuses. It is precisely on this type of situation that experts in soft biometrics have subsequently concentrated their research. The actual algorithms can draw from the system's experience and reconstruct an approximation of a face based on patterns within facial images, with as little as six pixels between the eyes of a suspect.

Soft biometrics for face recognition, c. 2015

that toy with typographical and syntactical microblogging codes.[22] Occasionally it even happens that multiple bots enter into conversation amongst themselves. *Tom Armitage* realized as much when he created four bots based on characters from the game *Left for Dead*.[23] Unfolding before the reader's eyes is the text version of a sort of strange play in which the characters express themselves, help each other out or are wounded just as they are in the game.

This logic of bot programming extends to many other ventures beyond just Twitter. *The Death of the Authors* by Constant V Z W (2013) is a combinatory literature project that automatically generates novels based on the texts of James Joyce, Henri Bergson, or Virginia Wolff. With a single click on their website one can generate phrase combinations drawn from these classic works. Multiple musical projects are also moving in this direction. To mention just one, *Dadabot*[24] selects pieces automatically generated on the basis of preexisting cultural elements.

In the field of photography, *Every Face in the Americans*[25] by Dafydd Hughes (2010) modifies the work of Robert Frank, extracting from it only the faces detectable by iPhoto's facial recognition system, which incidentally results in the disappearance of several of the portraits. In Ed Key and David Kanaga's video game *Proteus*, a subjective point of view explores a richly colored island in which each component of the universe as well as the movement of the creatures deployed therein is generated piecemeal in an randomly fashion by a program, including even the soundtrack, which is assembled following the movements of the protagonist. The experience it generates is singular, and more contemplative than rhythmic.

→ p.107

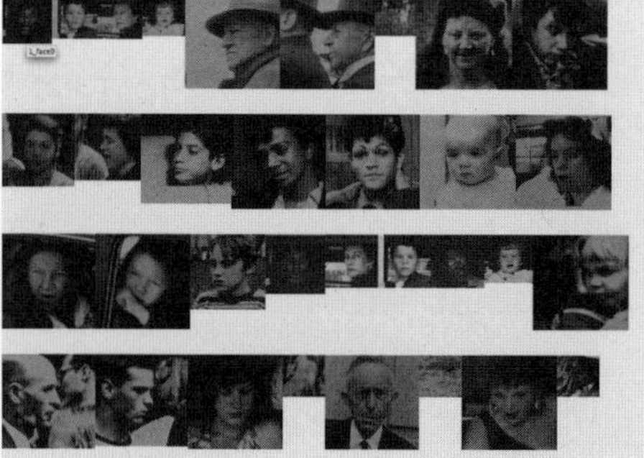

Robert Frank, *Every Face in The Americans*, 2012
Faces from photographs selected by Iphoto

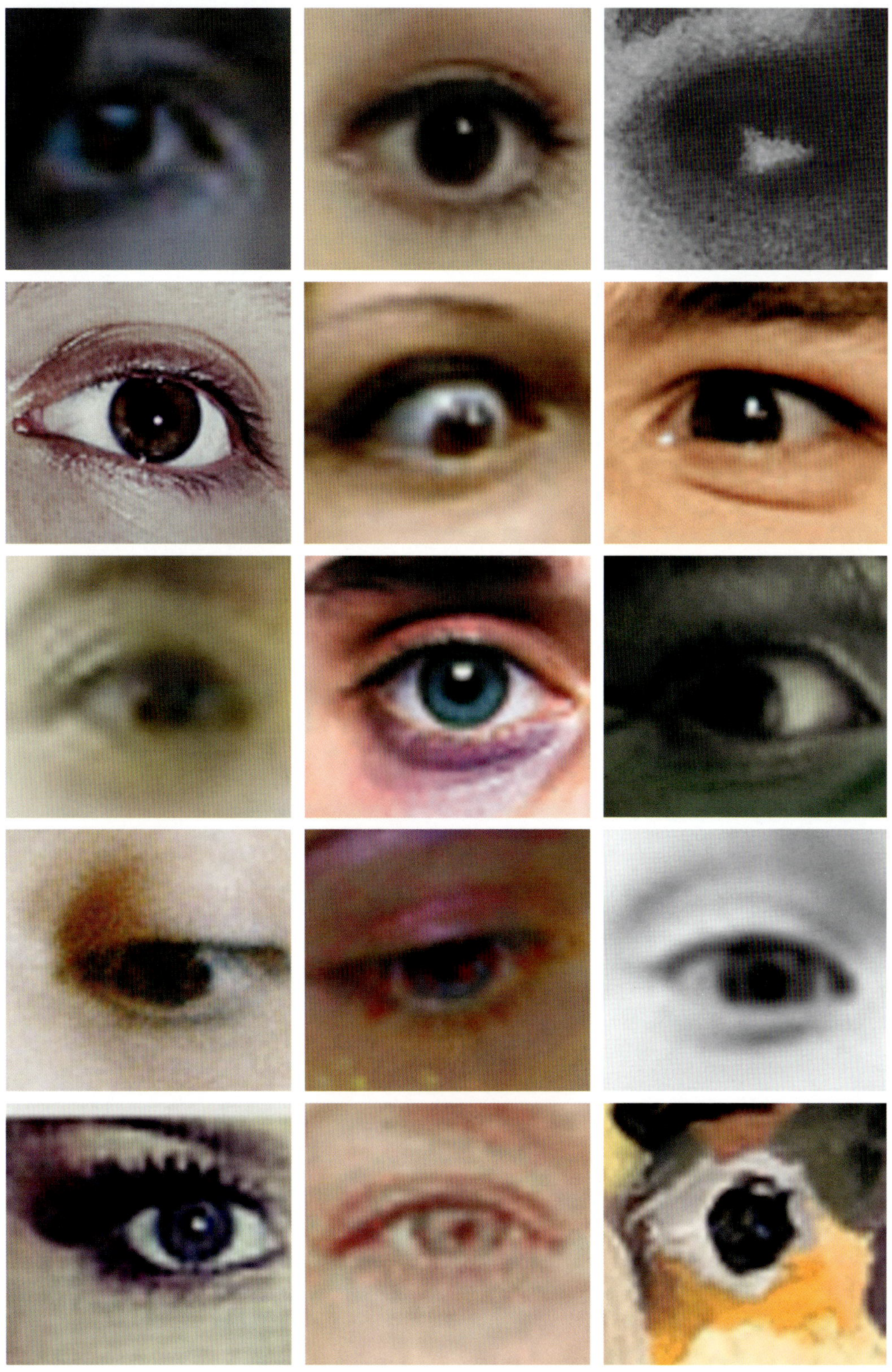

 Matthew Plummer-Fernandez, *All Eyes*, 2014– ongoing. The project software downloads eyes images tagged with metadata such as "selfie," "portrait" and "face," and uses computer vision to detect the presence of faces, cropping the image around the most notable eye.

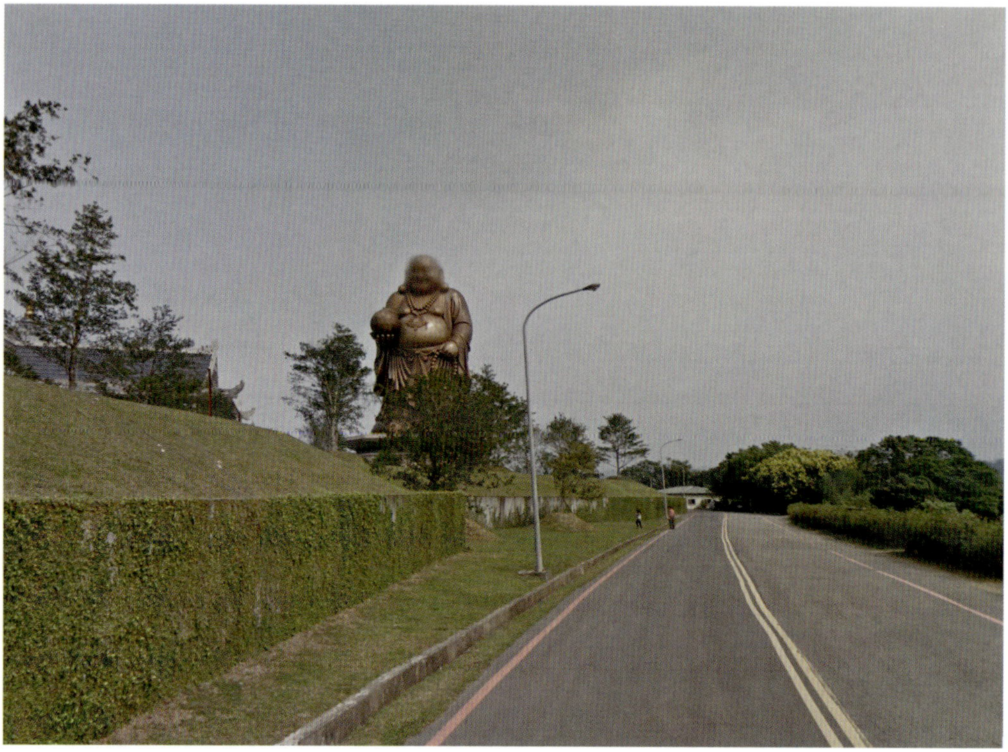

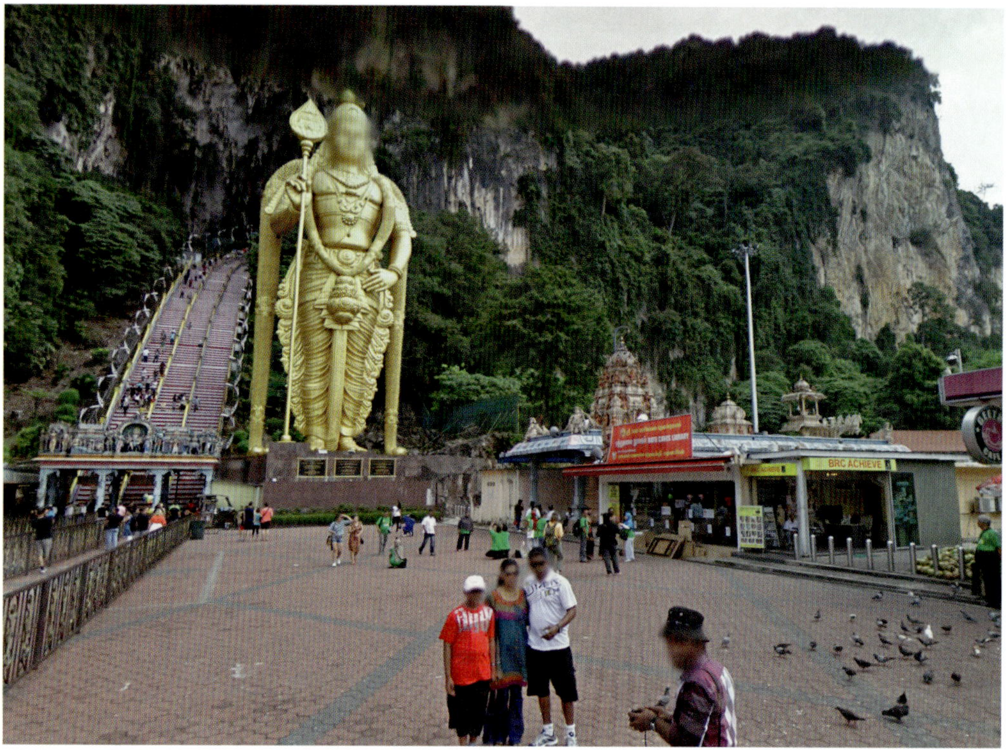

Marion Balac, *Anonymous Gods*, 2014

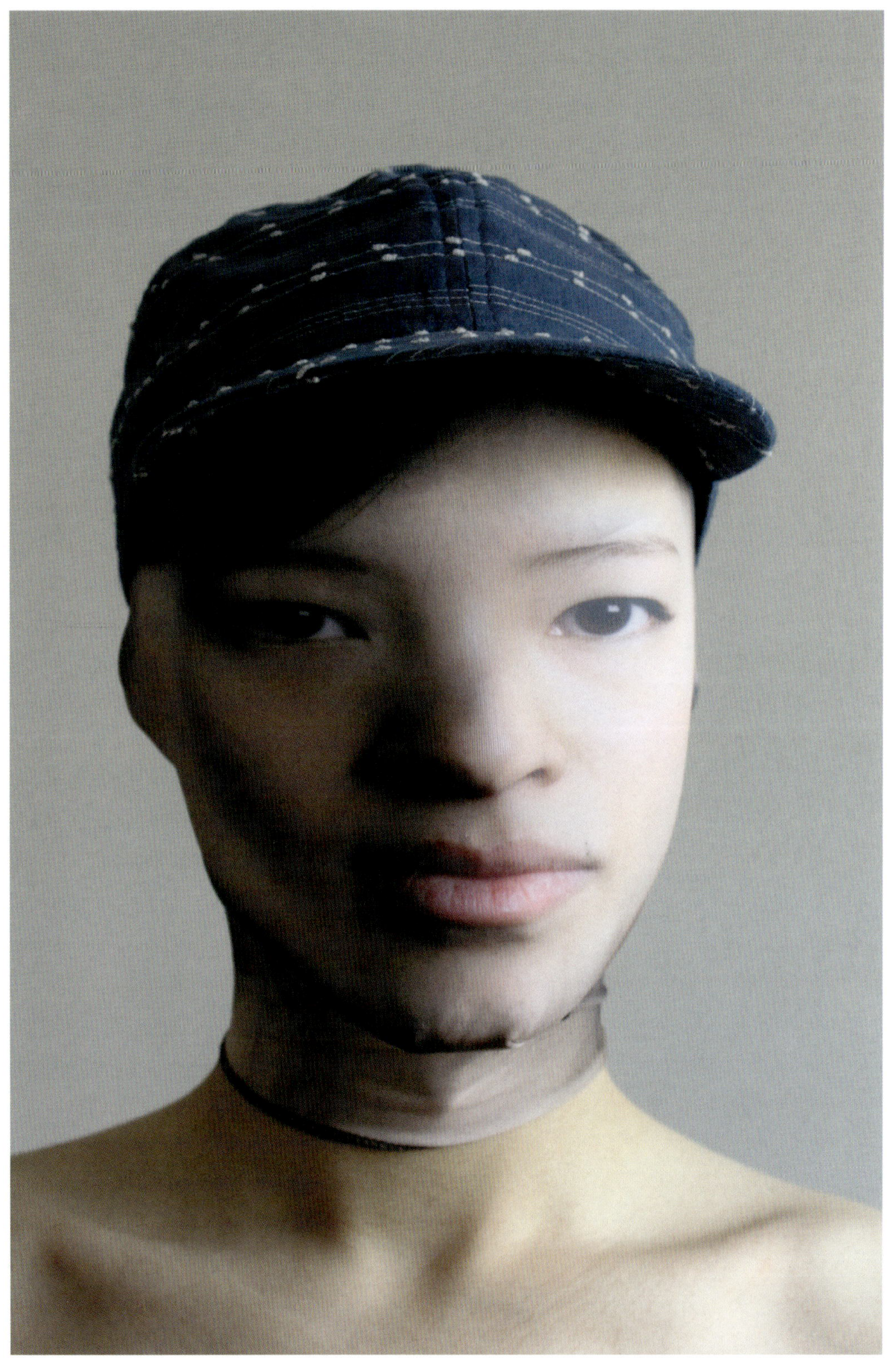

05   My-Lan Hoang-Thuy, Face printed on a cowl, 2014

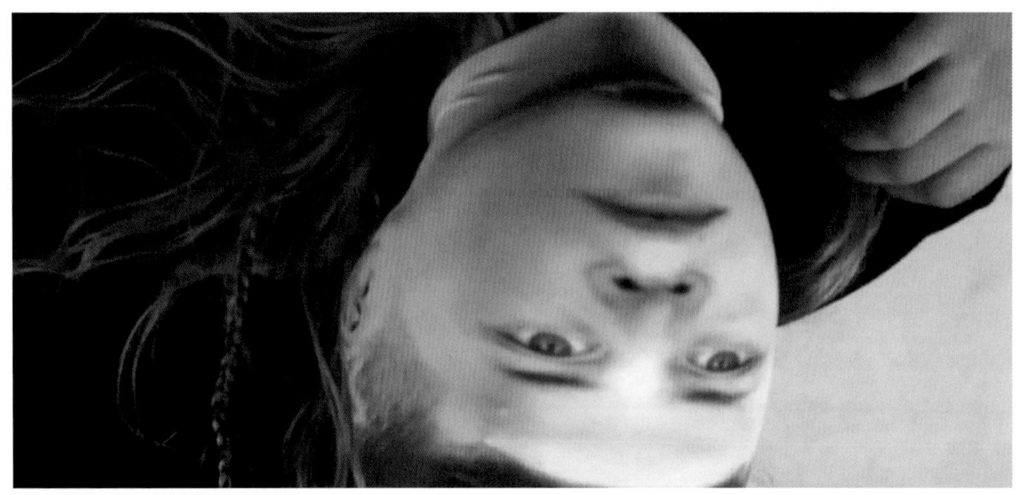
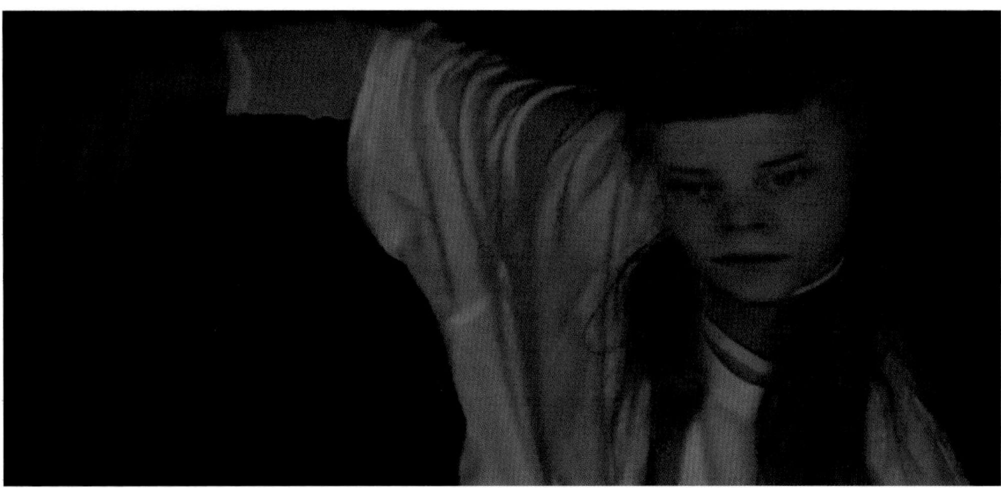
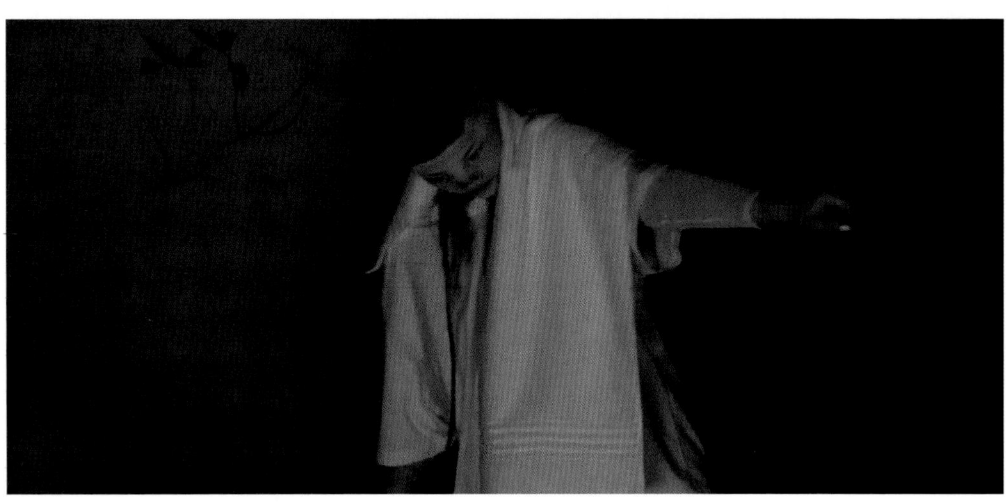

My-Lan Hoang-Thuy, Yung Lean, *Volt* (video stills), 2014

Generative Culture

Whether scheming, cryptic or mischievous, though these projects may not always be coherent, they are emblematic of a digital culture constructed from the fragments of pre-existing cultural elements. Regardless of their beauty or harmony, such explorations serve above all to highlight the place of processes and tools of chance in the production and diffusion phases. Such experimentation figures routinely in generative art, i.e. content produced automatically by digital programs.[26] Think, for example, of Brian Eno's *Generative Music 1* with SSEYO Koan Software, the title of which makes mention of the program used to produce it. The same is true of texts automatically generated by French author Jean-Pierre Balpe, whether they be novels (*Trajectoires*), operas (*Trois mythologies et un poète aveugle*), or poems (*Technopoèmes*[27]). The algorithmic musical programs designed by David Cope allow one to analyze recurrent motifs within existing compositions and to use them as a base for modeling new symphonic compositions. Although a wide array of such works have appeared over the past forty years,[28] the main difference today lies in the profusion of data accessible through digital networks. The latter forms a potentially infinite matrix from which it is possible to randomly and indefinitely generate new contents.

Variability

Another characteristic of these algorithmic cultures, and in particular those of new media, derives from the fact that every cultural object can potentially undergo an array of modifications.[29] Depending on the cultural field in question, the author, the designer, the composer, the graphic designer, the architect or even the user can modify cultural elements. Changing the words to a song or the colors of a painting, speeding-up a musical sample, adjusting filters on Instagram, etc., → p.123

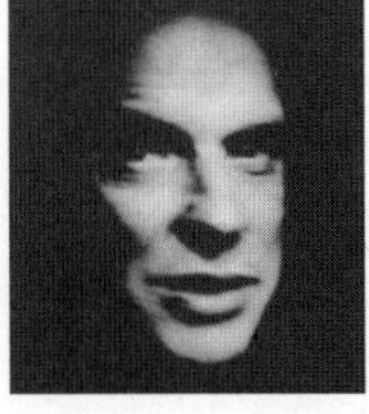

Brian Eno, *Generative Music 1*, 1996

Motern Media, Matt Farley

Matt Farley applies the principle of the long tail theory for his creative process. His concept is simple. If you write a song about every kind of topics, ranging from childish words to scientific research, it will always have a tiny ratio of people who will make a research with this words and, potentially, buy the song. Under more than 70 different aliases, he wrote around 17,000 songs, with names like Barack Obama Farts, Papaphobia, Gotta Poop, Puke & Pee (Simultaneously), Boston Girls are Wicked Awesome or The Greatest Guinea Pig Song Ever Made, all available on Spotify. He recently declared he would continue his prolific songwriting until 2018, when he will have reached 20,000 songs.

Q: How do you proceed to make a song?
A: I make lists of topics for each album. Then I make a song for each topic. If the song is just piano/vocals, I often make up the music and lyrics as I'm recording. For more complicated songs, I will prepare the music and lyrics.
Q: Do you make improvisation?
A: Yes, many of the songs are improvised. But not all. It's probably 60% of songs are improvised and the rest are prepared.
Q: What is the place of softwares in your creative process?
A: I use a Tascam 24-track digital recorder.
Q: Do you rely on presets?
A: When I write a new song, I sometimes use the music tracks again on songs for other albums, where I'll sing new lyrics over the old music.
Q: How long does it take to make a single track?
A: Anywhere between 5 minutes and 1 hour.
Q: How do you manage to be so prolific?
A: I simply force myself to keep producing more and more songs. Instead of sleeping late or watching TV, I make music!

Liste of Motern media artists

Moes Haven
Papa Razzi and The Photogs
The Passionate & Objective Jokerfan
The Toilet Bowl Cleaners
The Singing Animal Lover
The Singing Film Critic
The Paranormal Song Warrior
The Hungry Food Band
The Vampire & Werewolf Experience
The Strange Man Who Sings About Dead Animals
The Guy Who Sings Songs About Cities & Towns
The Guy Who Sings Your Name Over and Over
The Family Party Song Singers
The Best Birthday Song Band Ever
The Smokin' Hot Babe Lovers
The Very Very Awesome Song Band
The Best Friend Song Fun Band
The Wedding Proposal Music Song Band
The Prom Song Singers
General Cordswainer
The Athletic Sports Band
The Atlanta Sports Band
The Baltimore Sports Band
The Boston Baseball Band

The Boston Basketball Band
The Chicago Sports Band
The Cincinnati Sports Band
The Cleveland Sports Band
The Detroit Sports Band
The Extreme Left Wing Liberals
The Farley Flower Band
The FL Love Song Warriors
The Green Bay & Milwaukee Sports Band
The Los Angeles Sports Band
The MA Love Song Warriors
The Miami Sports Band
The Minnesota Sports Band
The Name Project
The New England Football Band
The New Orleans Sports Band
The New York Sports Band
The New York Sports Fan
The NH Love Song Warriors
The Oklahoma City Sports Band
The Philadelphia Sports Band
The Pittsburgh Sports Band
The RI Love Song Warriors
The River Mud Warriors
The San Diego Sports Band
The San Francisco Sports Band
The Seattle Sports Band
The Singing Texas Sports Fan
The Spoiled Chefs
The Sports Band of Denver, Colorado
The Sports Band of Indianapolis, Indiana
The Sports Band of Phoenix, Arizona
The St. Louis Sports Band
The Ultra Right Wing Conservatives
The Washington Sports Band
The Birthday Band For Old People
The Sorry Apology Song Person
The Boston Sports Band of New England
The Odd Man Who Sings About Poop, Puke, and Pee
The Very Nice Interesting Singer Man
The Great Weather Song Person
The Motern Media Holiday Singers
Projection From The Side

Interview with Holly Herndon

Q1: Where did you study and what are the important moments /experiences that influenced your approach?
A: Most recently I am pursuing a doctorate in the music department at Stanford University, working closely with CCRMA (the Center for Computer Research in Music and Acoustics). Prior to that I studied an MFA in Electronic Music at Mills College—both places have incredible histories, and are distinct in their experimentalism—which has been and continues to be a great influence on my work (and confidence). That being said, a great deal of my ideas and inspirations have been borne out of simple and lengthy participation in independent musical cultures. School has afforded me resources and support in refining my work, however the seeds of many of the things I am attempting to pursue began to germinate at noise shows and clubs. I really don't think there is any substitute for participation. While I was living in Berlin, there was a resurgence of interest in experimental and abstract music (particularly noise), and it has been interesting to see how subtle differences in interest have matured into gulfs of focus in the work of many of the artists active at the time.

Q2: San Francisco has a very strong history in experimental music. How does this legacy shape the actual soundscape of the city, what is special about being a musician in SF?
A: I won't lie, it is very hard to be a musician in SF. It has become one of the most expensive cities in the world and there is an intense land crush as a result of the booming tech industry (and idiosyncratic local laws). So many artists have been pushed out. If you don't have a professional or academic reason to be here, it makes a lot more sense to go to a place like NY or LA, where there is such an established cultural infrastructure and far more opportunities for artists to build a name for themselves. That being said, because of the odd confluence of advanced technological research and brain trust in

the Bay Area, the artists that do make it central to their practice tend to be pretty incredible—and really distinct from artists from other parts of the world. In that sense it can be greatly inspiring, if a little isolating. There is a huge legacy of people producing groundbreaking work here, and in my experience the place fosters a wonderfully approachable and welcoming form of intellectualism. California can be it's own special kind of smart. On the flip side, there is the reality that in order to maintain a presence on a global level in something like the music industry, I need to sit on a plane for over ten hours regularly, sometimes multiple times a month. It's a privilege, and a sometimes exhausting juggling act. There are many artists I have known in the Bay Area who have unfairly suffered from this lack of proximity to the critical aspects of the art world, and so being in SF necessitates being a nomad.

Q3: To what extend groundbreaking propositions by pioneers like Donna Haraway or Pauline Oliveros and/or others, affected your generation of female artists?
A: I cannot speak for anyone but myself. I am definitely familiar with many people taking inspiration from Pauline's work, less so Donna Haraway—which may change over time, and is necessary—if only to push past this common characterization that there is anything useful to the observation that many different artists and individuals happen to have been born female. I find Haraway's work most interesting in it's capacity for liberation from gender classification, with a focus on the hybrid/cyborg identities that we choose to construct.

Q4: You were recently invited to take part to *Ada Project* that consisted in the creation of musical pieces that use a robot as a primary source of inspiration. Could you tell us more about this project?
A: My collaboration with Conrad Shawcross actually took place in June 2013, however it has been shown in multiple iterations since. Ada Lovelace is considered by many to have

developed the first computer algorithm. Conrad and his team have constructed a system whereby a robot is able to perform set choreographies to music composed by guests. I composed a piece that attempted to augment and abstract the mechanical sounds of the physical movements in homage to Lovelace's own augmentation of the mechanical device she was presented with.

Q5: More generally, what is your position regarding auto generated compositions? Do you have some artists or specific projects that you find are opening interesting perspectives in this way?

A: I feel there is still a place for it. A lot of work has already been done exploring the generative and recursive possibilities of digital music, and so I tend to switch off a little when that is the primary focus of the exploration—as often it tends to illustrate little more than the emergence of pleasing patterns and symmetry. I do think that auto generated techniques can be amazing in the creation of a palette, in much the same way that free improvization can bring forward suggestions that you may not have considered had everything been meticulously planned out. I think it begins to get interesting when the automation itself assumes some form of critique—my regular collaborator Mathew Dryhurst developed a system where he can automatically construct compositions from his daily browsing experience, in the form of an economic critique on both the contemporary necessity of artists having a day job, and also the implicit work involved with participating in the internet. In a similar vein the artist Jonas Lund has done a lot of amazing work in automating the production of art works in accordance with trend analysis, as a critique of the formulaic nature of transactions and tropes in the art world. Lars TCF Holdhus is also doing some interesting work with algorithmic processes, and automating his own musical output and presence online. A lot of culture is served to us as a process of targeted automation, and so it is a very pregnant field for exploration.

Q6: I have been lucky to assist at your performance in the St. Johns Church in London. The way you played with the acoustic of the place was really impressive. What role plays the spatial dimension in your approach?

A: Well that was a very special show, and special space! I have done a fair amount of work involving spatialization, ambisonics and such—and it is something I find interesting to explore as I have always been drawn to the physicality of live music. It is challenging, as even if you are privileged enough to be able to write pieces for multichannel arrangements, it is rare to get the opportunity to present them—as most venues are simply not equipped to do it. In this sense I would find it hard to make it a primary focus of my work as it limits the ability for the public to engage with it. One major theme of my work is empathy and direct communication, which is part of the reason I am so focused on using the human voice, and so while I may pursue such ideas for research purposes I am concerned about rarifying my work to the extent that most people have no way to experience it.

As a computer musician, my instrument does not end at my soundcard, instead the speakers become an extended part of the instrument. This varies dramatically from place to place, so I like to take my time and figure out the sound of the room. Often the places i play were not designed for a live microphone—ie a function one stack facing my head :P So it can involve some maneuvering with the sound engineer. My friends Scott Arford and Randy Yau have a project called Infrasound where they play the acoustics of a room, it find the nodes and resonate them according to a score. I appreciate this performance because while initially it appears to be a dry computer music performance—two serious looking dudes typing on a computer—it quickly becomes very physical and intimate. They resonated my friend's bra off one time :)

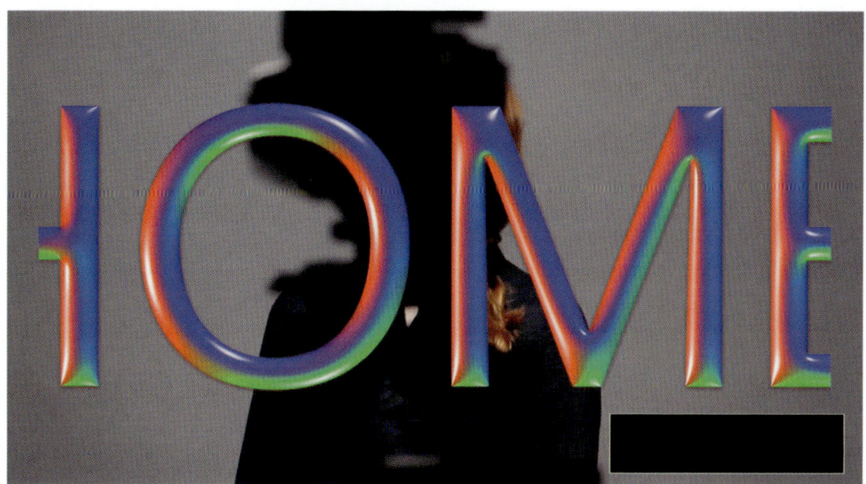

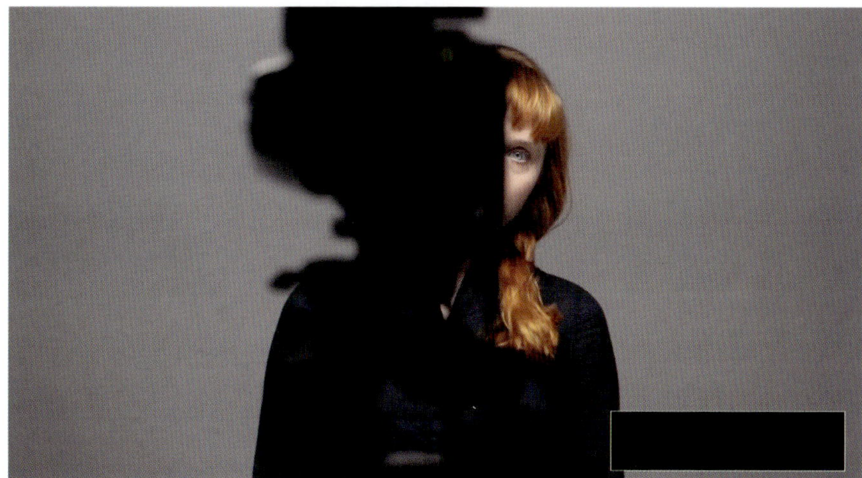

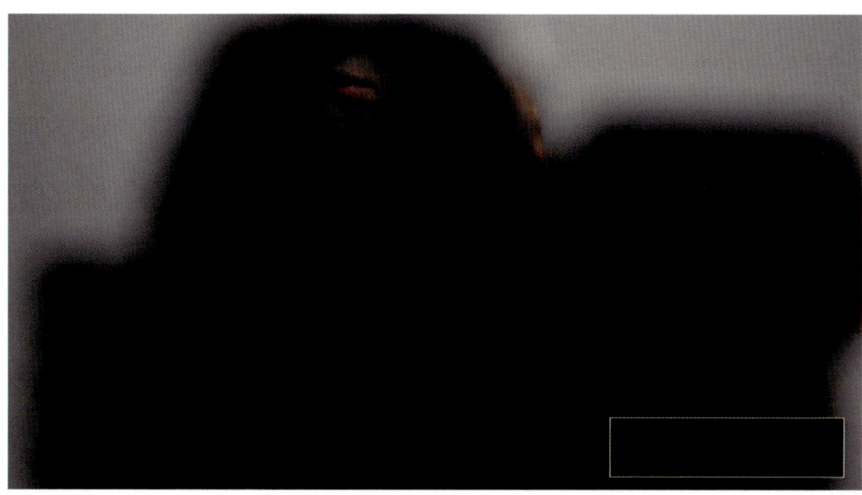

5   Holly Herndon (in collaboration with Metahaven), *Home* (video stills), 2014

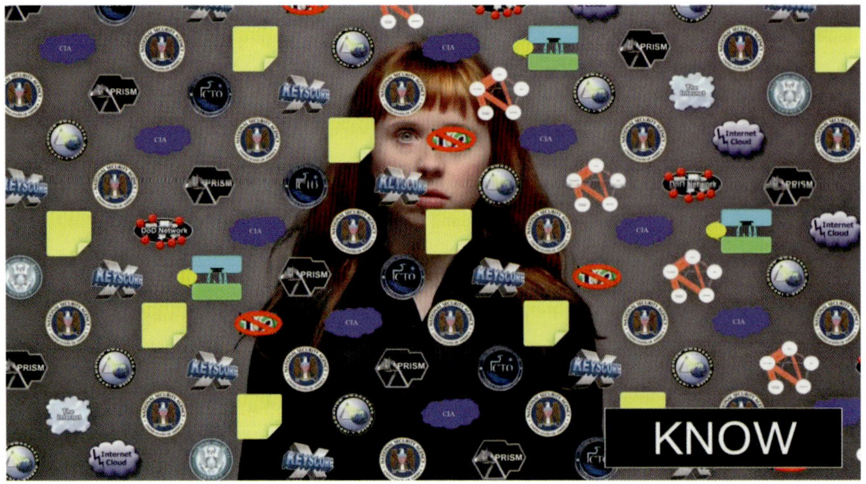

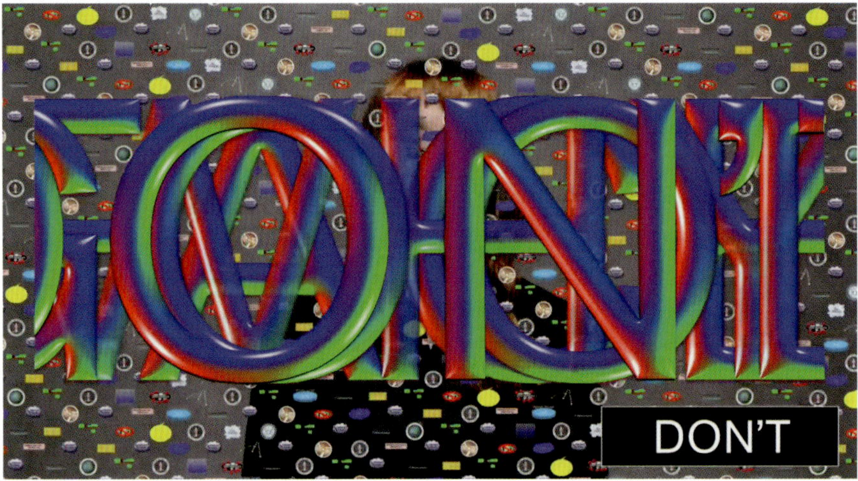

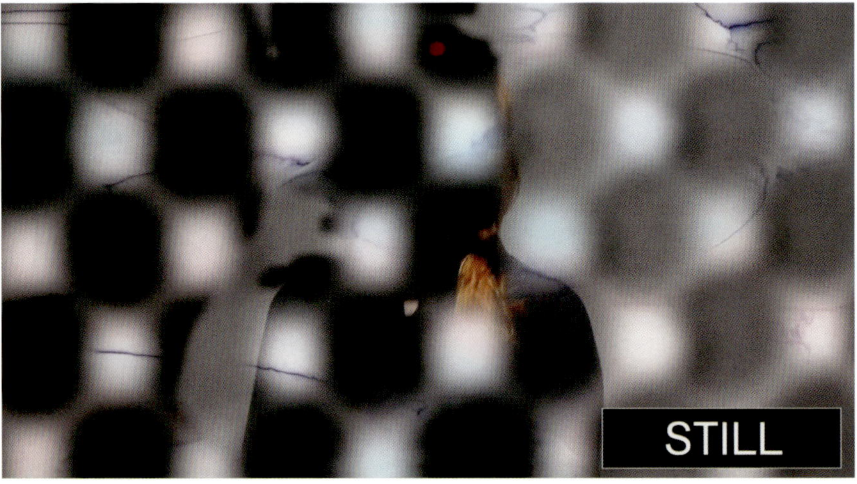

Holly Herndon (in collaboration with Metahaven), *Home* (video stills), 2014

Q7: The photographer Trevor Paglen recently stated: "I think about a 'script' as the basic and obvious function of an imaging system, its 'style' of seeing, and the immediate relationships (between seer and seen, for example) it produces, and the obvious ways in which a seeing machine sculpts the world. To put it crudely, a script is all of those things that a given seeing machine 'wants' to do, how it 'wants' to see the world, and how it does what it's designed to do." There are a lot of debates about diapositives that intensifies the automatisation of the visual regime but what are the "scripts" and the styles of contemporary Sounding Machines? or paraphrasing the title of Mitchell's book, What do Sounds Want?

A: That's a new question for me! It's interesting to contrast visual imaging technologies with sound recording technologies, in so much as there is far less utility ascribed to sound recording—the technologies that Paglen (who is incredible BTW) refers to have limited sonic analogs, to my knowledge. The closest analog I can think of are things like the the linear predictive coding algorithms that services like Skype use to be able to discern speech from cluttered signals. I was just recently asked to produce a response to Paul Lansky's *More Than Idle Chatter* which originally utilized this technique, and thought it was prescient in the sense that "Chatter" is a term used in signals intelligence regarding the amount of communications intercepted by surveilling bodies. In this treatment, sounding machines are looking for the voice, which can be used to generate empathy or facilitate suspicion. I have been doing a lot of self surveillance/sousveillance, using Mat's techniques and my own, as I do think that it is important to develop an understanding of the logics behind these dragnet technologies, and perhaps also uncover their potential for resistance.

Q8: Could you describe your engagement regarding the political and philosophical dimension of sounds/noise?

A: This is something I have been thinking about a great deal.

An appropriation and absorption have occurred, where despite the fact that we live in a time that is open to very abstract sounds, it seems like the radical agenda or momentum behind such ideas has disappeared. I can not remember a time when music felt so politically inconsequential. This is a topic worthy of a book, rather than a paragraph, however my first inkling in how to address such a condition is to simply alter my practice to become more collaborative, working with artists and other groups who are politically engaged and open to at least attempt to restore some political significance to the field. My work with Metahaven has been hugely invigorating, as a large aspect to their practice was also addressing the problematic of inconsequentiality in their own field of design. What I am convinced about, though, is that in order for music to assume such a transformative role, it must adapt and respond to the conditions and media relevant to the time—I think we have accomplished all we can accomplish through the affectations of loud guitar music as we know it, ghettoized subcultures from the 80s and intellectualized rave melancholy. New challenges call for new strategies, and one only has to look towards Wikileaks to understand that projects that internalize and exploit the radical potential of new infrastructures and behaviorisms can catalyze remarkable results of political significance. Music has a long way to go—the first step will be to disenthrall ourselves with the noble, but failed experiments of the past half century. We need to talk about money, we need to identify a new audience and new ways to engage with them, and not patronize others and ghettoize ourselves. New ways to love.

Q9: And, how does utopia sound like?
A: I think i'll leave it at the last question :)

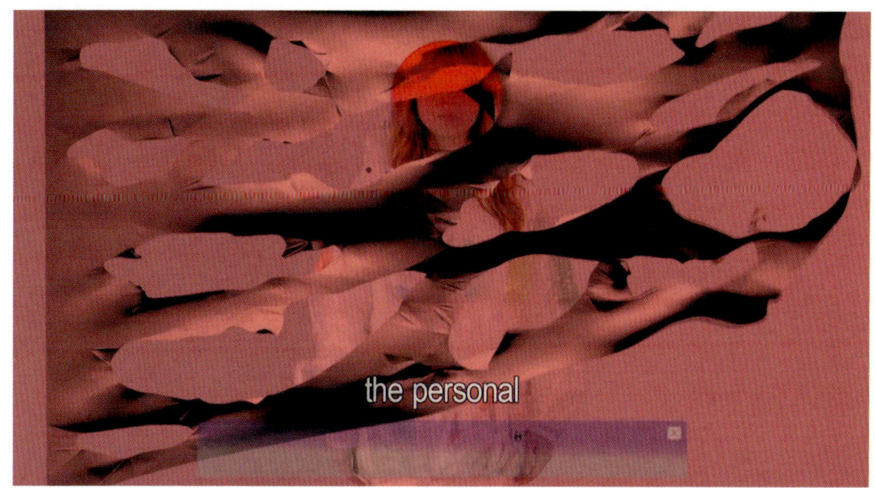

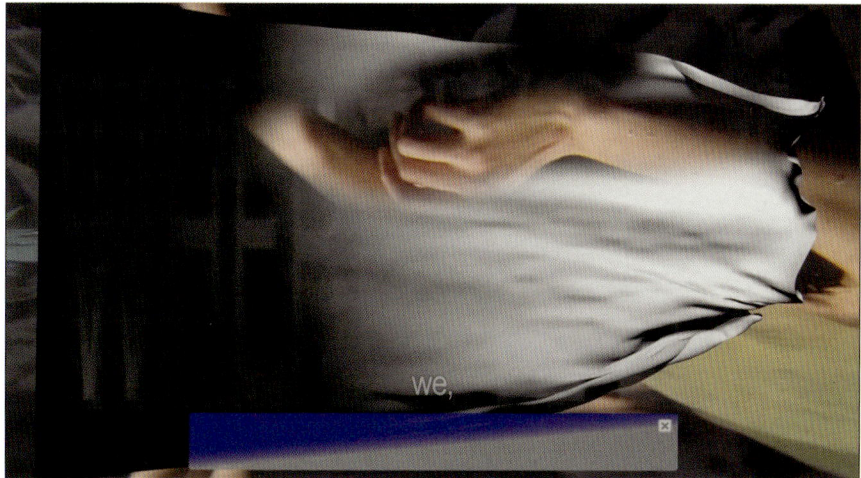

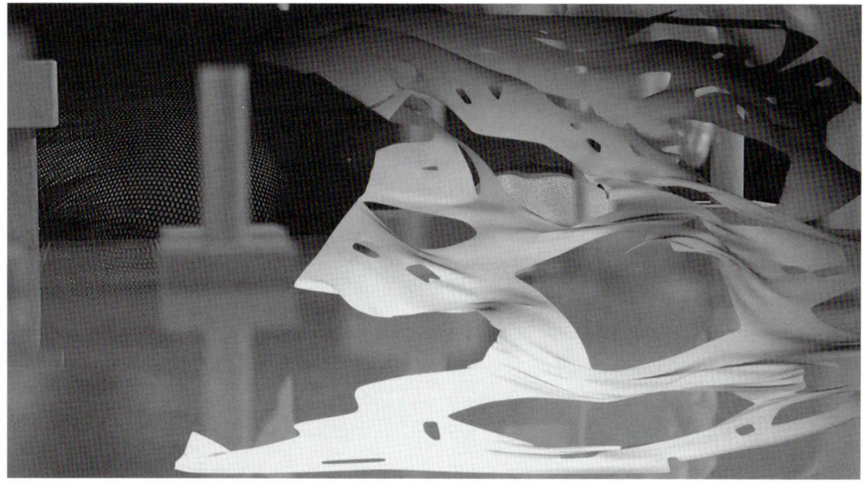

  Holly Herndon (in collaboration with Metahaven), *Interference* (video stills), 2015

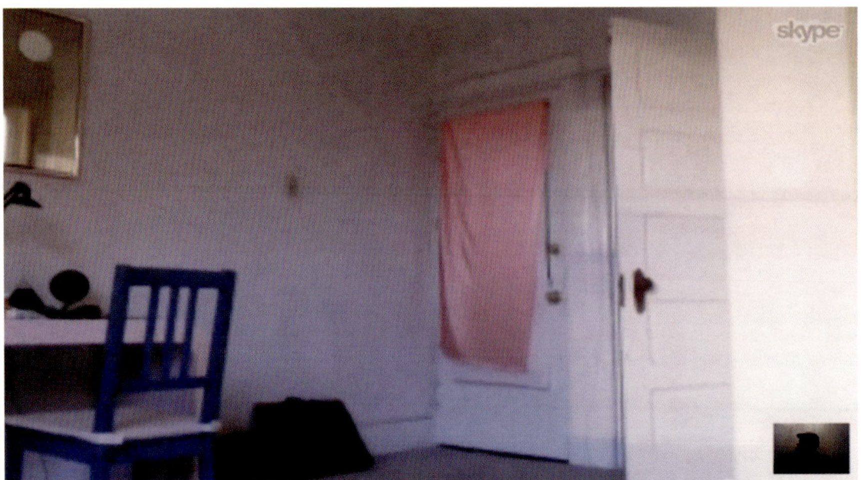

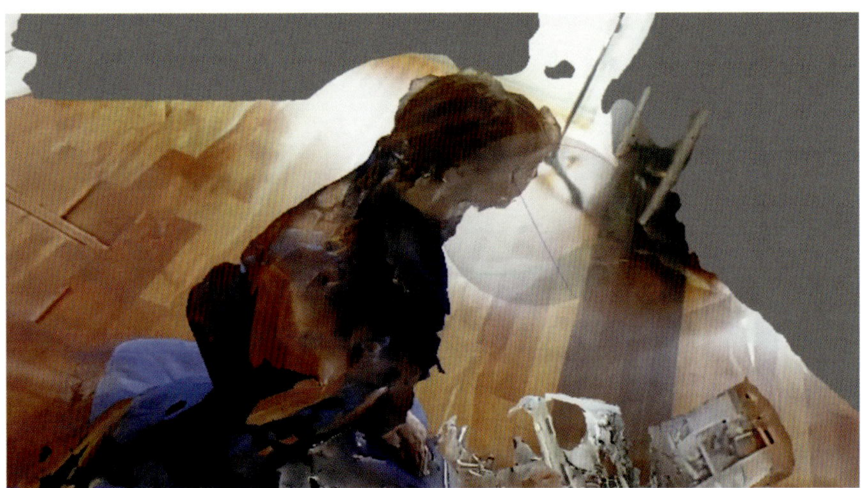

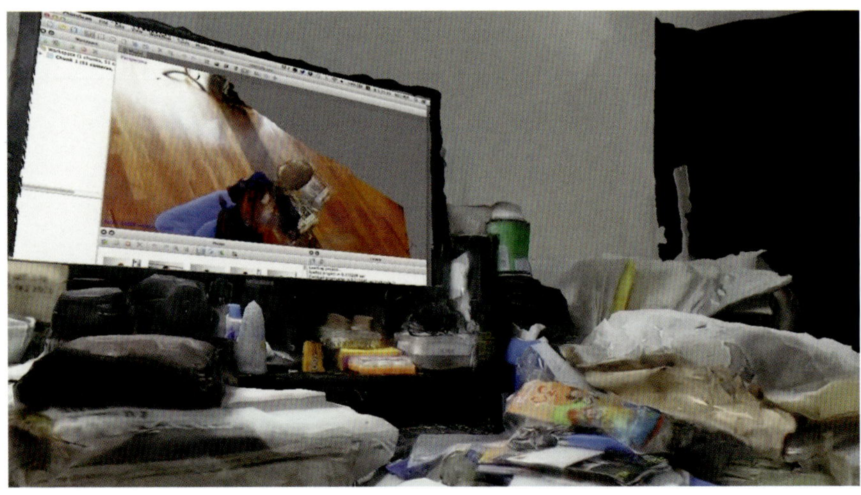

Holly Herndon (in collaboration with Akihiko Taniguchi), *Chorus* (video stills), 2014

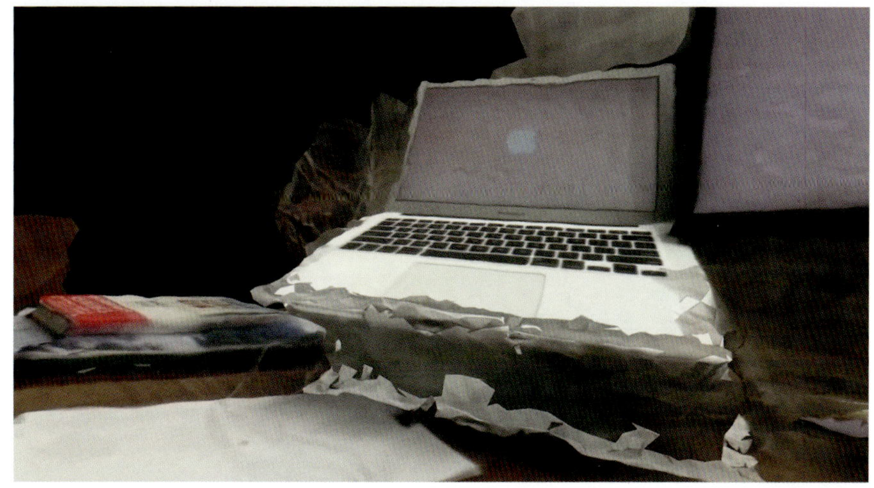

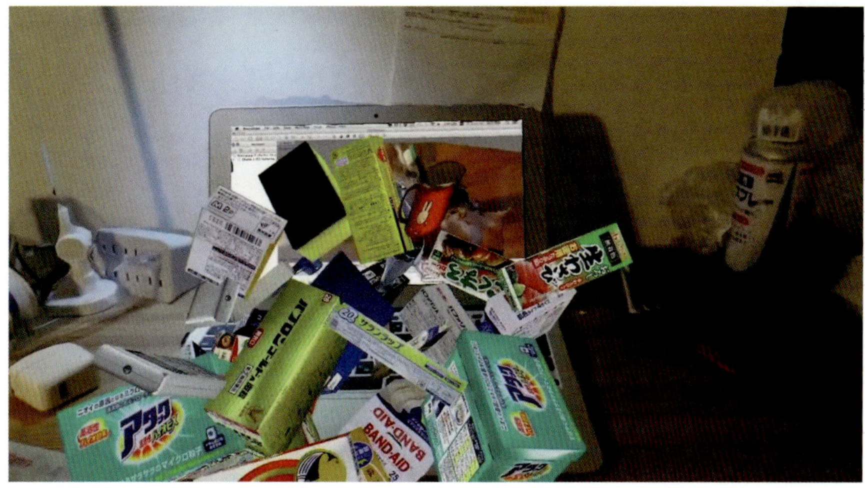

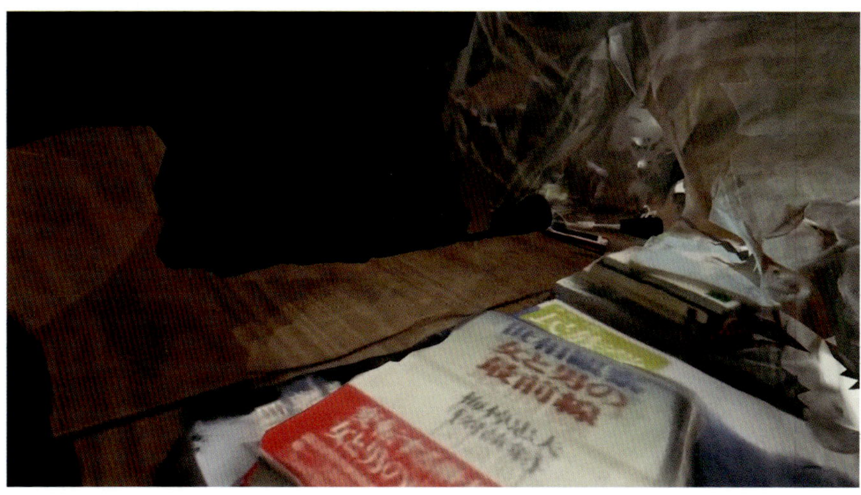

  Holly Herndon (in collaboration with Akihiko Taniguchi), *Chorus* (video stills), 2014

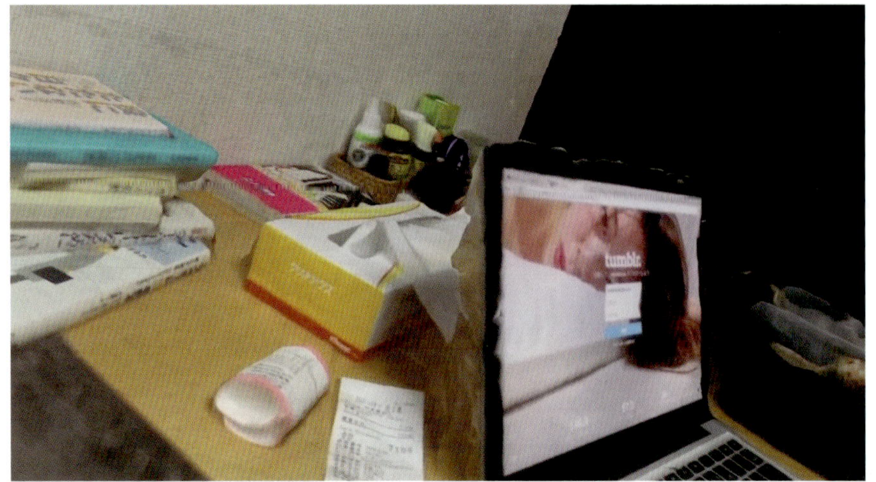

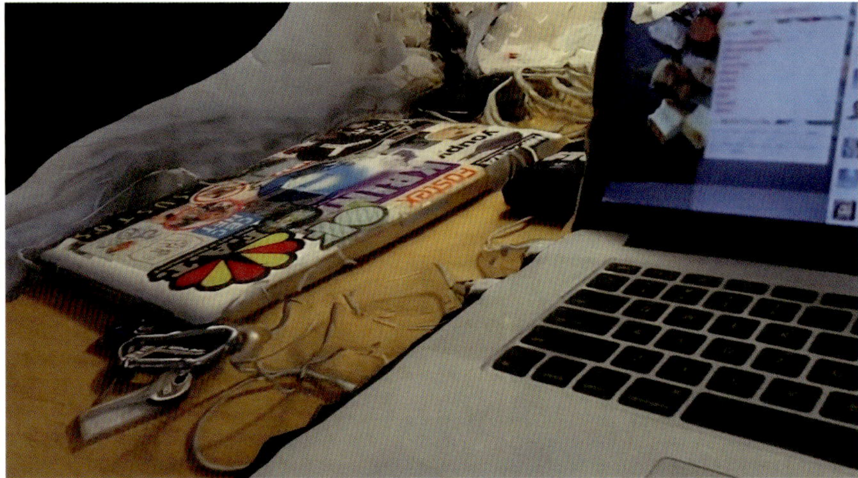

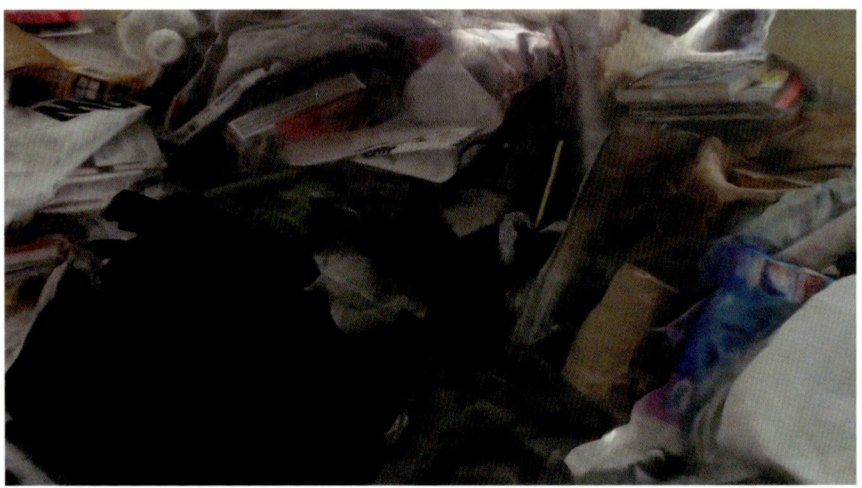

Holly Herndon (in collaboration with Akihiko Taniguchi), *Chorus* (video stills), 2014

is possible thanks to the precision of the algorithms handling the processing, presentation, and manipulation of complex data. Even where these operations are activated by a human user, this presence is obsolete, since each operation can be effectuated independently of the user's request. Automatic focus on digital cameras, suppression of "red eye" or the centering of a face detected in the captured scene are familiar examples of this implicit automation.

Remediation

In addition to those changes voluntarily implemented by the user, machines and software employed by users can also influence the content itself.[30] Technical objects convey cultural elements or ethnocentric components that directly affect the creative process. For example, Jace Clayton, a.k.a. DJ Rupture, developed Sufi Plug-ins as a means of questioning and subverting the latent ethnocentrism of electronic music. He thus conceived of an interface designed specifically for musical traditions emerging from Maghreb and the Middle East. For Clayton, this desire to alter the functions of digital softwares pursues the same ambition that once animated the pioneers of hip hop or techno when they re-appropriated machines to invent musical patterns.

Khalid Al Gharaballi and Fatima Al Qadiri's comic *Mahma Kan Althaman* [*Whatever the Price*][31] published in *Bidoun Magazine* presents yet another example of the influence of digital logic on cultural content. Part photo-novel, part collage of faces, it comprises a series of images overlaid with dialogues in the form of speech bubbles, and composed in non-standard Arabic. The Arabic employed is of a mixed sort—an "Arabix," as Fatima Al Qadiri has dubbed it—one transcribed into a Latin alphabet. Formed of both numbers and letters, it resembles the jargon that circulates among

→ p.127

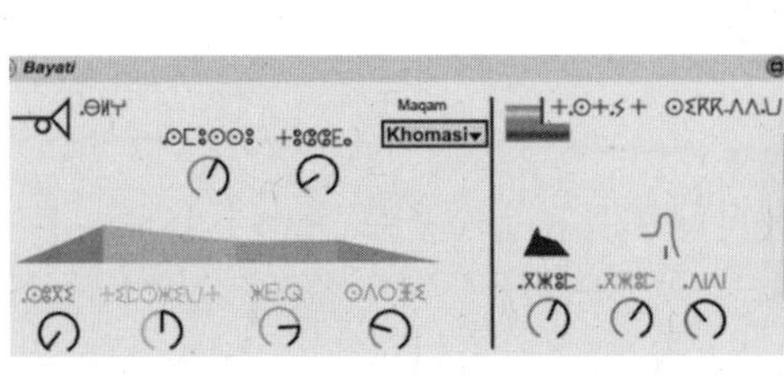
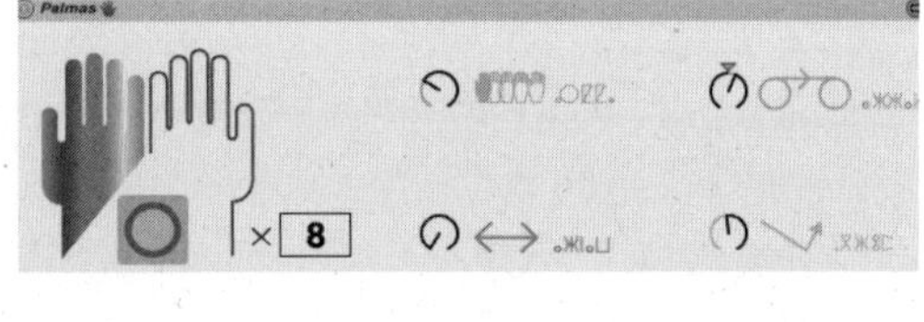

Jace Clayton, *SUFI PLUG INS*, 2012

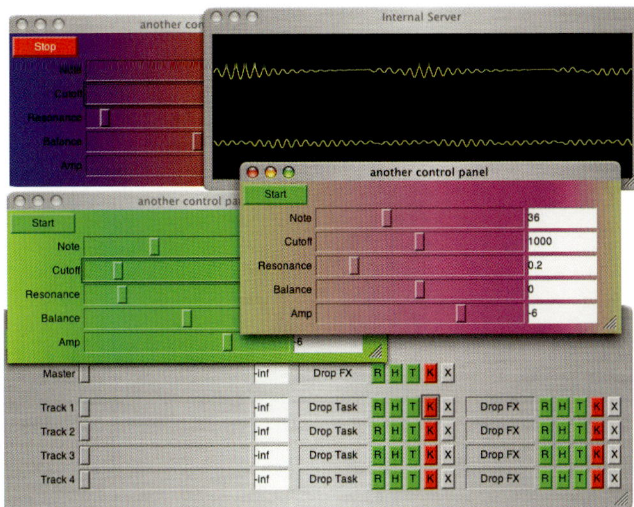

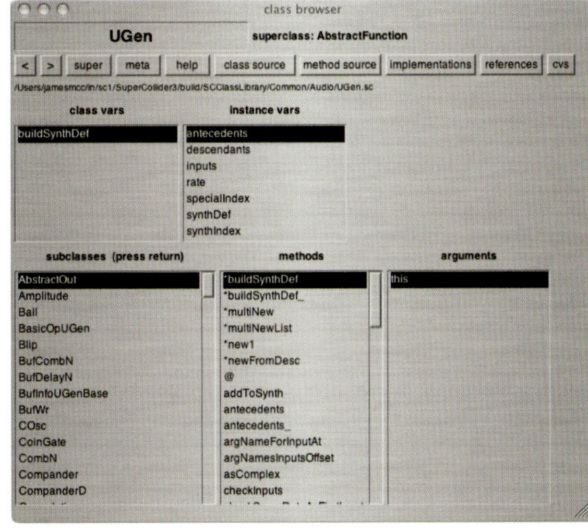

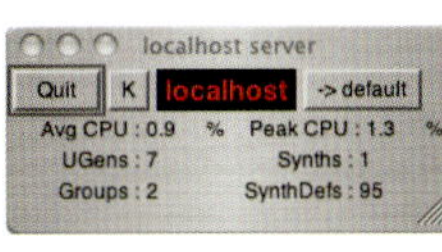

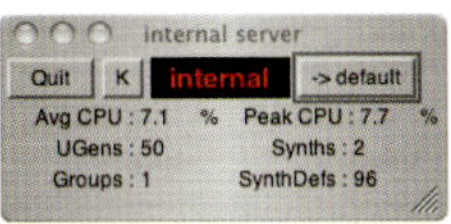

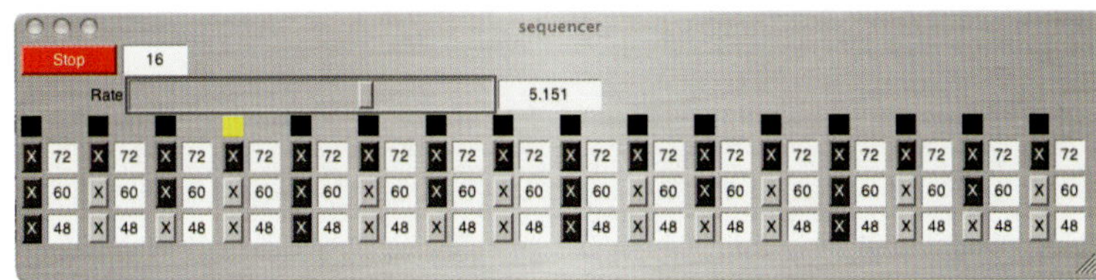

SuperCollider has been evolving into a system used and further developed by both scientists and artists working with sound. It is an efficient and expressive dynamic programming language providing a framework for acoustic research, algorithmic music, and interactive programming.

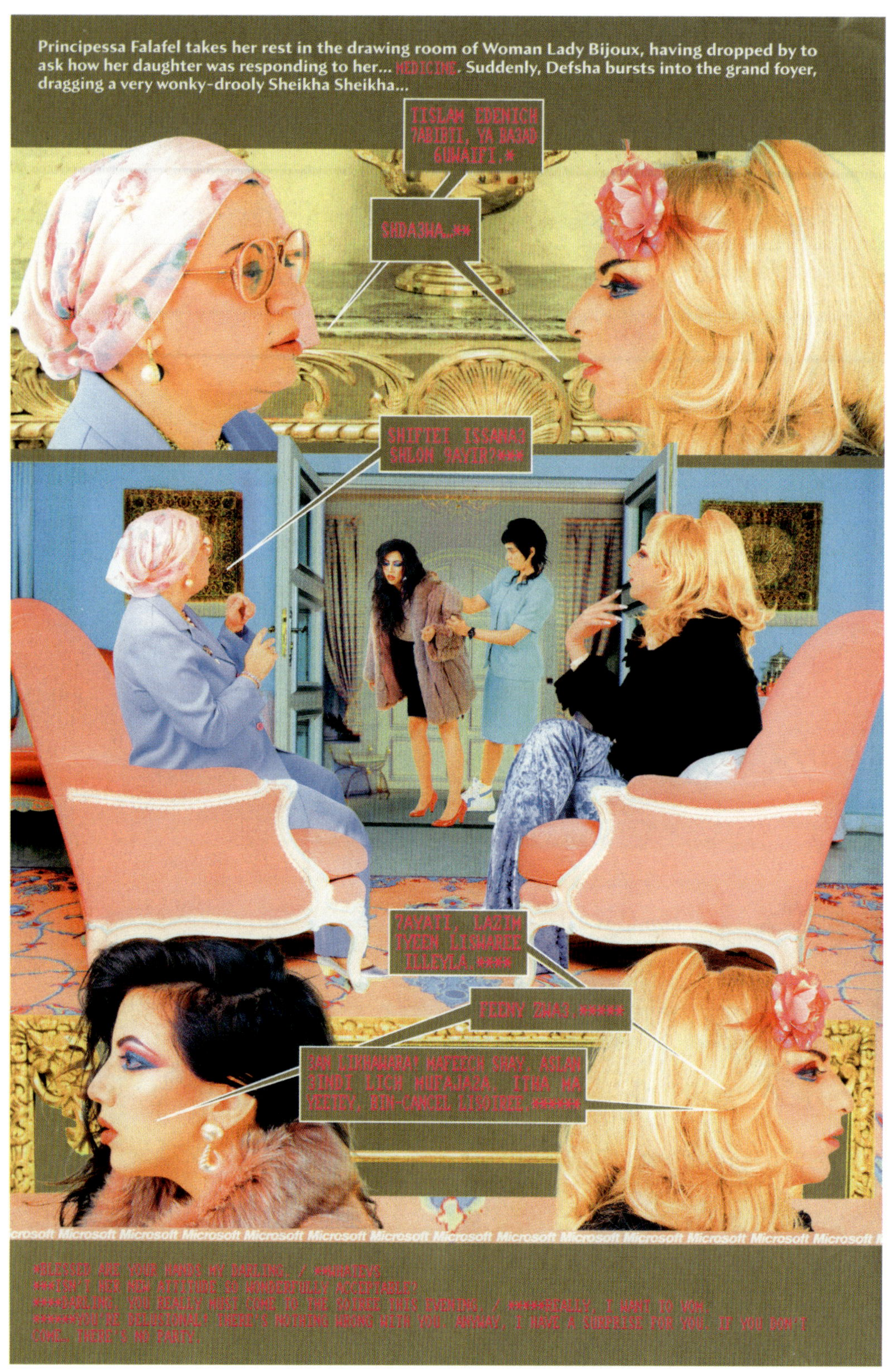

Khalid al Gharaballi & Fatima Al Qadiri,
Mahma Kan Althaman, Whatever the Price, 2010
Published by Bidoun magazine

mobile phone and social media users. Finding it impossible
to use Arabic within the technical interface, such users have
been compelled out of necessity to invent their own idiom. In
an article devoted to such cultural transformations, Fatima
Al Qadiri theorizes the existence of these alphabetic "trans-
gressions," and their persistence in cultural content to come
(Al Qadiri, 2013).

Put otherwise, technical objects—hardware and software—
can transport cultural elements and logics that steer the creative process. In other word, they remediate cultural elements
(Bolter and Grusin, 2000). Following in the footsteps of Basile
Zimmermann, who demonstrated this insight in numerous
cultural fields, one of the present authors took up another
case of this machinic influence, mainly that of 8-bit reggae.
The latter consists of reggae music that has been remixed
and recomposed on 8-bit video game consoles such as Game
Boy and Commodore 64 (Nova, 2014).[32] Musical productions
in this genre are singular, given that reggae and video games
combine to produce a quite specific aesthetic entirely different from their original creations.[33]

Towards a Machinic Creolization?

The examples described above demonstrate that we have sur-
passed the simplistic logic of the remix and the mashup. Even
if these practices continue to persist, the originality of algorithmic cultures resides in the potentialities emerging from
the processes of automation taking place between ever more
active bots. Additionally, the cultural elements widely available online, form a massive and novel material resource for
such programs. In a parallel fashion, the logic of modification
brought about by algorithms and the machines that execute
them shows that the cultural forms they produce are more
than a mere reorganization of existing cultural elements.

→ p.145

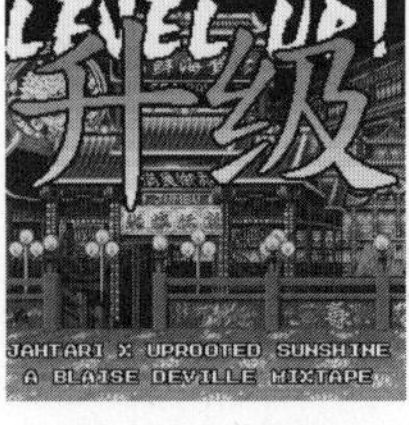

Blaise Deville, *Level Up!* album cover, 2014

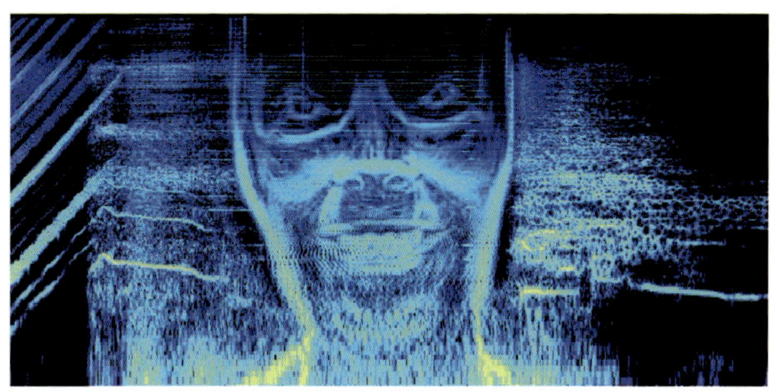

A spectrograph is an instrument or program that is used visualize the sound spectrum. Additionally, there are also programs, such as Coagula and Metasynth, that allow users to easily convert any image into an audio file. Musicians can then take these "image-to-audio" files, mix them into a track and if you were to run that audio through a spectrograph you would suddenly see images like the ones featured.

 Aphex Twin, *[Equation]*, 1999

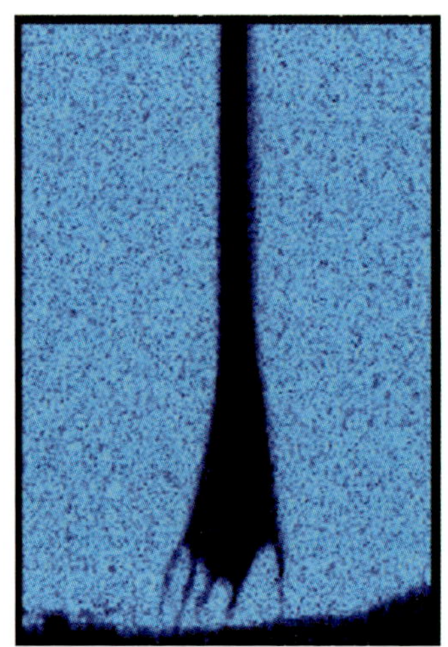

Nine Inch Nails, *My Violent Heart*, 2007

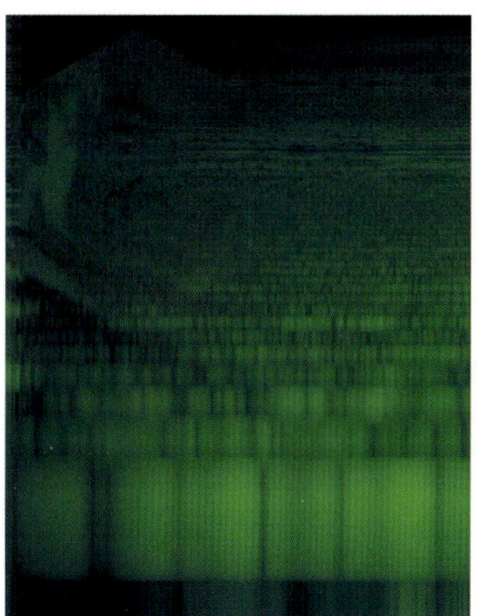

131 Disasterpeace, *Beyond*, FEZ Soundtrack, 2012

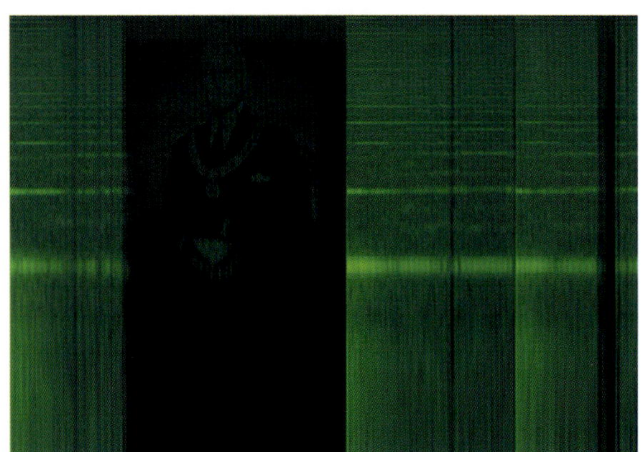

Disasterpeace, *Flow*, FEZ Soundtrack, 2012

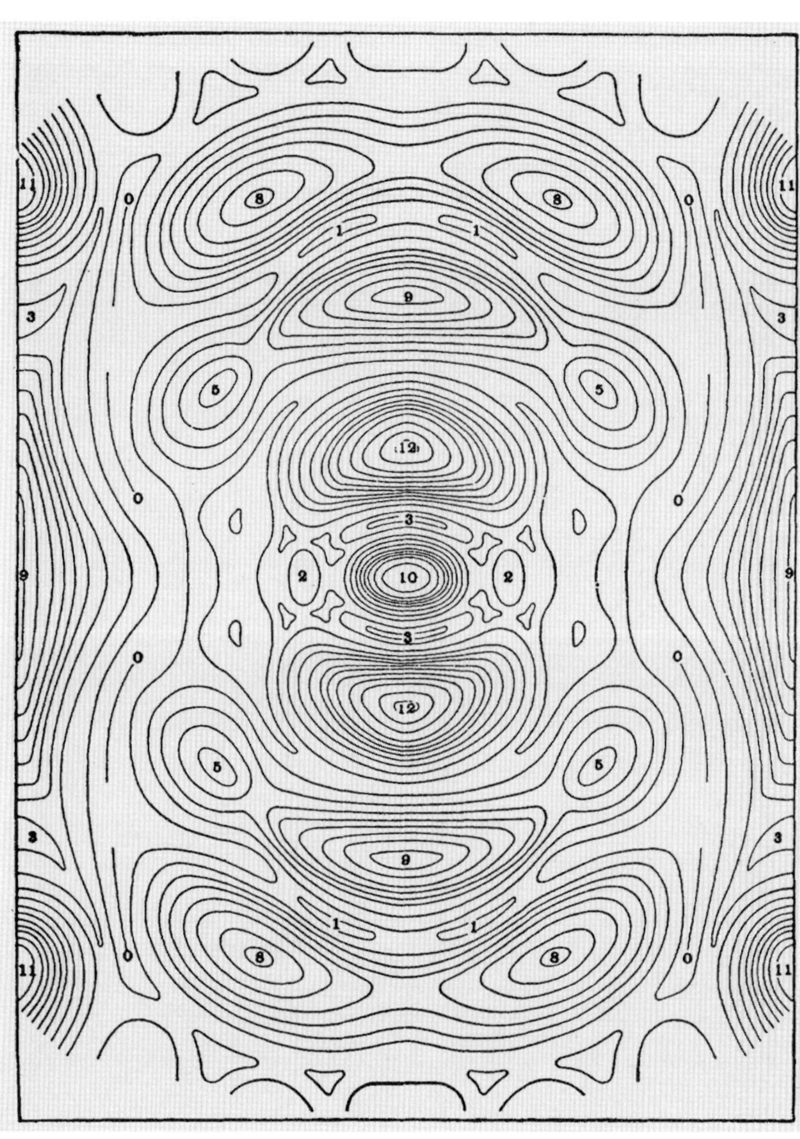

By using various techniques, in particular drawings and shadowgraphy, Wallace Clement Sabine managed to fix the evolution of sound waves emitted theaters. Once materialised on these documents, he was able to transform the fluctuation of acoustic flux into tools of knowledge. By marking their distinct features aural phenomenon left their archaic consonances for entering the modern regime of visuality.

 Wallace Clement Sabine,
Collected Papers on Acoustics, 1922

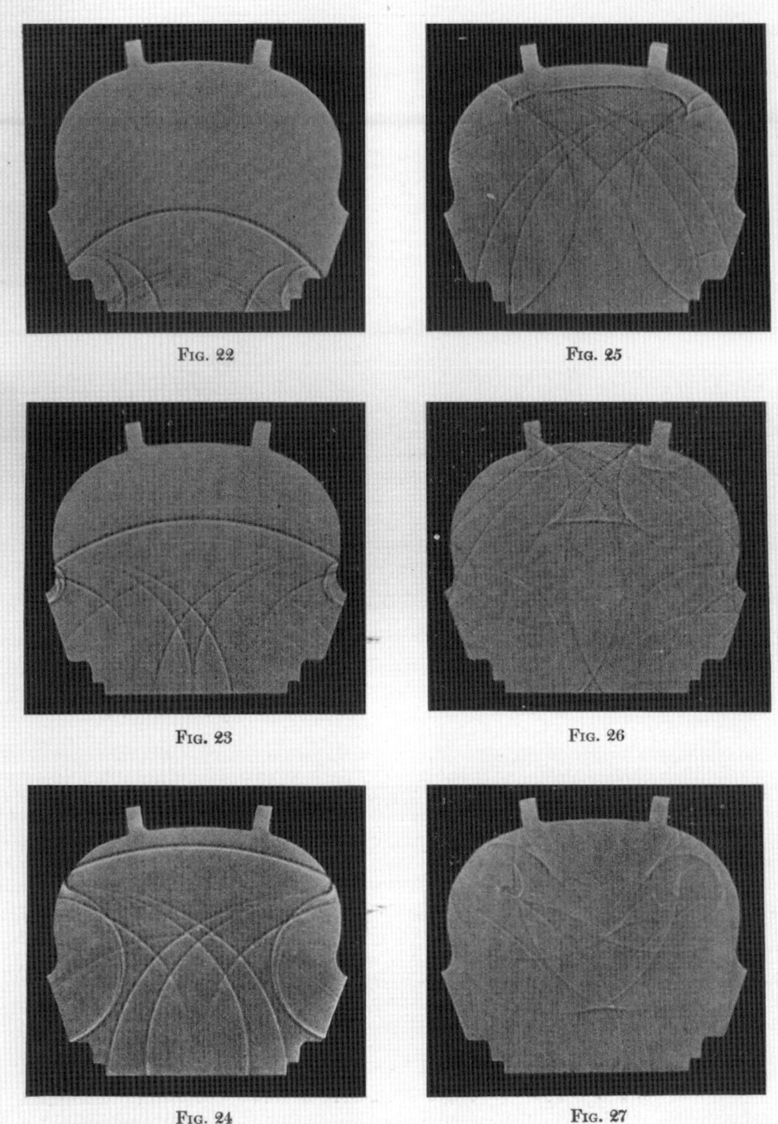

Photographs showing the reflections, in a vertical plane, from the sides of the proscenium arch, the plain wall below the actors' box, and the rail or screen in front of the boxes. The photographs taken in numerical sequence show the progress of a single sound-wave and its reflections.

Wallace Clement Sabine's representations allow to surface the interferences, reverberations, echoes and other vibrations embedded into photographs. Thanks to their mere presence, these ghostly silhouettes are also an attempt to poetically recharge photography at a time when it seems to have unveiled all its mysteries for want of being overexposed.

Wallace Clement Sabine,
Collected Papers on Acoustics, 1922

Interview with Florian Hecker and Dimitri Bruni (NORM) about *Chimerizations*

Q1: Could you explain what led to your collaboration in the publication *Chimerizations*?
A: Yes, technically, on January 6 2011, I received an email by James Hoff, who together with Miriam Katzeff, is doing Primary Information: "Dear Florian, I hope this note finds you well. I'm writing at the urging of ••••••••. I am a big fan of your sound work and told ••••••• as much. I wanted to get in touch to say hello. As you may know, I run a small press in New York devoted to Artists' Books. Up to this point we have mostly been re-printing out-of-print work, but we are now beginning to publish work by contemporary artists. While we don't have a formal invitation/proposal process, I wanted to invite you to propose any ideas for projects should you have any and be interested. At present we have projects lined up with Elad Lassry, Seth Siegelaub, Rhys Chatham, Destroy All Monsters, and Lutz Bacher. We are particularly interested in artist's writings. Oh yeah, the name of the press is Primary Information (www.primaryinformation.org)." I'm not producing writings myself and at the same time was aware of NORM's work through their work with Décosterd & Rahm for the *Physiological Architecture* publication in 2002 and I asked if they would be interested.

Q2: This project echoes the early stages of pictorial abstraction when artists of the *avant-garde*, in particular Kandinsky, tried to find a way to translate the potential parallels between sonic vibrations and pictorial tones. What are the criteria you had to consider for fixing the unruly flux of aural experiences into an editorial format, is it possible to hear with the eyes?
A: Even the most unruly flux as you call it has, in my way of working, has a formal, structural and methodological way of being put into it's unruliness and putting formalized music into a format is something I am working with on a daily basis.

It seemed appealing to do the thing as a book and clearly not as a book with a sound storage support attached or the other way round. While I've been working on *Chimerization* (MIT Project) at the Massachusetts Institute of Technology in 2011, I became aware of Antonio Torralba's work and we got In touch if there would be a contemporary process which would take certain features of one image, exchanging these with another. The SIFT Flow process he's been researching on seemed a particular way to second that in the images—installation or performance stills—something is going on which is not depictable as such, the lack of capturing a core of the work, was beneficial to deal with it as images.

Q3: How did you select and distort your visual documentation and what is the place of (auto-)generative techniques in this process?
A: The book documents all the auditory chimera works till the time of its production. Each chapter deals with a piece that has a textual, a vocal and a narrative element. What ones sees in each chapter stems from a series of installation, performance or production photography as its source material.

Q4: How did you come with the idea of this evolutive typeface and what does it tell us about the role of interferences in any forms of communication?
A: At the beginning of the project, our first idea was to consider the book as an integral entity of chimerization. In this way, all the elements that were included in it could then be subject to the same symptoms. A pandemic chimerization taking over physical aspects (papers, format), page setting (grid), graphic principles and typography. It finally transpired that it were best for the project to settle instead for graphic principles with a structure that was rigid, structural, linear and functional.

Q5: Do you agree that fonts provide a kinetic effect and should be examined through their ability to vibrate?

A: In its original drawing, the *Replica* font presents some aspects which, from a formal point of view, are reminiscent of a genetic modification. For the page setting of Reza Negarestani's text, the Programmer, Ben M. Jordan generated 99 degrees of perturbation, thus modifying the original font drawing. This intention not only implies a progressive reading degradation, but also joins up the reading of the images in the book. In 1989, *Letterror* (Just van Rossum and Erik van Blokland) had already considered this issue with the *Beowolf* font. The programming and the use of *Replica Chimera Light* has been conceptually unavoidable within this project framework.

Q6: By developping the Gothic Futurism, Rammellzee aimed to liberate the letters from the alphabet's printed form. Is there any kind of Wild Style ethos in your approach?
A: The intention is not linked to a "Wild Style" idea, but instead to that of a synthetic and disruptive approach. The typeface colour is black. The vibration issue is something that is detected between the quantity of white, the quantity of black and their respective shapes.

Q7: In an article called *The Amateur Photographer and Photography*, 1923, Alfred Stieglitz wrote an interesting statement about his groundbreaking series *Equivalents*: "I wanted a series of photographs which [when] seen by Ernest Bloch (the great composer) he would exclaim: 'Music! Music! Man, why that is music! How did you ever do that?' And he would point to violins, and flutes, and oboes, and brass, full of enthusiasm, and would say he'd have to write a symphony called *Clouds*." What kind of equivalences did you create through *Chimerizations*?
A: The "chimerized" images suggest rather an absence of the urge of completion via an auditory hallucination. Something is missing in these images.

Q8: Knowing that a photograph makes visible the light-reflection of something, or somebody, in front of the lens. Can we also expect that the same process happens with the reflection of noises bursting during the shot?
A: The process here is reversed—a bottom up synthesizing one, not one of capturing something real. The sonic material, besides the original human voices recorded in anechoic chambers or audiology booths, is completely synthetically generated.

Q9: By using technique of shadowgraphy invented by August Toepler in 1864, Wallace Clement Sabine, who was a physicist in Harward, managed to fix the light refracted by sound waves emitted in models of theaters and auditoriums. Once photographed, it was then possible for him to isolate and identify the effects of certain acoustic events in a given space. Extrapolating from this early experiments in acoustics, do you think that our readings of photographs is influenced by the symptomatic presence of sonic events?
A: There is a certain typology of images that directly allude to sound and are perceived as such, even if they are not directly referring to it in their representations. The images in *Chimerizations* are a good example of this. Their repetition and the sequence of images, all alike while also being all different, conceptually suggest a morphological variation, thus implying their relation to sound in a more explicit manner. Generally speaking, the series plays a decisive role in preparation for this perception.

Q10: Is *Chimerizations* dealing with the idea of hauntology?
A: No.

 Florian Hecker *Chimerizations*; Primary Information, New York, 2013

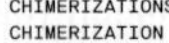

168

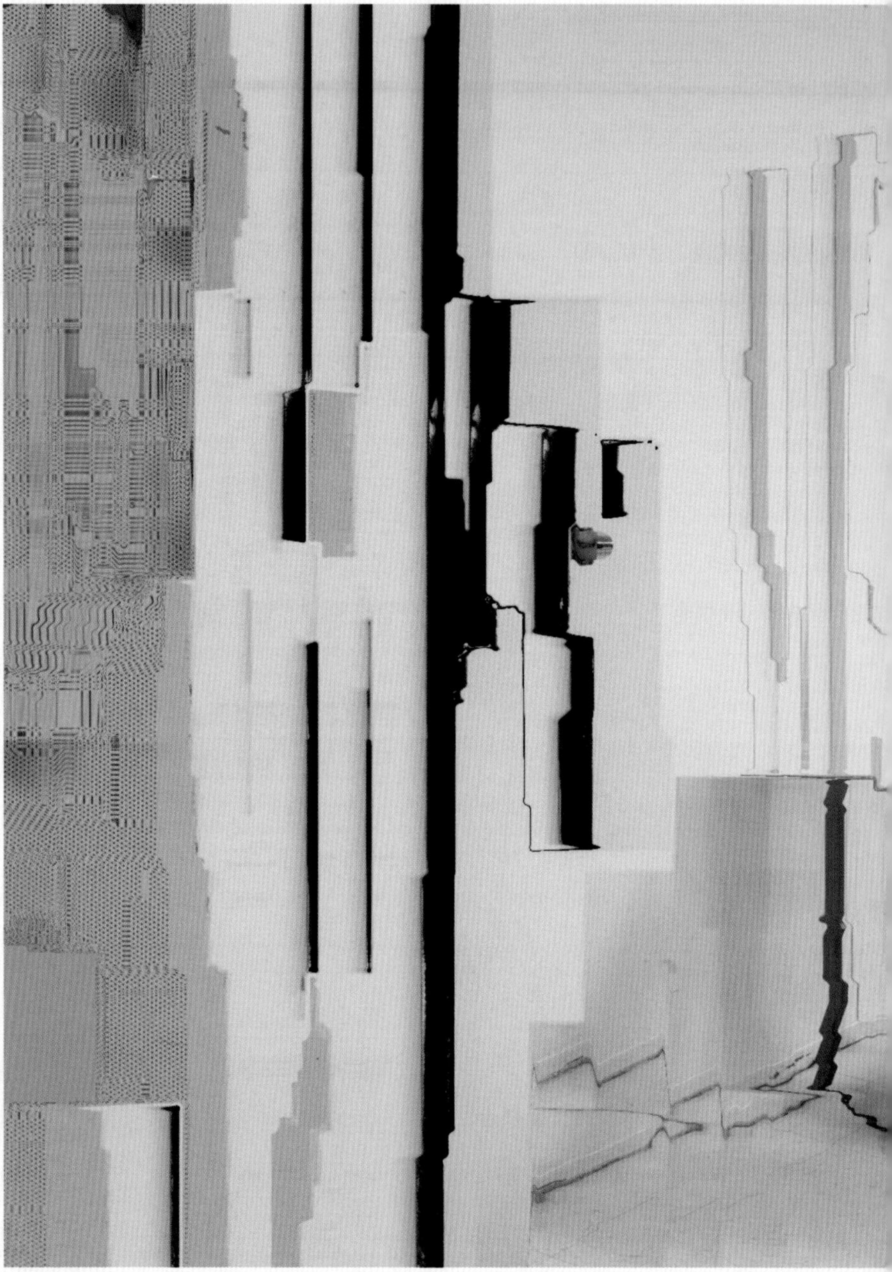

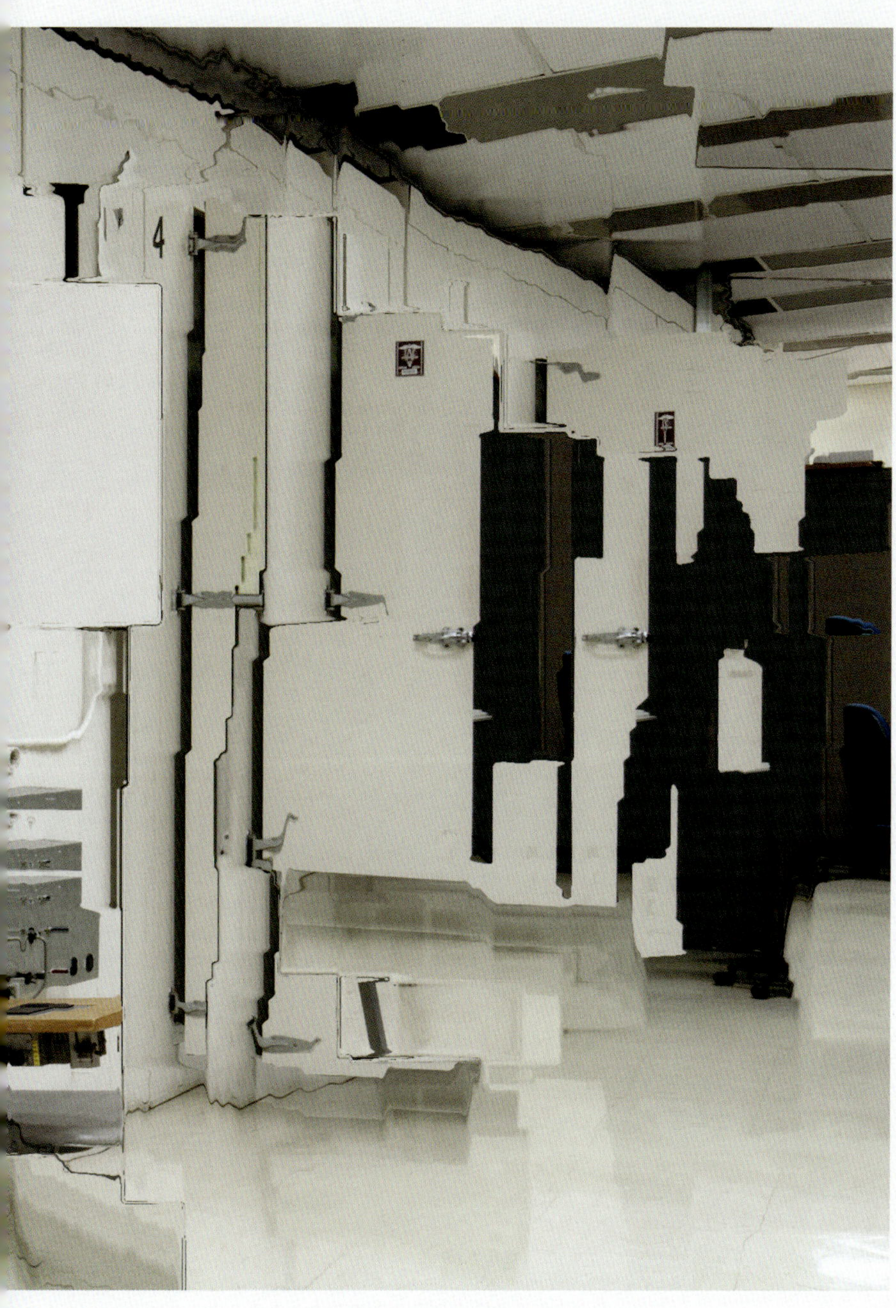

Snake and Ladder   *All brought about by the continuous and unbound relation of the abyss/nature to itself.*

We call this modern player that reflects the geometric schema of the abyss in the externally distinct voice of Man in nature and re-navigates the local horizon of Man and its voice in terms of a geometric perspective into the abyss, chimera.

Snake   [illegible]

Ladder   [illegible]

Snake   [illegible]

Ladder   [illegible]

Snake and Ladder   At the same time.[8]

[illegible]

THE SNAKE, THE GOAT AND THE LADDER
[illegible]

HOW TO START THE GAME

[illegible]

PLATFORM AND INTERFACES

[illegible]

[illegible]

216

217

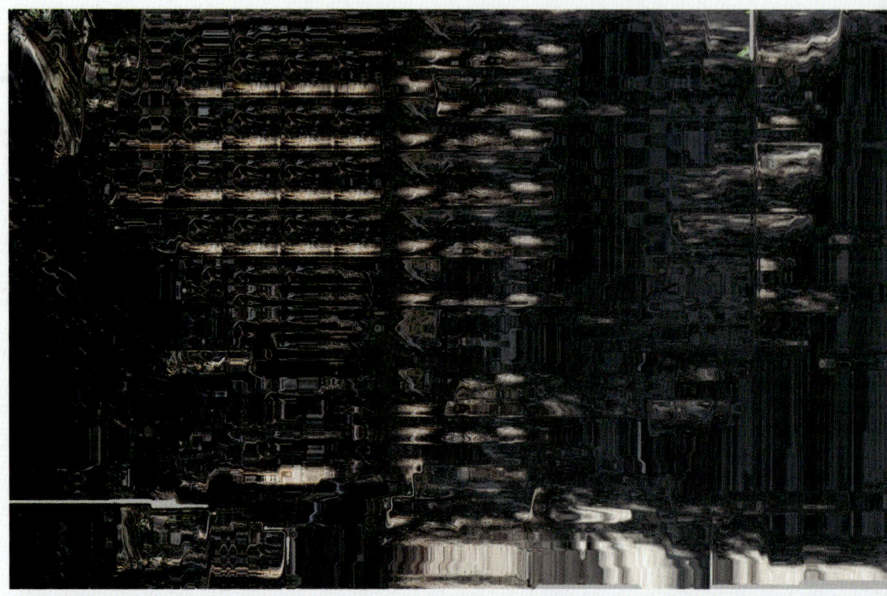

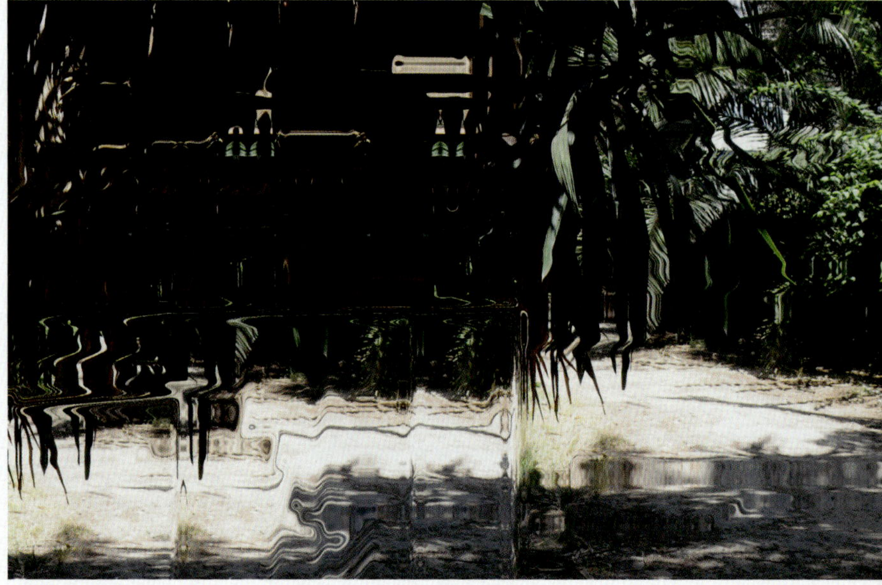

260   SIFT FLOW (E04)^(E07) WARP   MAX FLOW 1658.2415
             ELAPSED TIME 5.957019 SECONDS   FLOW RANGE U = -634.402 .. 1050.042; V = 999.000 .. 1560.463

Florian Hecker *Chimerizations*, p.260; Primary Information, New York, 2013

Their constituent elements are transformed in and through these mixtures, producing new and singular contributions. Put otherwise, it is like listening to a remix whose samples were transformed organically in the course of the playback under the influence of the algorithms of the program.

Such a dynamic evokes a cultural phenomenon wellknown to linguists, anthropologists and poets, mainly that of creolization. As Edouard Glissant describes it, the term refers to the "meeting of multiple cultures, or at least of multiple elements from distinct cultures, in a single place in the world, resulting in the emergence of something new and totally unforeseeable when considered only as the sum or synthesis of its elements."[34] Without delving into the complex history of the word creolization, we may simply recall that the notion derives from the use of the word "creole" which, during the 16th century, served to designate those individuals born from the collision and mixture of populations in the American and Caribbean New World. Over the course of time, the word "creolization" came to refer to the process of intercultural exchange giving rise to a new language, one influenced by the original maternal languages of the people in question (Mühlhäusler, 1997). Such is the case with Haitian Creole and Jamaican Patois. The term creolization has since been used by historians and anthropologists to describe and understand the intercultural exchanges that go beyond simple linguistic matters, as in the intermixing of alimentary or musical traditions arising through a logic of mutual entanglement and transformation of constituent elements. The term creolization may be defined as a conjoint process of hybridization and transformation of cultural elements leading to the production of a new and unforeseeable result. The notion is employed by anthropologists precisely in order to overcome the simple logic of the remix or combination of existing forms.[35]

→ p.149

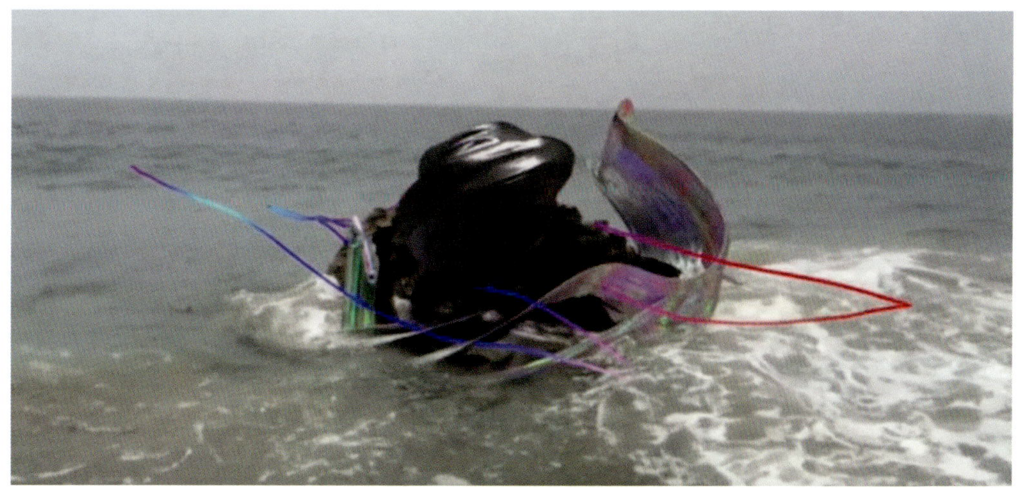

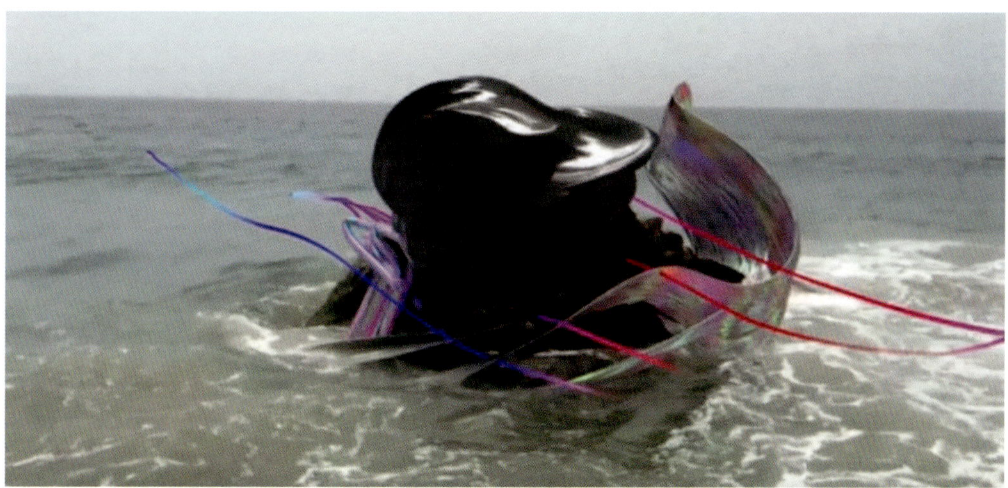

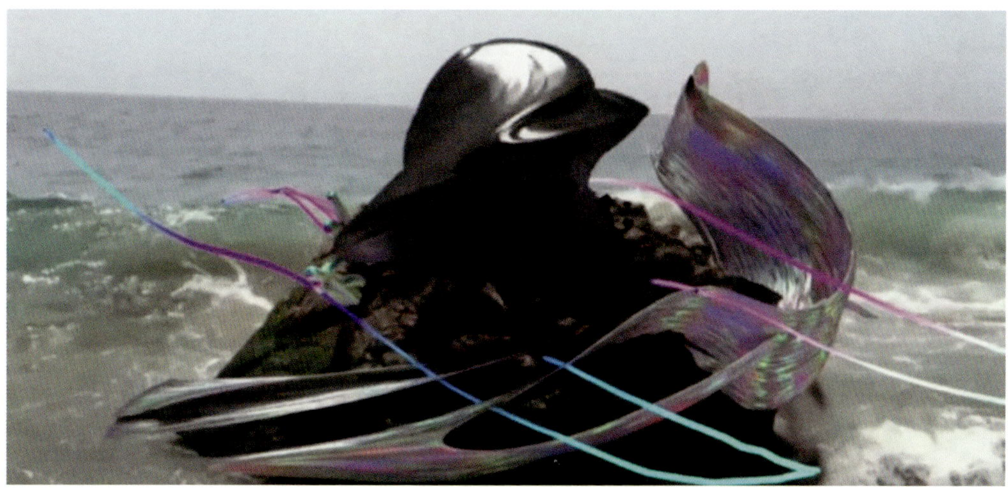

147 Vince McKelvie, *Untitled*, 2014

Yet, as we have seen, given their reliance on computers and the omnipresence of algorithms therein, current uses of digital technology add yet another layer of supplementary complexity to "creolizing" situations. We are aware that such a transposition of the term is not uncontroversial. Are we really dealing with the same process? Any application outside of its original postcolonial context is potentially problematic and it remains an open question. And yet the very idea of creolization suggests that the analysis of current cultural productions is not confined to the customary analytic tools endorsed by the Western canon. Whether it be the omnipresence of samples and mashups, the influence of presets and autotune, the circulation of glitches and memes, the strange humor of Twitterbots, etc., the algorithmic mechanisms at work in all of these projects outstrip the common idea of hybridization. The notion of creolization seems to us better adapted to evoke this "emergence of something new and totally unforeseeable" through the use of machines in the creative process today.

→ p.155

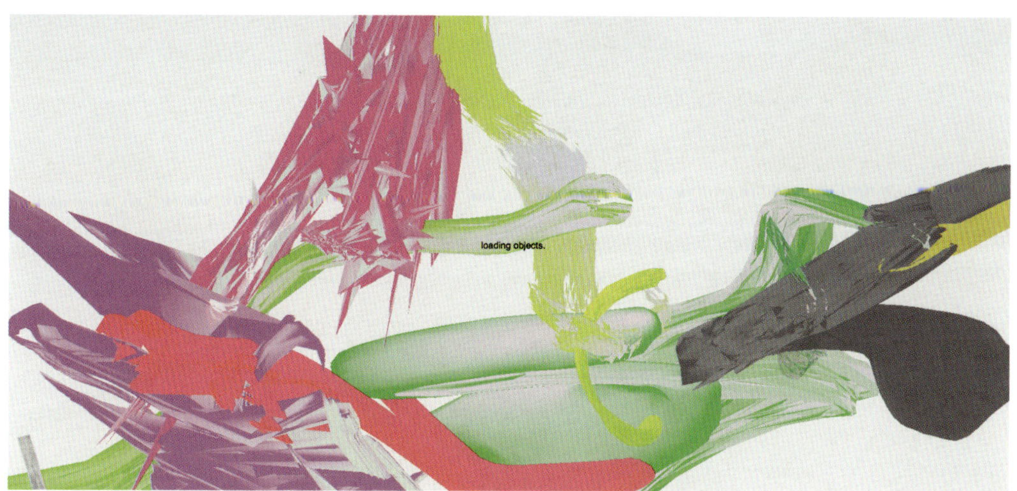
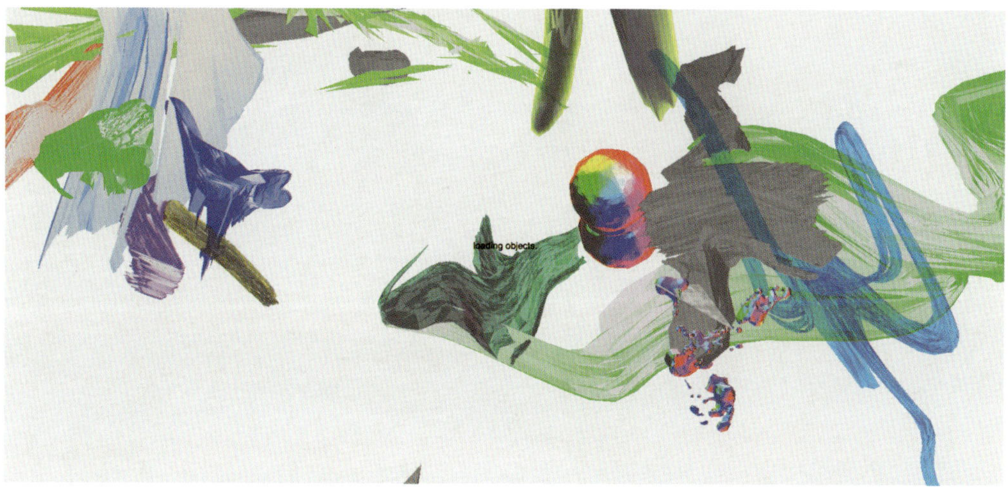
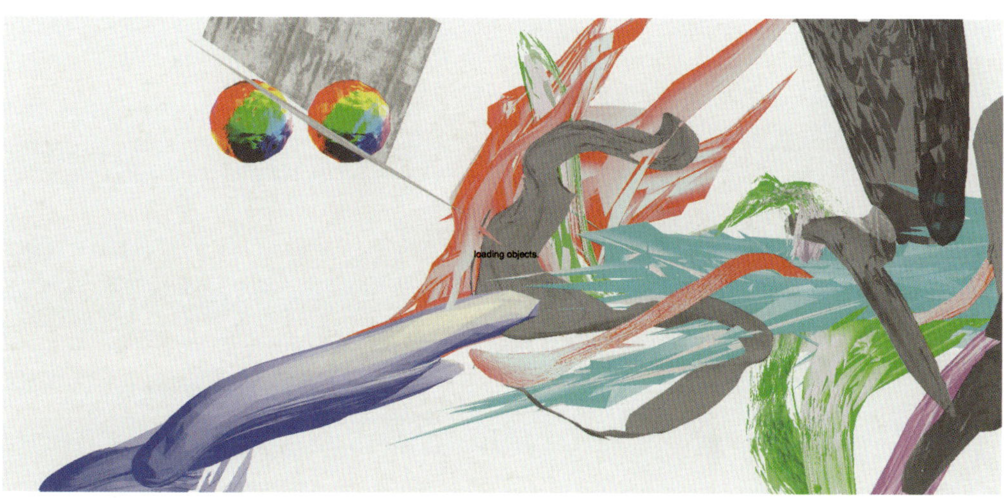

1 Vince McKelvie, *Orthographic Camera*, 2014

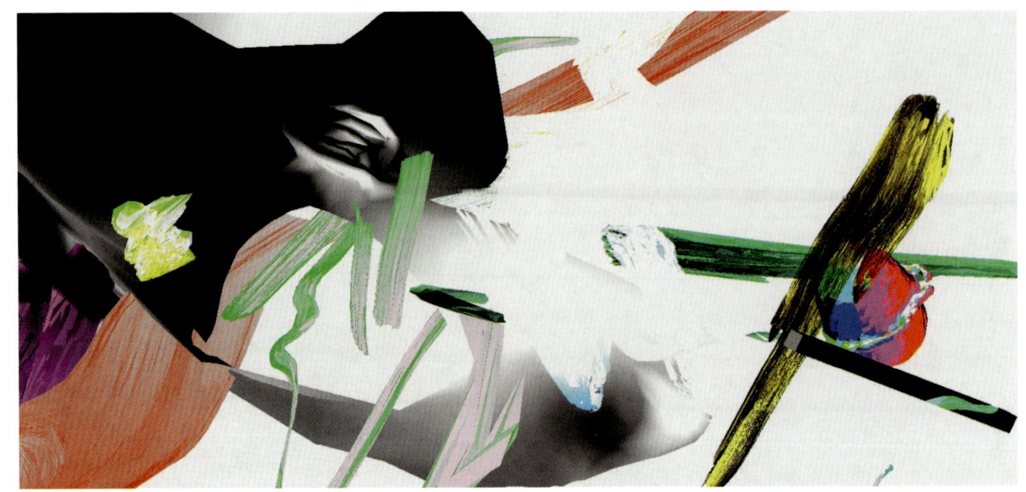

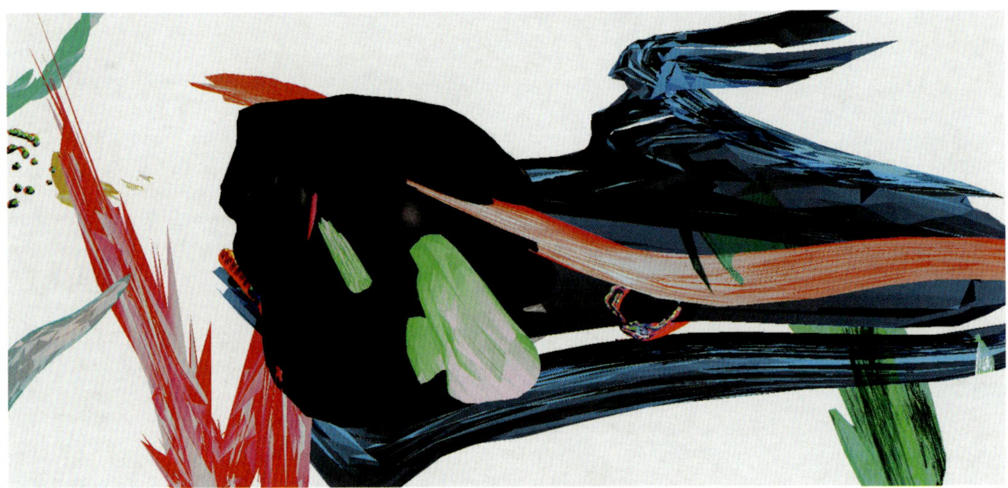

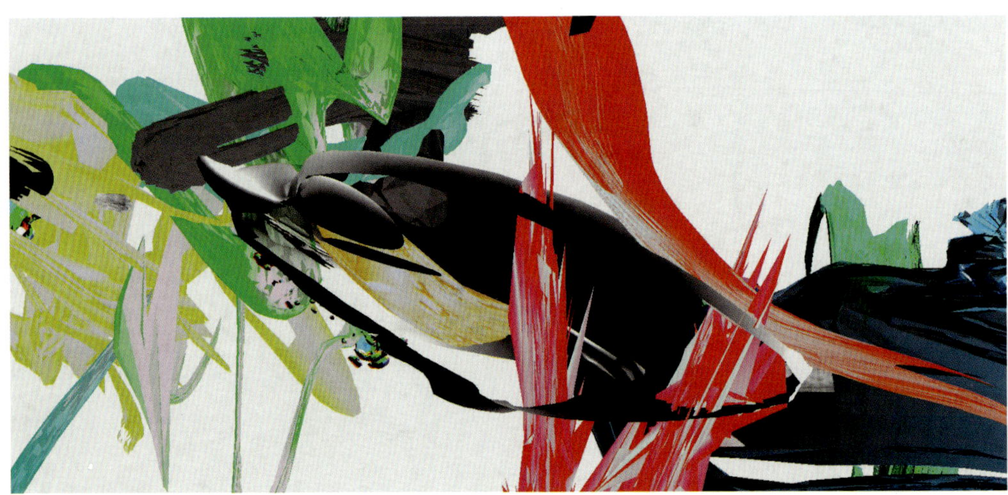

Vince McKelvie, *Orthographic Camera*, 2014

None of the aforementioned projects are a perfect fit for the notion of creolization. Nonetheless, they testify to the presence of a logic within algorithmic cultures, and offer some paths along which its evolution within automated production may potentially be understood. This can take the form of fictions produced by bots that reassemble and transform fragments of events or dialogues into a new and coherent narrative, or books created on the basis of actions carried out in a video game, from the passages in spoken languages to turns of phrase and syntactical mistakes generated by algorithmic productions, etc.[36] What is at issue is a turning point in contemporary culture. We thus propose the hypothesis of a "machinic creolization," that is, the constant automation of hybridized and altered cultural elements. With this term, we wish to underline the fact that "creolizing" processes of creation can be carried out by machines and algorithms entirely on their own. This is a globally novel situation.

These phenomena by no means imply the disappearance of earlier forms of cultural production. What we are instead witnessing is the advent of projects that transgress and intensify the sorts of collaboration possible between human and non-human entities. We are also seeing new forms of coexistence between automated and non-automated modes of creation. What physical and symbolic forms will this take in the future? Without offering an answer here, the projects presented in this publication should feed the debate by offering a singular perspective upon the transitory state of creation in the 21th century.

• Notes   → p.195
• References   → p.201

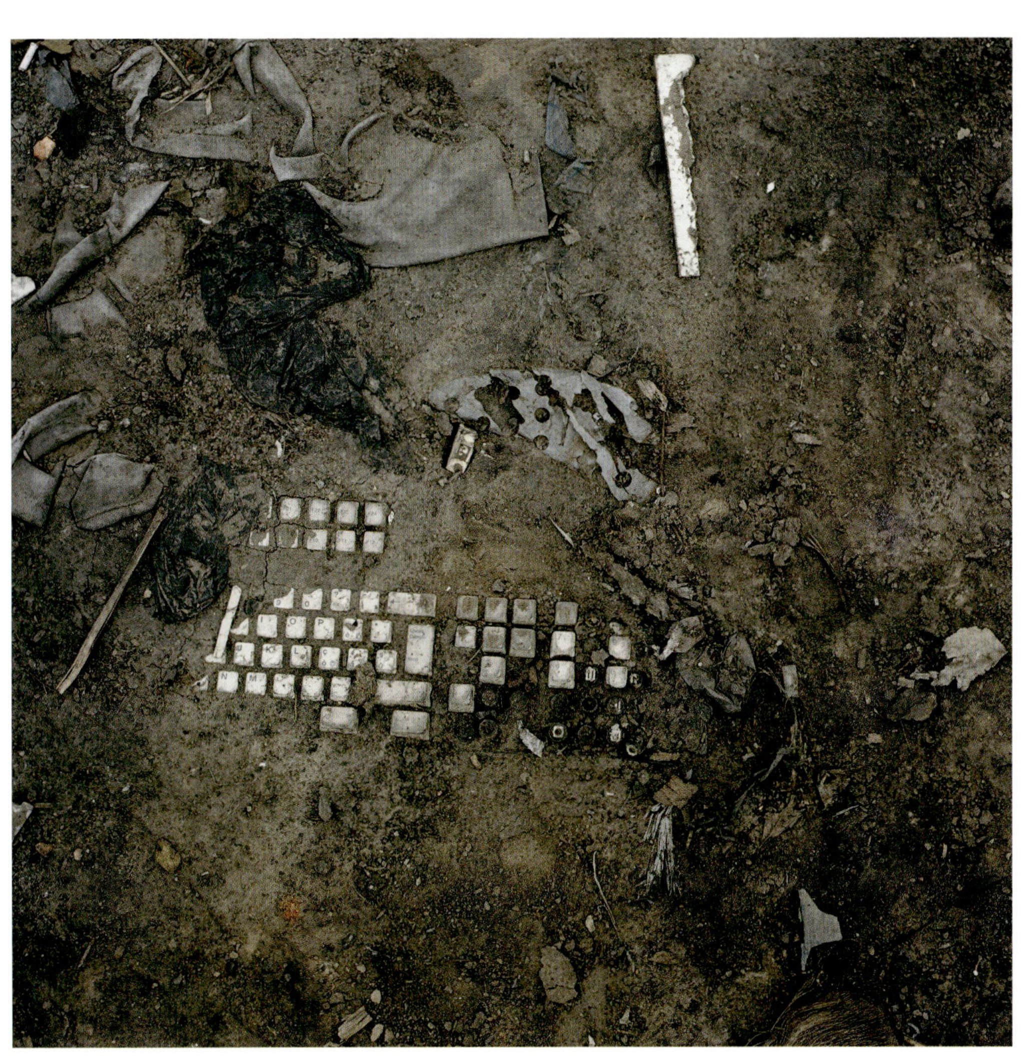

  Pieter Hugo, from *Permanent Error*, 2011

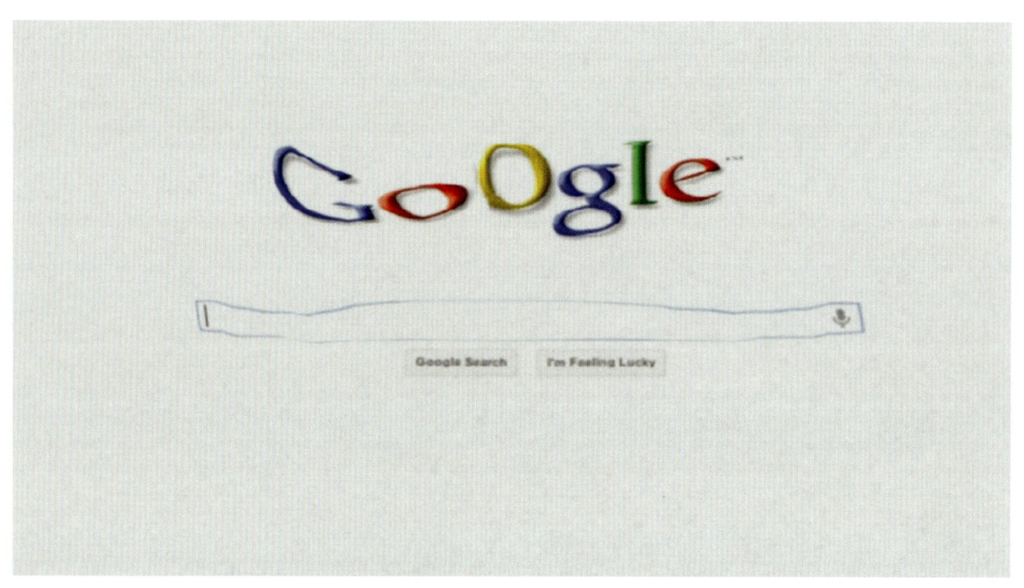

Constant Dullaart, *Terms of Service* (HD video), 2012

Interview with Constant Dullaart

Q1: How did your *Jennifer in Paradise* project come about?
A: What I was really interested in was the background of the Photoshop tool, which has become so important for the manipulation of the representation of reality. It is so influential that it leaves a cultural mark. And I wanted to know more about its heritage; who had made the filters, who had decided how to name and how to structure the tool.
While researching Photoshop, I came across interviews of one of its founders, John Knoll, as well as this re-enactment video of the first demonstration that he did to present his product to potential customers.
In one of the interviews, he talks about the first image that he used: a personal image of his girlfriend Jennifer, half naked on a beautiful beach. I thought this was such a *cliché* image. I also felt it was strange that this picture of the person dearest to him was what he offered his customers to test his product. It is a very masculine and Western way of thinking. It is also a clear cultural artefact. It is obvious that what we have here is an American software, and not an Asian software, for instance.
It is also important to realize that you're working with the software of somebody that chose this as the first picture. He didn't choose a turtle, or a man, or a child. He didn't choose a tree or a house. He chose a woman without a bikini top on, holidaying on a luxurious island, all of which representing money.
I tried to locate this historical, original image online, but no luck. I wrote to the founders as well, but they did not respond. Instead, I restored it from a screen grab of the above mentioned video. I then upgraded it through Photoshop. Finally, I decided to incorporate steganography into it, because I thought this is a story where the image is already so important that it will distribute.

Q2: Tell us a bit more about steganography.
A: Let's say you and I were to meet in physical life and agreed on a password. I would then continuously upload images to an enormous message board. Once in a while, I would include a message locked with our password. You would then download all the images and you would try the password each time, then maybe once a day, while you have this loop running, like a program scanning through the images, you would actually get a message. So it would be a way of having an anonymous encrypted communication without a clear sender or a clear receiver. It's an inventive way to hide and secure your communication.
The distribution is public but this other layer is private and this privacy becomes a commodity. We are almost paying to increase our privacy and our freedom. I thought this is something which will become normal in our society. This led me to do something similar in arts. There is a message in the *Jennifer in Paradise* image that I restored. And there are three different versions of this image and they all have a password. This is what is on sale at the gallery. If you can buy the password, you can have access to these files and you are able to read the files differently from how everybody else can read them. Of course, this is still very experimental for art galleries: buying a password as a commodity, in other words your access key to something becoming a value.

Q3: In some of your other projects, you play with software default standards.
A: I am interested in these default standards, in the study of software anthropology; how you understand the defaults of a software, its title, its name.
In my *HEAL* project, I took images from disasters, for example the earthquake in Japan, and I then applied the healing brush to them. I made the healing brush really big and clicked on the whole image, so the whole disaster got healed. Why did they call it the healing brush? If you talk about a healing brush, you

are implying that something is sick. So I healed something. I took away a disease, I took away something negative and I made it better.

This is why I was thinking that if I healed the whole image, I would end up with the best image you can get, because it is completely healed. You take away all the sickness from the image. Actually, this means that all the details go away and you are left with this beautiful color spectrum that's completely healthy.

This kind of idea of being visually pleasing, being positive and better is something that YouTube also uses. On YouTube, you can "improve you video." This means taking away the shaking, improving the color, etc. One of the ideas I had was to upload earthquake videos and "improve them." As a result, the earthquake doesn't shake anymore, because it is "improved." These are the kind of standards that I am trying to work with.

Q4: Can you explain the concept of balconization.
A: I was getting more and more aware of the fact that we all have machines around us that can potentially always listen to us. It's the same as if you were on a balcony. There are passers by that can always hear you. If you're on a balcony, somebody can stand under your building and can overhear you. But it also feels private, it feels like you are in your own house. So that's what we mean when we say: "we are all on the balcony." You feel in your own private atmosphere, yet somebody can listen.

If you're going to have children, you should be aware that they're going to be born on the balcony, they're not going to be born in private anymore. The whole web already consists of spatial analogy: chat room, superhighway, the web itself. There is all this spatial representation of information. You're being put on this balcony, it's not your choice but you should act as if you were very aware that you are on this balcony and that you're also making use of it.

Q5: We have never been surrounded by so many images, yet we are so blind to the actual nature of these images and the tools used to process them.

A: You might say that we almost get distracted by the normal visual markers. But I think we are all educated. When I was young, there were analogue images; my father had an analogue camera and this is how I related to images. I think that children who are born now have a completely different understanding of images. They grow up and understand much more and are aware that there is an algorithm which decides that you see a particular image because other people like that image. There's a way of understanding and a way of archiving. There are images in the newspapers because they look a different way and not because a person selected them. Right now, many newspapers are using algorithms to analyse all the images that come in. They look at a certain composition, a certain colour. Human decision is taken away from reading and selecting images more and more.

But who writes those algorithms, what type of decisions are made? I would say that the people who create these algorithms are the magicians of our time. They are creating these proprietary things that people pay a lot of money for. Yet we don't have access to them. There is no social attribute to stipulate that it needs to be shared with everybody.

From my perspective, this is the most radical change that needs to happen: these algorithms, or these ways of looking at how information is sorted, should become public. They should be made more available while also being kept more under control or under scrutiny. This again becomes a political decision.

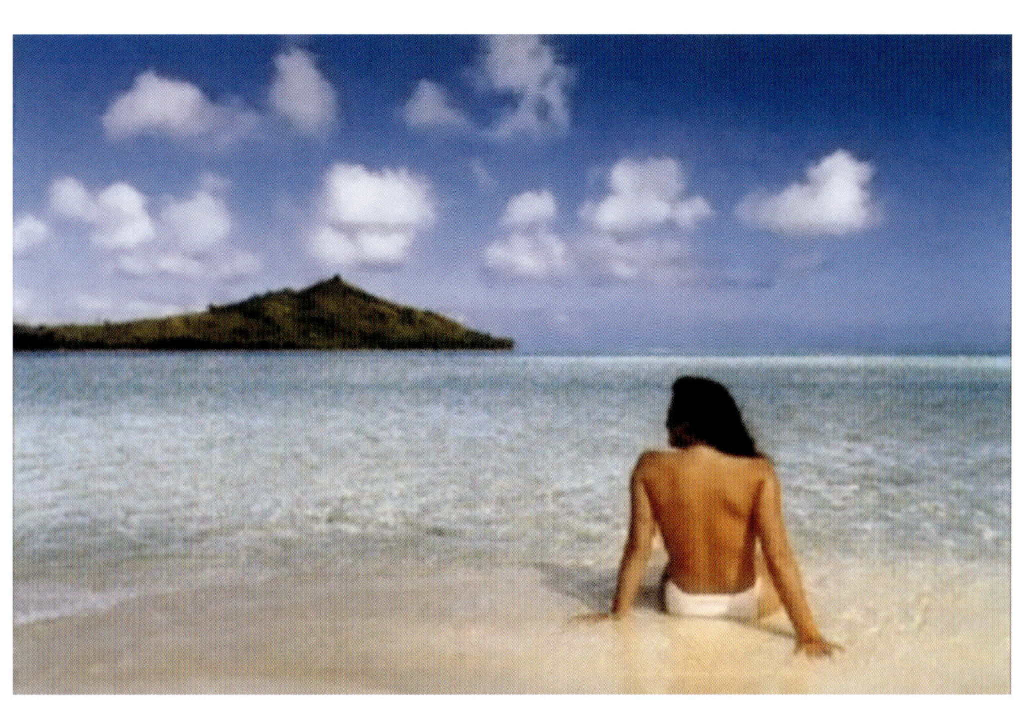

3   Constant Dullaart, *Jennifer in Paradise*, 2013
Framed archival pigment print with a steganographically
encrypted payload, 30 × 45 cm

Constant Dullaart, from *HEALED* series, 2011–ongoing
Lambda print

Q6: These algorithms that you mention, how wide spread are they?

A: There are algorithms already catering your news feed on Facebook or your Instagram feed. The newspaper algorithm already existed, but the difference now is that there is no human eye to check it.

If you build these algorithms to just confirm your cultural position, then doesn't this become a very hermetic position? If you want to find the exception to a culture, if you want something that is critical against the cultural position that you are developing, then it becomes harder and harder to find or even to accept this critical point. The people or whatever it is that offer this critical voice end up falling outside of the algorithm, outside of the regular path. They are not in the mainstream, they are automatically secluded, because it is much harder to fight.

I think it's very dangerous that our culture is inhibited by the fact that you have to go up to certain measures to fall outside of this mainstream. The gap will keep on widening. Mainstream will become even more mainstream and subculture will become even more subculture and hidden, under the radar and easier to be perceived as dangerous.

Q7: We just have to find a way to get a good set up on the balcony.

A: Yes, I think that you have to find communities of people who have other solutions. The same way that you make conscious, ethical decisions about what food you eat and buy, you should also make similar conscious decisions about how you read images, how you interact with friends, how you behave in the world. This is something normal. You are not an activist!

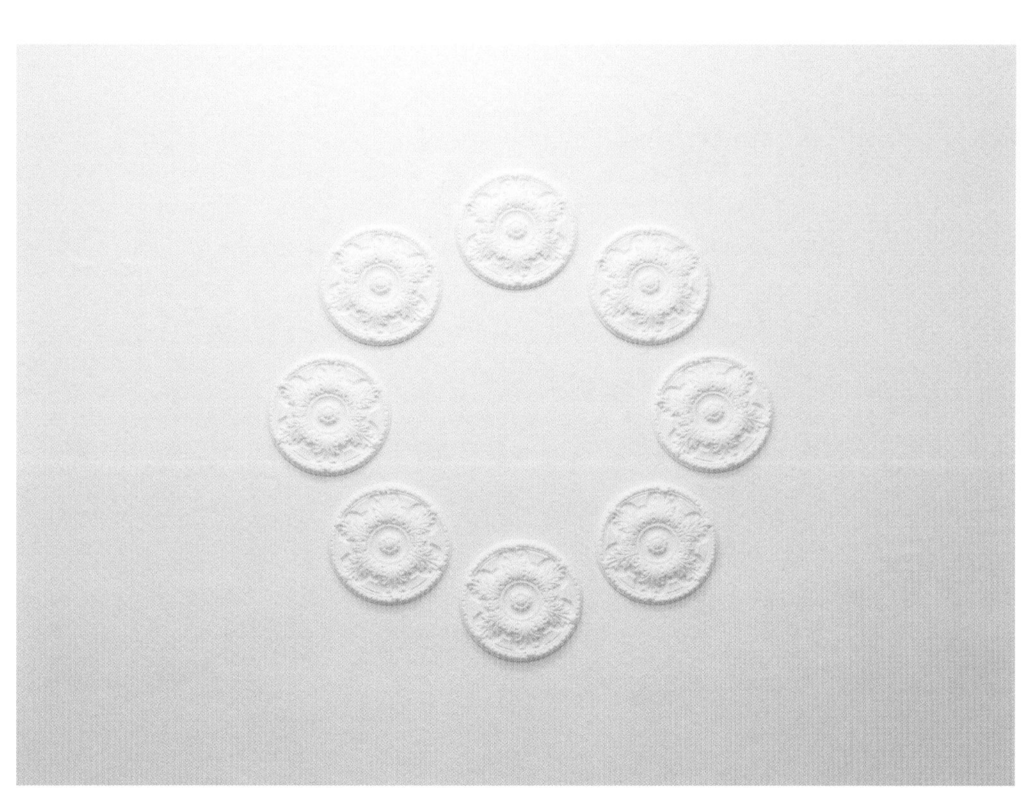

 Constant Dullaart, *YouTube as a Sculpture*, 2013
8 moulding patterns

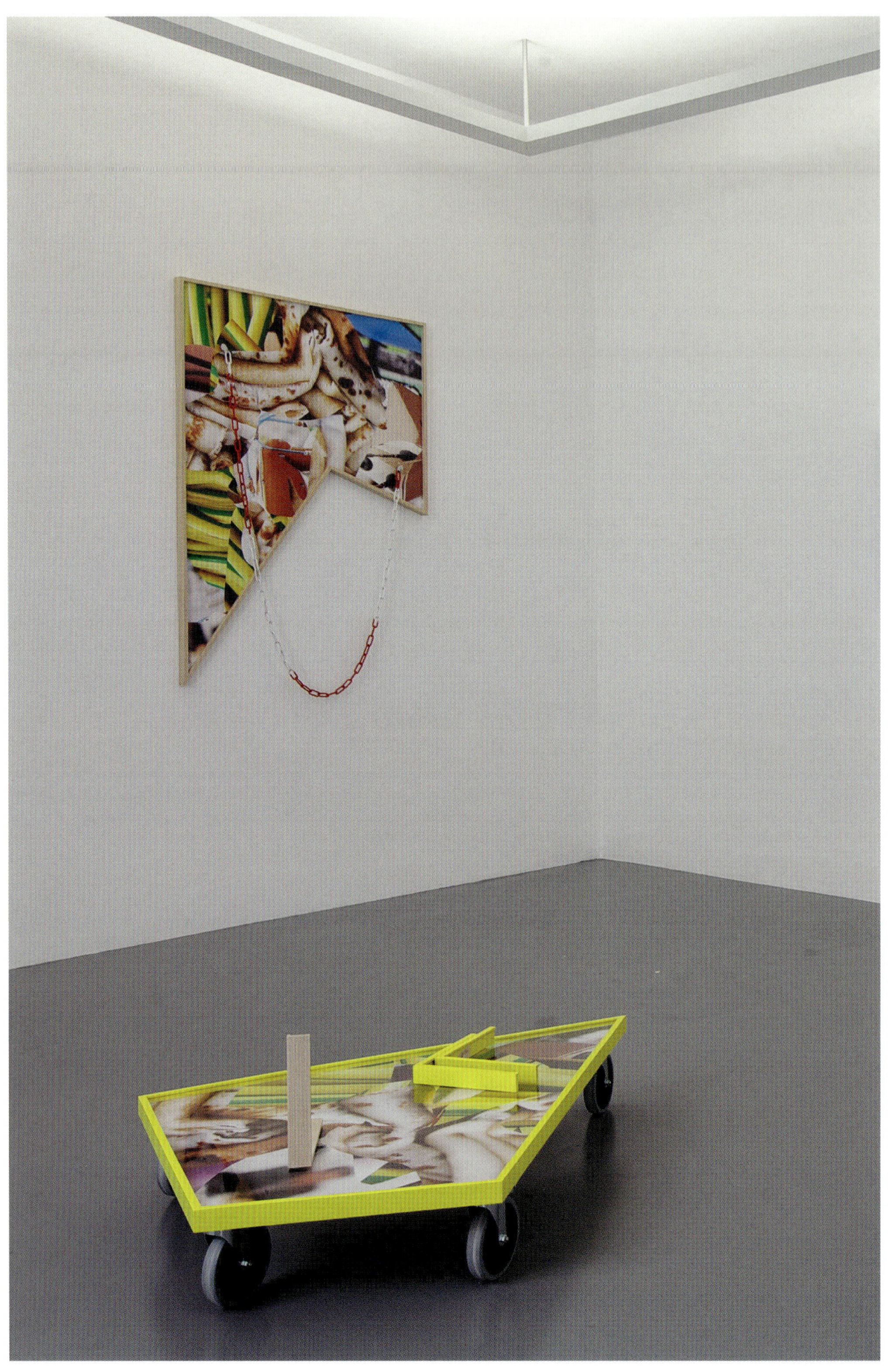

Kate Steciw, *Actife Plassity*, installation view, 2014

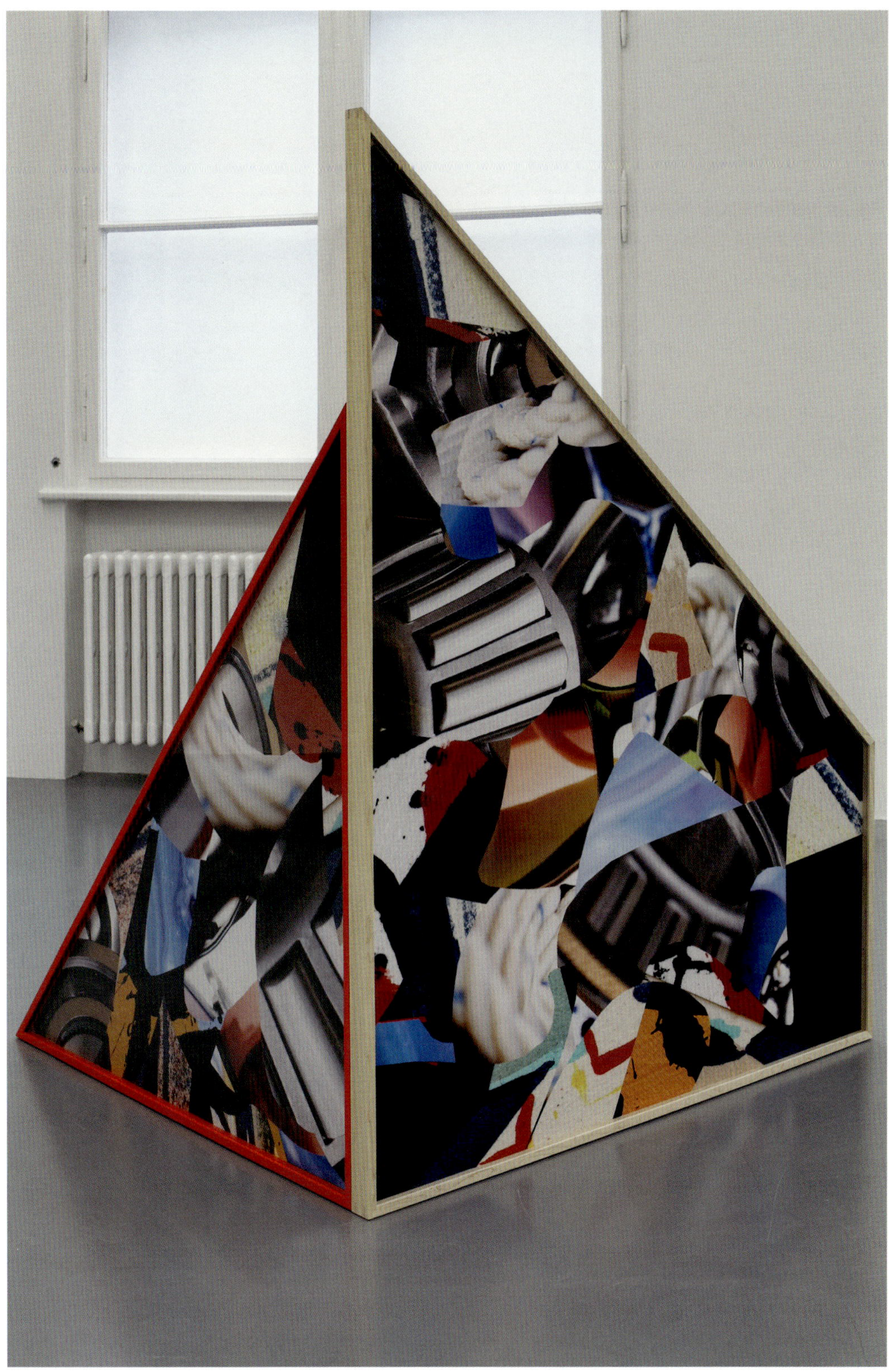

Kate Steciw, *Composition 012*, installation view, 2014

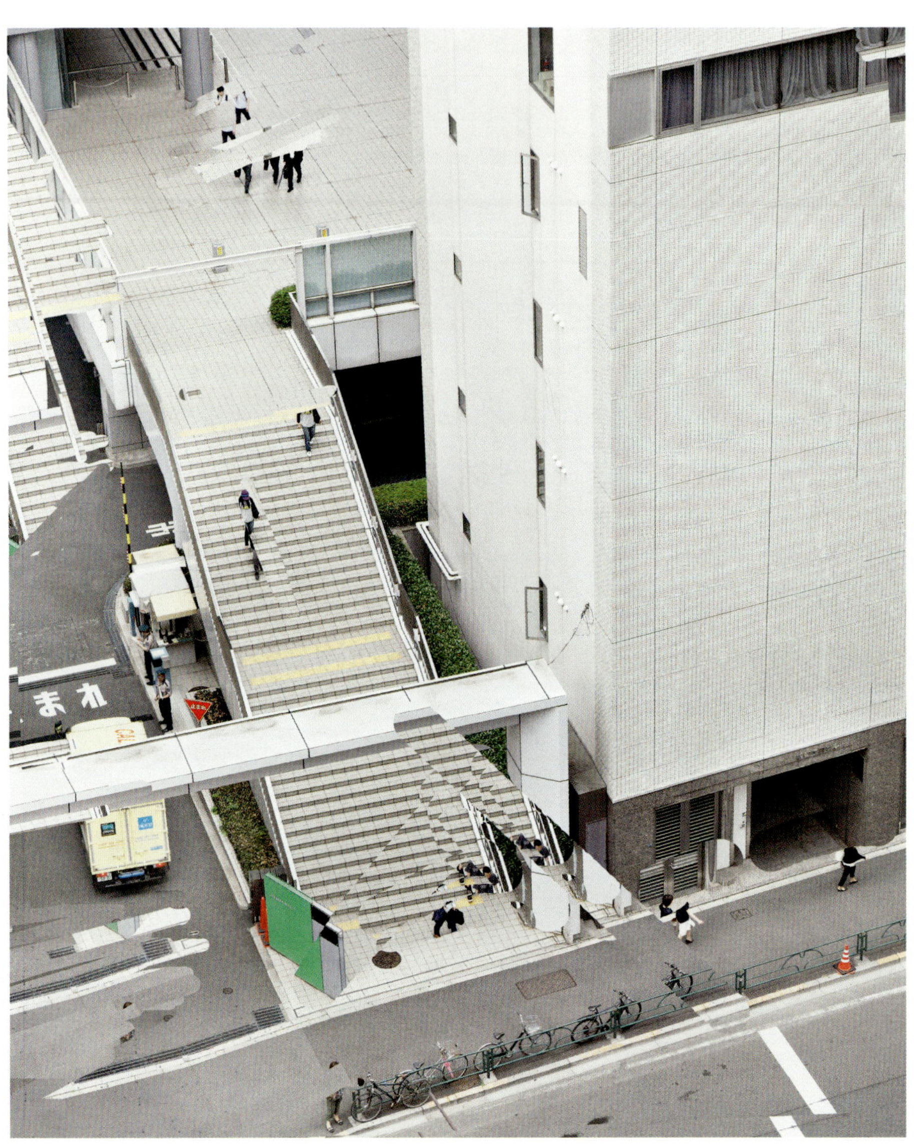

Daniel Everett, *Untitled*, 2013

The New Plastic Malleability
Maxime Guyon

Digital software and media have assumed a prominent role in the visual artistic practice of photography. For both professional photographers and the general public, they have become the principal tools for the creation, editing, and design of images, with Photoshop remaining the most emblematic among them. Lev Manovich asks, How do software applications change our conception of what "media" is? How does software for viewing/managing/remixing media affect our experience of media and the actions we perform upon it? How do software applications shape our worlds and our imaginations?[1]

Our relation to images is certainly not what it used to be, and to say that programs have exercised a determining influence in this process would be a fairly facile observation. In fact several typologies of media exist: on the one hand, older technologies have been simulated or augmented (e.g. the paint brush tool in Photoshop), extending physical techniques into virtual form; on the other hand, there are techniques specific to digital media, such as those emerging from new medias, (e.g. the "swap color" command, history functions, etc.). These new functions give new direction to photography. Although every new tool must be subjected to critique, it is also important to take account of the new malleability that such software affords photographic practice.

Of this new generation of living photographers, Christopher Schreck was among the first to remark that they are living through a "crisis of photography." Exploring the plastic [plastique] malleability of these new media technologies, he shows how certain photographers and artists have made use of digital manipulation in order to liberate photography from its perpetual search after the veracity inscribed in images.[2] Fred Ritchin's *After Photography* adopts a similar approach:[3] In the nascent digital era, the photograph was already extant and the magic was in modifying it. No longer was it the slow emergence of the 'trace' or 'footprint' that was 'directly stenciled off the real,' as Sontag had put it, which was captivating, but the manipulation of the images themselves." The most flagrant illustration of these observations comes from artists like Lucas Blalock, whose works conspicuously display typical Photoshop modifications. For his part, Darren Campion has argued that, "more prominent too in recent work are the layers of digital intervention that extend Blalock's concern with the studio as a site of production into the virtual realm. He is, in effect, using the implicit 'seamlessness' of the technology against itself."[4] In the same spirit, Kate Steciw's work departs from collages and photographic manipulations drawn from online image banks: "Her work draws heavily upon the artist's day job as a retoucher at Art + Commerce in its concentration on manipulating images in post-production, examining the extent to which Photoshop can double as an expressionistic application."

This confirms once again that software can serve as an extension of the means of production of photographic work. An increasingly significant number of photographers have developed this suggestion over the past five years. For example, Daniel Everett explicitly links his research in aesthetic architecture to digital manipulation; Michael Bussel has developed digital modifications that evoke painterly gestures; Andrey Bugush blends scraps of test samples and copies drawn from photography catalogs, which evoke the abstraction and contingency of digital reality. Such examples seem to confirm the notion that photography is essentially a "composite of separate parts."[6] Though such software remains limited by the algorithmic programs within it, we may postulate

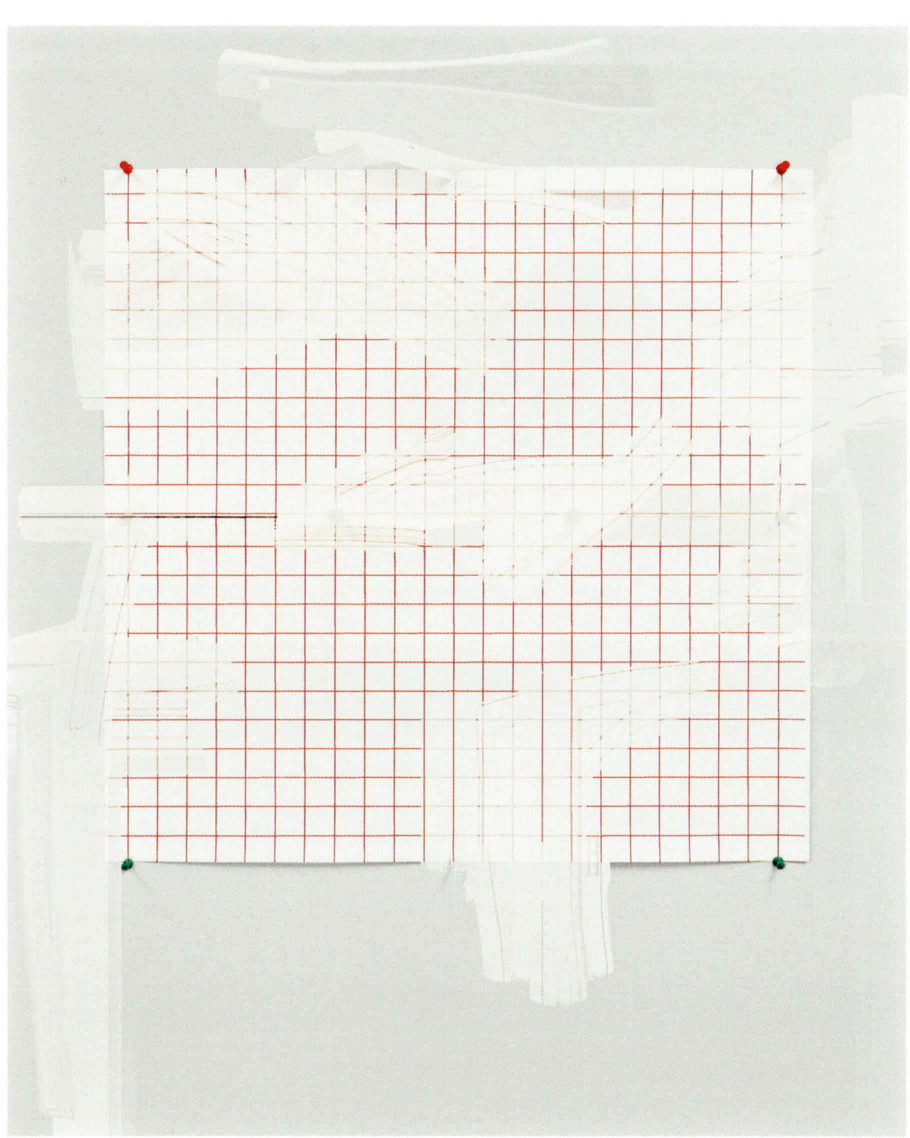

73 Daniel Everett, *New Existence (Array 2/∞)*, 2013

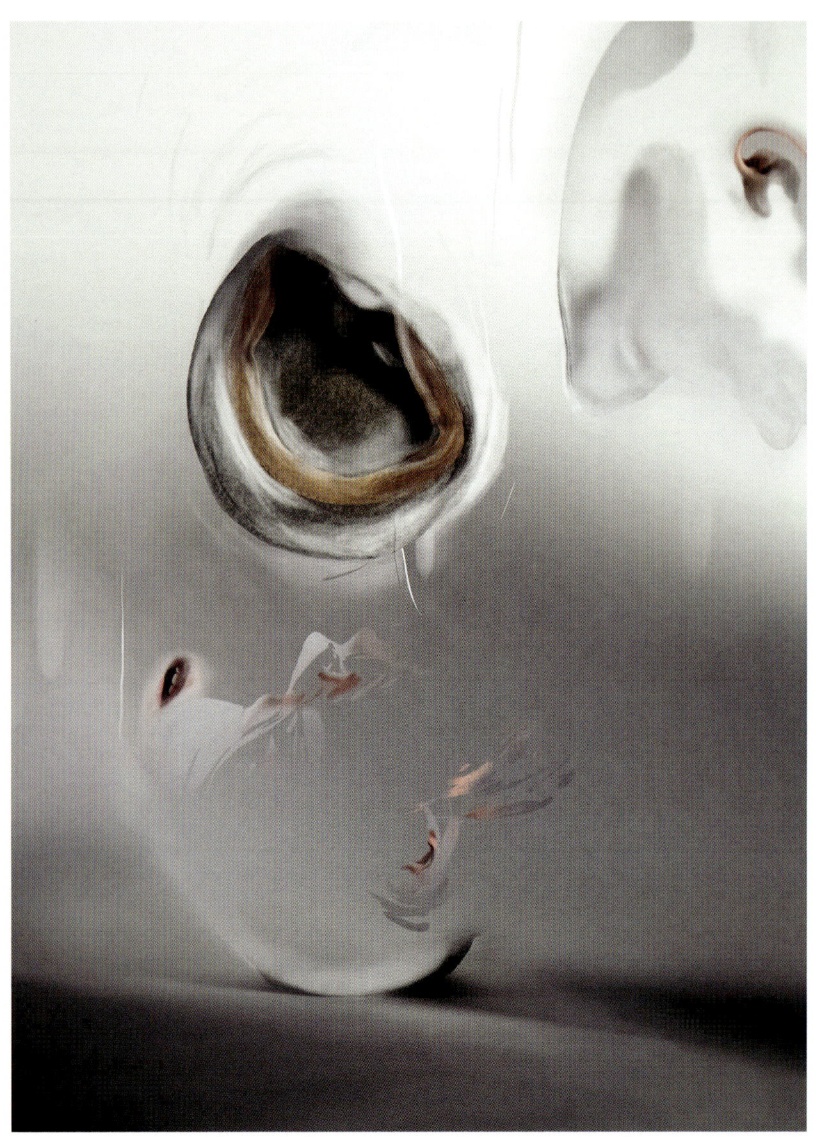

Michael Bussell, *Threshold II*, from series titled *Object Affect* (2013–2014), 2014
Archival pigment print mounted on Sintra in maple frame

that these technologies stimulate artistic production and inspiration in effective ways.

Other approaches related specifically to this software attempt to exploit the inherent flaws in such tools. Mishka Henner sees an example of such digital contingency in the censuring of Google Earth by the Netherlands, who requested that their visible army bases be obscured. These mosaics are not accidents per se, but rather constitute an unintentional aesthetics. In an entirely different context, Clément Valla investigates the flaws in Google Earth through his *Postcards from Google Earth* project: collecting images sourced from Google's 3D navigation simulator, our attention is drawn to visual discordances in bridges and roads unfolding within the cartographical frame. The calculations on which this navigation software is based are nevertheless not errors: what Valla's work calls into question is the relation between the literal and the Cartesian interpretation of vision that Google Earth presents to us.

Diego Collado uses *Data Recovery* software to rescue images erased from hard drives, by means of a technique that recreates the calculation of the image, and on this basis is able to partially reconstitute its digital vestige. The images reinterpreted in this way by the software comprise metaphorical representations of digital photographic traces, highlighting the flaws in the photographic message and its inscription in time: "The software generates designs, textures and colors, which confer a surreal continuity to the section of the image that was recovered. The quintessence of the project is the metaphor of what occurs with the neurological mechanisms of our memory, which in time leaves gaps that need to be completed. In other words, *Data Recovery* creates an image of a kind of amnesia."[7] This contingency is equally present in the work of Travess Smalley, who creates photo-collages drawn from images that have been scanned, cut-up printed out, and edited in Photoshop, in this way establishing a dialog between the physical and the digital. For Carol Squiers,[8] Smalleys works are unique in that, having passed through multiple digital and analog versions, they are therefore impossible to identically reproduce, owing to the complex production processes that make it impossible to reconstitute the color tonalities and frame characteristics.

The specific consequences of these new media techniques have changed our photographic comportments, as well as our expectations of photography as such. The photographic medium evolves alongside technology, and as always is in an intimate relation to it. It is hardly surprising that software applications play an important role in the evolution of the practice. For Wendy Hui Kyong Chun, "Software, or perhaps more precisely operating systems, offer us an imaginary relationship to our hardware: they do not represent transistors but rather desktops and recycling bins. Software produces 'users.'"[9] Chun goes on to describe the imaginary relation we entertain with our digital materials and, by extension, with the digital images that we stockpile in the "libraries" of our computers. What is the nature of this relation? Are we destined to digitalize the tools and sites of photographic creation? Is this a reduction of photographic practice, or should we see in it a form of "progress?" Such are a few of the problems posed today by the new plastic malleability.

01   Lev Manovich, *Inside Photoshop*, computationalculture.net/article/inside-photoshop , November 2011.

02   Christopher Schreck, *Still Life New Wave*, photography.glossom.com/2012/02/on-the-still-life-new-wave, February 2012

03   Fred Richtin Christopher Schreck, *Still Life New Wave*, photography.glossom.com/2012/02/on-the-still-life-new-wave, 2012, *After Photography*, 2008

04   *Improvising Eye: An Interview with Lucas Blalock*, paper-journal.com/interview-lucas-blalock, 2013

05   Ashley W. Simpson, *Kate Steciw, Distorted vision*, interviewmagazine.com/art/kate-steciw-love-my-way#_

06   Lev Manovich, *Inside Photoshop*, computationalculture.net/article/inside-photoshop), November 2011

07   Joan Fontcuberta, *Data Recovery*, lensculture.com/articles/diego-collado-data-recovery), 2014

08   Carol Squiers, *What is a Photograph*, January 2014

09   Wendy Hui Kyong Chun, *On Software or the persistence of visual knowledge*, in *The Visual Culture Reader*, 2013

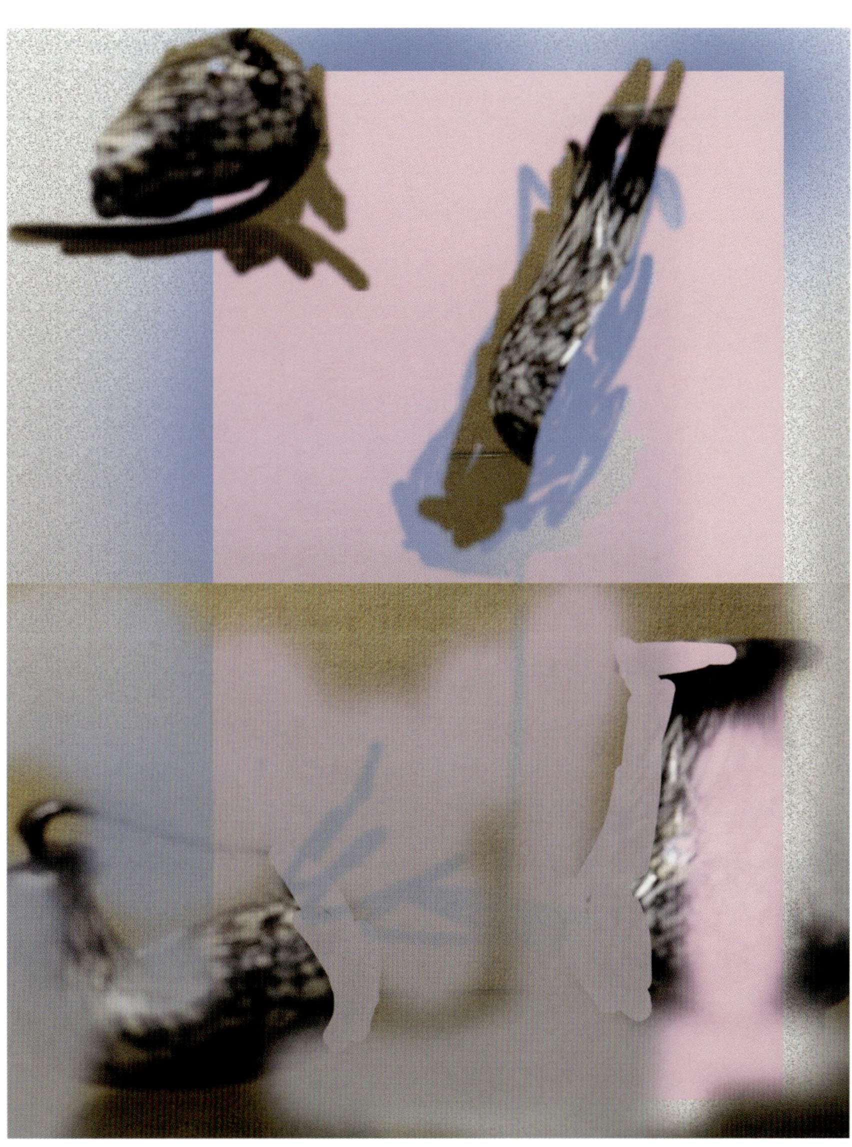

 Andrey Bogush, *Proposals for museum room, duplicated head and green*, 2015

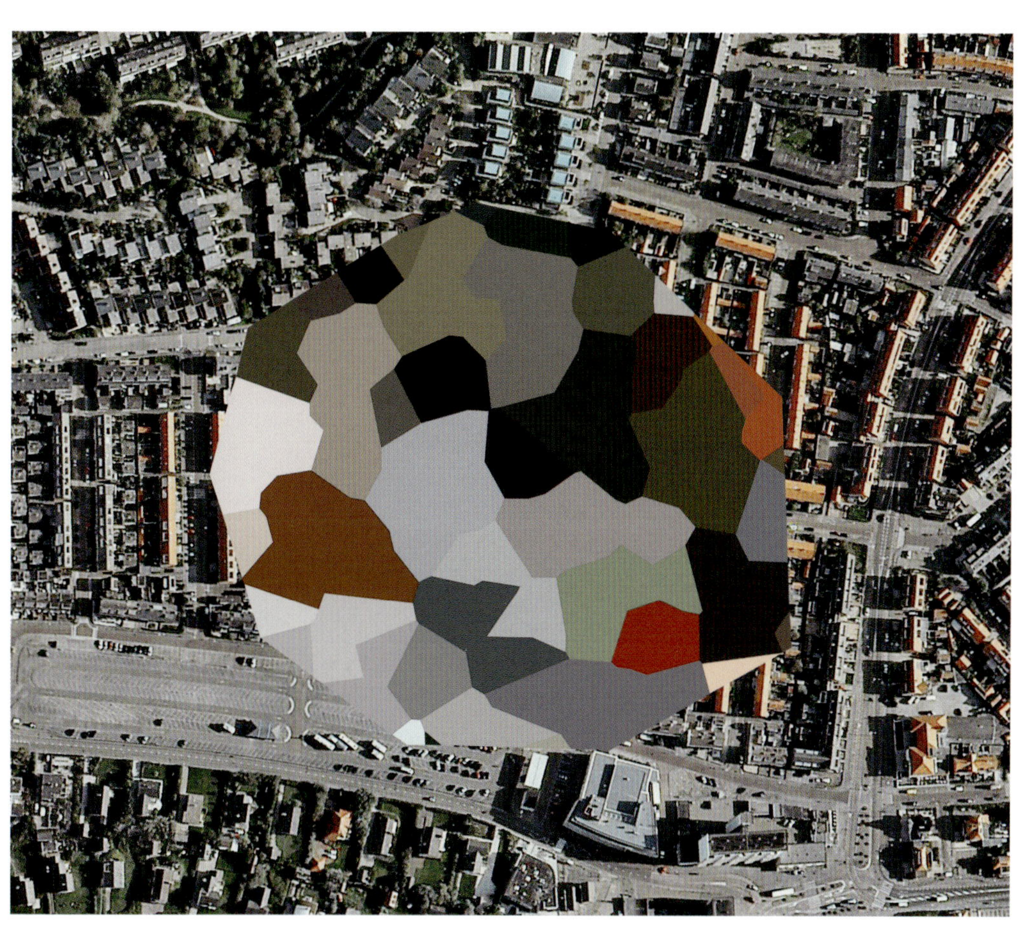

 Mishka Henner, from *Dutch Landscapes*, 2011

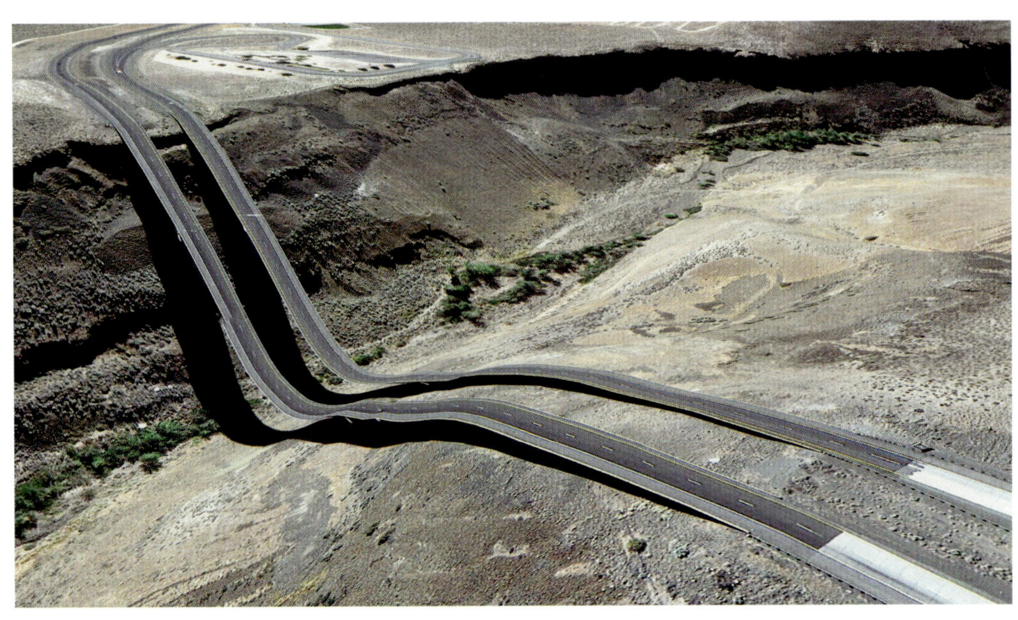

Clement Valla, *Postcards from Google Earth (46°42′3.50″N, 120°26′28.59″W)*, 2010

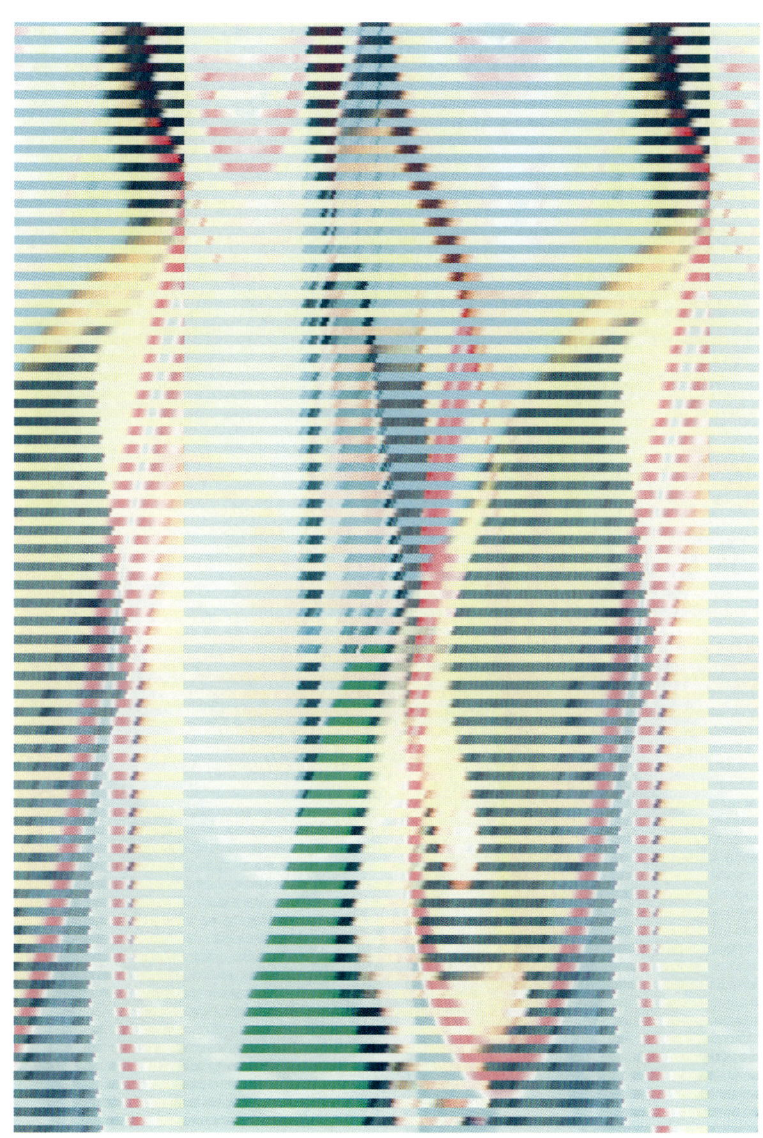

31 Diego Collado, *Data Recovery*, 2010–2014

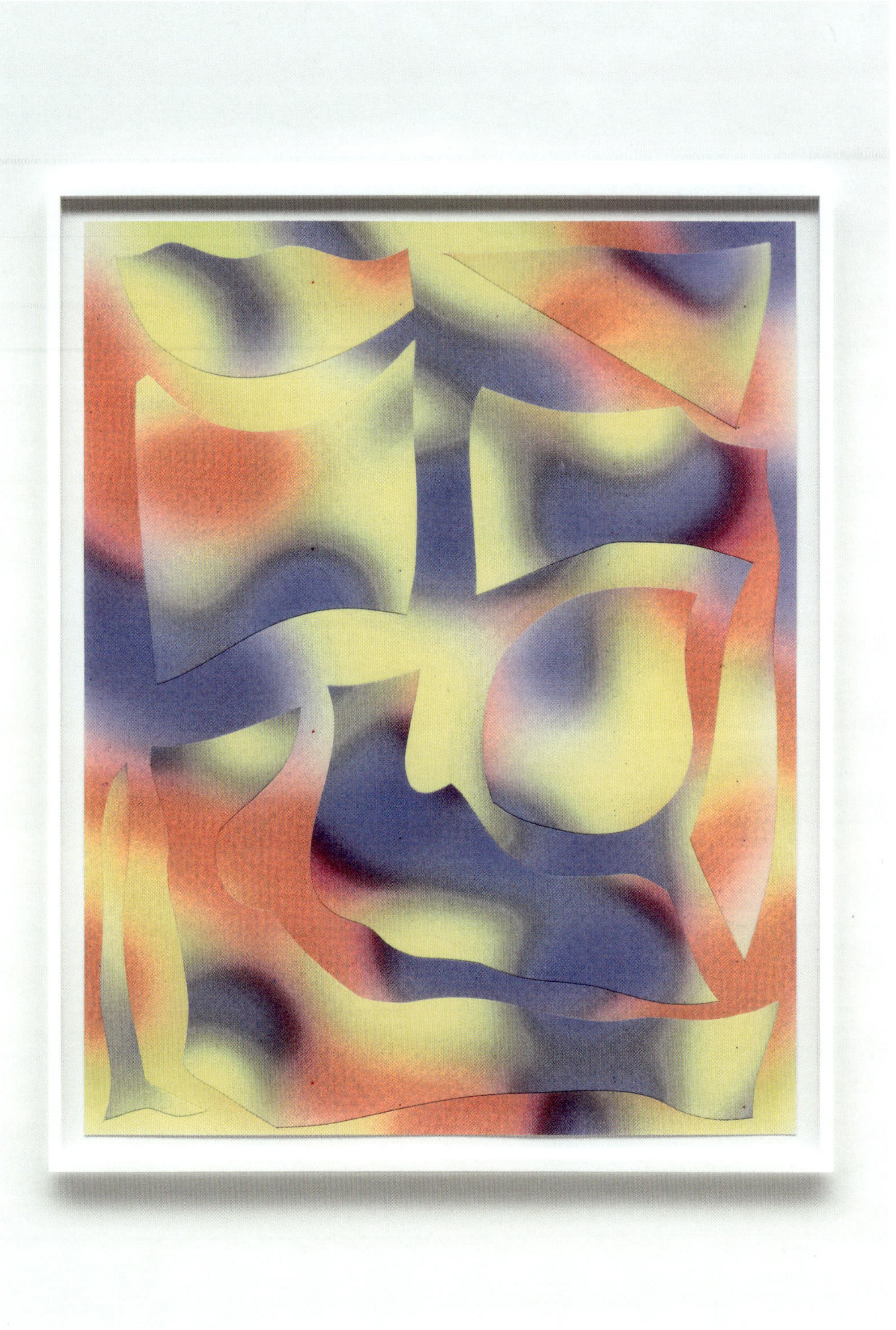

Travess Smalley, *Capture Physical Presence #49*, 2011–2013
Pigment print, New York

Amazon Mechanical Turk
HIT 334ZEL5JX5EWDMVI8X7W3IW1SQXSO7

Assignment (20.11.15)

Write an essay, fictional or/and real, presenting wh
advantages and the inconvenients of Amazon Me
Turk for a Writer following guidelines.

Guidelines

1. The text has to be divided in 5 parts, introduced by a title
• Part 1: the first part presents a general overview about
Amazon Mechanical Turks and what kind of services it
provides.
• Part 2: the second part presents the experiences and the
opinion of a student.
• Part 3: The third part presents the experiences and theopin-
ion of a profesionnal
• Part 4: The fourth part presents your own experiences and
you opinon.
• Part 5: The fifth part presents a synthesis together with
speculations about the future impact of Amazon Mechanical
Turks.
2. Each part stated in 1. should combine descriptions and
analysis (at times, it is possible to place sentences of reported
speeches).
3. The essay should provide an editorial credibility and a
stance similar to news magazines or websites.
4. All the places, names and examples provided in this essay
can be real or/and fictional.

Total length: 8,000–12,000 characters
Fee: 10$
Deadline: 8 hours

Amazon Mechanical Turk: The Post-Millennial Workplace

Just what is Mechanical Turk? It's an online marketplace in which people who need work done request jobs to be done who can select from an available pool. The work requester is responsible for setting the framework for the task and setting a reward amount and a time limit. The worker will accept the task and do whatever work is needed. This work is then submitted for review by the requester, who will then accept or reject the work. Upon acceptance, and after a small delay, the reward amount is deposited into the worker's Amazon Payments account, for the worker to either transfer to a checking account or use as credit on Amazon's websites. The kinds of jobs which can be found on Mechanical Turk can be extremely varied, with academic surveys, freelance writing, transcribing and so-called "batch" work being the most common varieties.

The many uses of mechanical turk for the student

Students are a group which may find the most reward from Mechanical Turk. For the cash-strapped student, doing odd jobs on Mechanical Turk as a worker is an excellent way to earn extra money without having to commit large chunks of valuable time. In addition, students make great use of Mechanical Turk in an academic capacity. Mechanical Turk makes it easy and affordable to conduct research using a large pool of demographically-variable participants. The economic cost and benefit of using Mechanical Turk in either role is an important factor, both in trying to find work that offers decent pay, and offering enough pay for requested work to ensure that one gets useful results (or any results at all).

Making crowdsourcing work for the professional
Mechanical Turk is a fairly customizable service, and some professionals put it to use in creative ways. Websites may put up hits to have people test features and functionality. A lawyer may have a large batch of names and information that workers will classify, one per HIT (human intelligence task; the Mechanical Turk term for a job). Professionals may put up audio or video files of interviews or conferences, asking a worker to transcribe the audio. The creative professional can find a way to get almost any kind of crowdsource-friendly work done, using the tools Mechanical Turk has to offer.

Continued on page 193

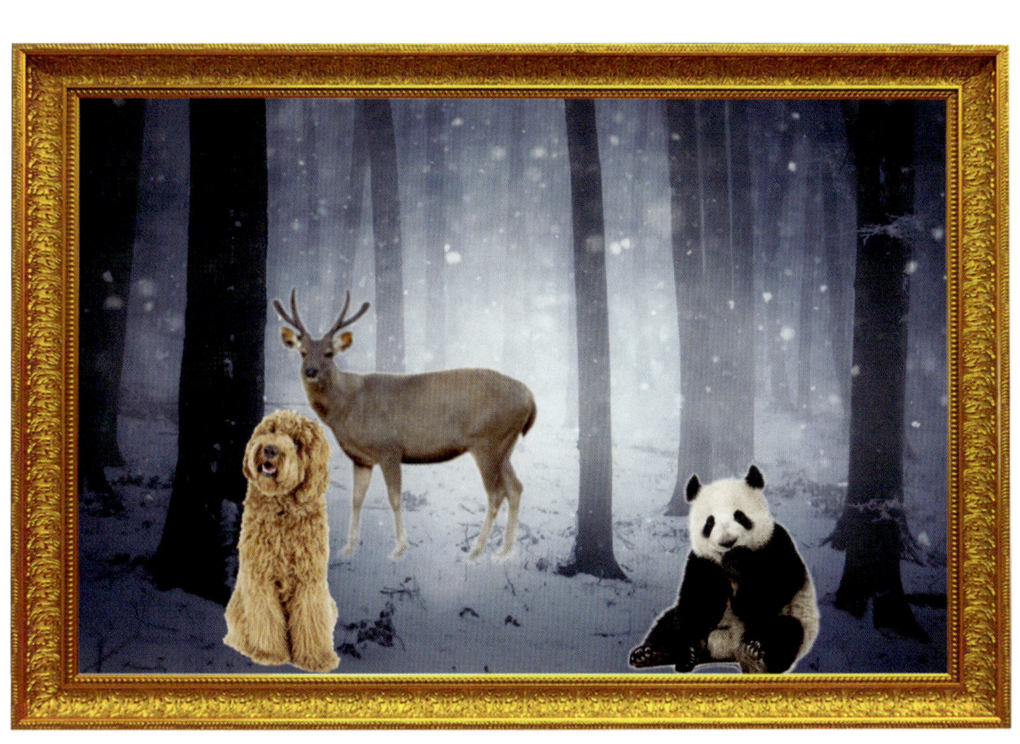

 20 × 200 × GlassView® (2014) is sold by size and bycontent See the convenient table to the left. Plenty of additional options and alternatives available

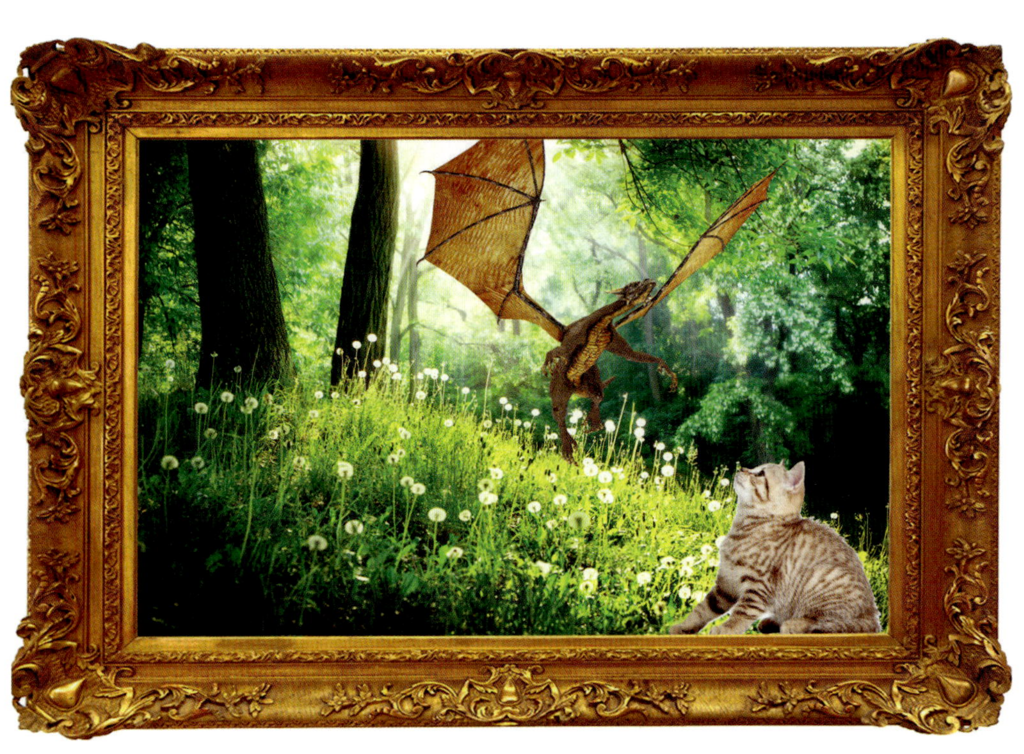

20 × 200 × GlassView® (2014) is sold by size and
bycontent See the convenient table to the left. Plenty
of additional options and alternatives available

Have You *Seen GlassView®*
and *20 × 200™ Parametric-Algorithmic Wall Art?*

The artisans of GlassView® have partnered with the ingenious distribution of *20 × 200™* to introduce—*20 × 200 × GlassView® Parametric Wall Art™*. The Art the you desi gn by spec-ifying the "parameters" directly. Now you can be the artist. Our aesthetate algorithm will create real, authentic art computationally. It ic not so-called "squiggle art" or anything that looks like it was done with a computer.
Specify parameters to create lovely output suitable for hanging. Every painting, photo-graph or drawing is almost unique.
Mountains, trees, wet cobblestone, forest animals, kittens or ferocious tiger. Create multi-sunsets, double rainbows or a fantasy scene with attacking golem, dragon, or cyclops and handsome knight to save the day. Or all of that in one epic scene for large walls.
You have seen our work in many, many places including big restaurant chains, hotels, airport, book library, cafe, car dealership, maybe even your friends house has our art and you don't know—until now.
20 × 200 × GlassView® is Art crafted by you for your tastes.

00.13	For base image per sq. Cm. Upto 2k sq cm
00.10	For base image per sq. Cm over 2k sq cm
01.00	Hoved animal
01.50	Paw animal
00.50	Human
01.50	Human crowd
01.50	Feathered animal
07.00	Sunset per sun
07.00	Moon any phase
02.00	Mountain peak
07.00	Dragon
01.00	Prince or princess
03.00	Attacking army
12.00	Atomic-like explosion
18.00	Urban scene
18.00	Animal herd
01.00	Cabin or lodge
01.50	Extra tree
02.00	Vintage look
17.00	Black&white, sepia, atonal, int'l grae
02.50	Old broken motor car in tall weeds
02.50	Old bicycle
01.50	Sunlight through tree
09.50	Winter time (december–january)
07.50	Spring time (february–march)
05.50	Summer time (april–november)

Additional options available.
Contact our algorithm directly.

Algoriture Publishing Fiction

Algoriture creates lovely works of matrix fiction, many resulting in NYT Best Sellers! Algoriture Publishing creates a guaranteed unique, custom book for you based on books you've read and enjoyed—and a matrix of genre specifications you provide. Each book is guaranteed unique and guaranteed enjoyable—or your money back. Only works of fiction. Genres: romance, technothriller, science-fiction, fantasy, thriller, young adult (incl. fairy tale), mystery and more.
No e-reader versions available to mitigate digital copying. Your book is guaranteed one of a kind. Sell your book! Marketing services available: SEO optimization, target market analysis, potential distribution (contact for prices). Algoriture Publishing reserves the right to produce any and all books that receive 40,000 page visits.

Product #ALG.131.629
USD 1.50/200 pages one archetypal setting, e.g. *The River, The Garden, The Wilderness, The Sea, The Island, The Mountain, The Wasteland, The Pasture/Field*, etc. Or mix and match setting archetypes. For archetype combinations add USD 1.50 per combination.

7.00 .... per genre/style, mix-and-match! + Character archetypes	0.79 ....Humor
4.50 ....Hero	0.72 ....Zombie
7.50 .... Outlaw	0.76 ....Legend
3.00 .... Jester	0.29 ....Metafiction
1.50 ....Lover	0.94 ....Mystery
0.50 ....Caregiver	0.12 .... Mythology
5.50 ....Everyman	0.19 ....Poetry
1.00 ....Innocent	0.98 .... Realistic fiction
3.50 .... Ruler/Power	0.83 ....Science Fiction
5.50 .... Sage	0.81 .... Short story
3.50 .... Magician	0.57 .... Tall Tale
0.3–0.99........................Creator	1.10 .... Biography
6.50 .... Explorer	0.12 ....Essay
	0.85 ....Narrative nonfiction

Next, configure a major genre basis

3.50 .... Drama	Add a target maturity level
3.75 .... Romance	1.50 .... AG–Y
2.10 .... Satire	1.50 ....AG–7
1.50 ....Tragedy	1.50 .... AG–G
3.25 .... Comedy	1.58 ....AG–PG
3.90 .... Tragicomedy	1.58 ....AG–14
	2.10 ....AG–MA
Add a common genre basis to the algorithm:	0.75 ....D–Suggestive Dialogue
0.89 .... Fable	0.75 ....L–Coarse Language
0.87 .... Fairy Tale	1.10 ....S–Sexual Content
0.92 .... Fantasy	1.19 .... V–Violence
0.91 .... Technothriller	
0.83 .... Database	
0.73 ....War	
0.79 .... Espionage	
0.69 .... End of World	
0.12 .... Folklore	
0.39 .... Historical fiction	
0.79 ....Horror	

Albatross
Algoriture

The Black
Zombie

114 min.
Read

Albatross
Algoriture

Outlaws
of the World

92 min.
Read

Albatross
Algoriture

Southern
Lovers

68 min.
Read

Albatross
Algoriture

Citizen
at War

107 min.
Read

Albatross
Algoriture

A Vampire and his Friend

238 min.
Read

Albatross
Algoriture

Teens of the North

44 min.
Read

A view from the ground floor
I have been a worker on Mechanical T
almost two years, and I've used the
most of my bills and pay for my
As a full-time worker, it has been
rely on the hard work and help of o
Mechanical Turk workers' communi
be accurate to think of Mechanical Turk
as a sort of libertarian social experiment. The
Mechanical Turk system is maintained and
operated by Amazon, but it is exceedingly rare
for Amazon to interfere with the business
they facilitate. Disputes between workers and
requesters are often left to the involved parties
to resolve on their own. To respond to an environ-
ment in which workers are basically left to
fend for themselves, strong communities have
formed, who help each other avoid unethical
or unscrupulous requesters, to find hits that
are "worth Turking for," and to create unofficial
add-ons to add functionality to an otherwise
spartan user interface. As a worker, it is
important to work with others and to look out for
yourself if you want to really make a go of
it. The community works together in a similar
fashion to how labor unions once empowered the
previously powerless. It puts both parties on
more of an even footing.

What Lies Ahead

The Mechanical Turk experience has changed over the years, in mostly subtle ways, and most of these changes have been the result of workers cooperating to make the experience better for everybody. There are requesters out there who will take work and reject everyone to avoid paying. There are requesters who get away with paying a pittance for the work they do. The community of workers must always be vigilant and watching each others' backs. Keeping requesters honest is to everyone's benefit. Workers can be sure that the work they are paying a bit more for is work they can rely upon, done by workers who feel more inclined to put more effort into what they are doing in appreciation for the generosity of the requester. Where the service goes from.

Notes

01   "Dada is a new tendency in art. One can tell this from the fact that until now nobody knew anything about it, and tomorrow everyone in Zürich will be talking about it. Dada comes from the dictionary. It is terribly simple. In French it means 'hobby horse.' In German it means 'good-bye,' 'Get off my back,' 'Be seeing you sometime.' In Romanian: 'Yes, indeed, you are right, that's it. But of course, yes, definitely, right.' And so forth. An International word. Just a word, and the word a movement." Hugo Ball, *Dada Manifesto, 14 juillet 1916.* Accessible here: en.wikisource.org/wiki/Dada_Manifesto_(1916,_Hugo_Ball).

02   A portmanteau formed from the artistic movement dada and bot, the diminutive for robot.

03   "As we begin using automation technology in July [2014], we will check each automatically generated report and then publish to the AP wire. As we work out any problems, we hope to move to a model of more fully automating the reports and spot-checking the feed for quality control." COLFORD, P (2014). "A Leap Forward in Quarterly Earnings Stories," Associated Press Blog. Accessible here: blog.ap.org/2014/06/30/a-leap-forward-in-quarterly-earnings-stories.

04   BACHMAN, J. (2010). *"Are Sportswriters Really Necessary?"* Business Week. Accessible here: businessweek.com/magazine/content/10_19/b4177037188386.htm

05   "Video games are games, yes, but more importantly they are software systems; this must always remain in the forefront of one's analysis. In blunt terms, the video game *Dope Wars* has more in common with the finance software Quicken than it does with traditional games like chess, roulette, or billiards. Thus it is from the perspective of informatic software, of algorithmic cultural objects, that this book unfolds" GALLOWAY, A. (2006). *Gaming Essays on Algorithmic Culture*, University of Minnesota press.

06   NOVA, N. (2014). *8-bit Reggae: Collision and Creolization*, Editions Volumique.

07   MENKMAN, R. (2011). *The Glitch Moment(um)*, Institute Of Network Cultures.

08   "A new media object may be a still digital image, a digitally composited film, a virtual 3D environment, a computer game, a self-contained hypermedia DVD, a hypermedia Web site, or the Web as a whole." MANOVICH, L. (2002). *Language of New Media*, MIT Press.

09   See "MANOVICH, L. 2013."

10   Metadata is data serving to define or describe other data. The most familiar example would be the GPS coordinates recorded inscribed within a digital photograph.

11   ZIMMERMAN, B. 2015

12   "An idea, behavior, or style that spreads from person to person within a culture." "Meme" in Wikipedia (16.11.14). Applied to digital culture, a meme constitutes a unity, typically an image, passed between individuals in a viral manner. Zimmermann abandons this notion, preferring the larger concept of a cultural element.

13   "What we are missing with 'culture' is an appropriate concept for its 'atoms:' lower-level elements, located sometimes in artifacts, sometimes in human beings, and sometimes traveling from one to another. [...] I will call these lower-level elements cultural elements." ZIMMERMANN, B. 2010.

14   "Most people wouldn't mix the rhymes of Notorious B.I.G. with the melody of Elton John's Tiny Dancer and expect an ear-pleasing result. But then again, most people don't have an ear like Pittsburgh native Gregg Gillis, better known as the one-man band, Girl Talk. The musical misfit and laptop magician broke into the mainstream with his 2006 hit album *Night Ripper*, whose 16 tracks sampled more than 150 artists, from Abba to 2 Live Crew to Aerosmith." M.J. Stephey in: *The Time*, 22.10.08

15   "Sound system culture redefines the meaning of the

term performance by separating the input of the artists who originally made the recording from the equally important work of those who adapt and rework is so that it directly expresses the moment in which it is being consumed." GILROY, P. in: *The Black Atlantic*, pp.217–218, 2002 (1987).

16   O'REILLY, 2005.

17   DERRIDA, 1993. The word is derived from the French term "*hanter*" (to haunt), referring to the imaginary of phantoms, "*anthologie*," which decribes a collection of selected literary or musical samples, and "*ontologie*," the metaphysical study of "*existence*." See also REYNOLDS (2011) or the work of musicians such as Burial or The Caretaker.

18   ZIMMERMANN, 2006.

19   "People's decisions, choices, mistakes, whatever we choose to call them, are stored within the technology. In turn, users, among them artists, are collaborating with the virtual presence of the (often many) people whose actions have been embodied, temporarily or permanently, inside the tools." ZIMMERMAN, (2005).

20   As formulated by Daniel Lopatin (aka Oneotrix Point Never): "The machines of the past contain prenatal patterns and unborn mythologies that eagerly await for their next chance. And when they storm back from the abyss of history, they are never the same. Action/adventure jams come back as devotional dirges. Mantras re-animated as new ageinal horizons" (skulltheft.tumblr.com/post/131570505/synthemas-and-notes-1).

21   "Early bots trawled through articles, fixing simple grammatical or stylistic errors—like capitalizing certain unique proper nouns. At present, some of the most active bots are those that review every edit made in real time, using sophisticated heuristics to revert blatant incidents of spam and vandalism." in Geiger and Ribes (2010).

22   "Conversational agents" simulate human reactions in instant messages, social networks, or automatic answering

machines, and are in general rather frustrating.

23   The majority of these Twitter accounts is engineered by bots. However, users are sometimes fall victim to such mystifications as well, as we saw during the controversy around the @horse-ebook account, which turned out to be managed by a human.

24   infovore.org/archives/2008/12/29/twit-4-dead

25   Whence this article draws its title.

26   "iPhoto's looking out for us. It knows just how many pictures we're taking these days, how much information we have to contend with, and it wants to help. In fact, it's so eager to help that it doesn't wait to be asked." www.everyfaceintheamericans.ca

27   For Philip Galanter (2003) generative art "refers to any art practice where the artist uses a system, such as a set of natural language rules, a computer program, a machine, or other procedural invention, which is set into motion with some degree of autonomy contributing to or resulting in a completed work of art." It should also be pointed out that this creative logic has long been present in the history of art, in particular amongst artists such as fluxus or Sol Lewitt (1971) who proposed precise instructions.

28   Published on Arte Radio.

29   Multiple digital languages have been specially developed to facilitate such generative creations. Design by Numbers (DBN), by graphic designer John Maeda, Processing, by Ben Fry et Casey Reas, or SuperCollider, a programming environment and language used for improvised interactive programming during performances.

30   MANOVICH, 2001.

31   This is what Lev Manovich (2013) has called cultural transcoding : "Since new media is created on computers, distributed via computers, stored and archived on computer, the logic of a computer can be expected to have a significant influence on the traditional cultural logic of media. [...] The

result of this composite is the new computer culture: a blend of human and computer meanings, of traditional ways human culture modeled the world and computer's own ways to represent it. [...] in new media lingo, to 'transcode' something is to translate it into another format. The computerization of culture gradually accomplishes similar transcoding in relation to all cultural categories and concepts."

32   *Bidoun Magazine*, #20 (2010).

33   NOVA, 2014.

34   In part because some melodies cannot be reproduced per se, due to the reduction of possible tonalities in such machines; or else, because the sounds are altered by the programs written for these machines (the speed of the processor can modify the sound effects)

35   GLISSANT, E. (1997). *Traité du Tout Monde*, Gallimard, Paris.

36   TONINATO, T., P. and COHEN, R. (2010). *The Creolization Reader: Studies in Mixed Identities and Cultures*, Routledge Student Readers (#5). London

37   This is Frédéric Kaplan's claim (2014), when he observes that the algorithms of the Google search engine tend to evolve our language by creolizing it.

References

AL QADIRI, F. (2013). *Future fictions*, *FRIEZE*, p.156
BOLTER, J.D. and GRUSIN, R. (2000). *Remediation: Understanding New Media*, MIT press.
DERRIDA, J. (1993). *Specters of Marx: The State of The Debt, The Work of Mourning and The New International*, University of California Riverside.
GALANTER, P. (2003). *What is Generative Art? Complexity Theory as a Context for Art Theory, in Generative Art Proceedings*, Milan 2003.
GALLOWAY, A. (2006). *Gaming Essays on Algorithmic Culture*, University of Minnesota press.
GEIGER, R.S. and RIBES, D. (2010). *The Work of Sustaining Order in Wikipedia: The Banning of a Vandal, Proceedings of the 2010 ACM conference on Computer Supported Cooperative Work*, Savannah, USA, pp.117–126.
GLISSANT, E. (1997). *Traité du Tout Monde*, Gallimard, Paris.
KAPLAN, F. (2014). *La Question de la langue à l'époque de Google*. In STIEGLER, B. (ed), *Digital Studies: Organologie des savoirs et technologies de la connaissance*, Fyp, Limoges.
MANOVICH, L. (2002). *The Language of New Media*, MIT Press.
MANOVICH, L. (2013). Software Takes Command, Bloomsbury.
MENKMAN, R. (2011). *The Glitch Studies Manifesto*, Institute Of Network Cultures.
MÜHLHÄUSLER, P. (1997). *Pidgin and Creole Linguistics*, London: Battlebridge.
NAVAS, E. (2012). *Remix Theory. The Aesthetics of Samping*. Springer-Verlag/Wien.
NOVA, N. (2014). *8-bit Reggae: Collision and Creolization*, Editions Volumique, Paris.
O'REILLY, T. (2005). *What Is Web 2.0 Design Patterns and Business Models for the Next Generation of Software*, O'Reilly weblog. Accessible at: im.ethz.ch/education/HS08/OReilly_What_is_Web2_0.pdf.
REYNOLD, S. (2011). *Pop Culture's Addiction to Its Own Past*, Faber & Faber.
TONINATO, P. and COHEN, R. (2010) *The Creolization Reader: Studies in Mixed Identities and Cultures*. Routledge Student Readers (No.5). London.
ZIMMERMANN, B. (2015). *Waves and Forms: Electronic Music Devices and Computer Encodings in China*. MIT Press, Cambridge.
ZIMMERMANN, B. (2010). *Redesigning Culture: Chinese Characters in Alphabet-Encoded Networks, Design and Culture*, 2(1), pp.27–43.
ZIMMERMANN, B. (2006). *De l'impact de la technologie occidentale sur la culture chinoise: les pratiques des musiciens électroniques à Pékin comme terrain d'observation de la relation entre objets techniques et création artistique*, Thèse de doctorat: Univ. Genève, 2006—L. 602.
ZIMMERMANN, B. (2005). *Technology is Culture: Two Paradigms, Leonardo Music Journal* 15, pp. 53–57.

Image index

Sources (captions)
P.004: Jane Wakefield, Google behind Webdriver Torso mystery, bbc.co.uk, 10.06.14
P.014: plummerfernandez.com
P.023: bergerstadelwalsh.com
P.030: Pinterest
P.034: silviolorusso.com
P.035: novel.coryarcangel.com
P.055: wwwwwwwwwwwwwwwwwww.bitnik.org/r
P.071: camouflage.csail.mit.edu
P.077: Facebook
P.081: emoji.ink
P.096: Wikipedia
P.099: en.wikipedia.org
P.100: Joël Vacheron, *Alpha (Predatory) Vision*, Verities Magazine, 2015
P.103: plummerfernandez.com
P.125: Wikipedia
P.129: twistedsifter.com
P.133–134: Joël Vacheron, *Protocol #2: The Sabine Equation*, Kunsthalle Luzern, 2013

Dadabot
Nicolas Nova, Joël Vacheron

Editorial concept
Nicolas Nova, Joël Vacheron, Raphaël Verona

Design and Typesetting
Studio This is not / Faure & Verona

Assistants
Guillaume Besson, Benoît Timothée Ebener

Typefaces
Clarendon Graphic, François Rappo, Optimo
Plain, François Rappo, Optimo
Millionaire, Raphaël Verona

Printing
PCL Presses Centrales SA, Renens, Switzerland

Published by Thierry Häusermann
IDPURE éditions
Switzerland
www.idpure-editions.ch

ISBN 978-2-9700992-1-5

Essay
Dadabot—An introduction to Machinic Creolization;
Lexicon; Mechanical turks: Nicolas Nova, Joël Vacheron

Interviews
Silvio Lorusso; Matthew Plummer-Fernandez: Nicolas Nova
Holly Herndon; Florian Hecker and Dimitri Bruni (NORM);
Constant Dullaart: Joël Vacheron
Transcriptions: Letizia Monti

Words
The New Plastic Malleability: Maxime Guyon

Translation
Kieran Aarons (Essay and Words)

Biography

Joël Vacheron
Joël Vacheron is a writer and cultural theorist based in
London. Besides various projects related to contemporary
culture, he is Professor and Researcher in visual communication at ECAL/Lausanne University of Arts and Design. He
is currently a PhD candidate in Visual Studies.

Nicolas Nova
Nicolas Nova is an ethnographer and design researcher,
working both as a Professor at the Geneva School of Arts and
Design (HEAD–Genève) and co-founder of The Near Future
Laboratory. His work focuses on observing and documenting
digital and new media practices, as well as creating design
fictions.

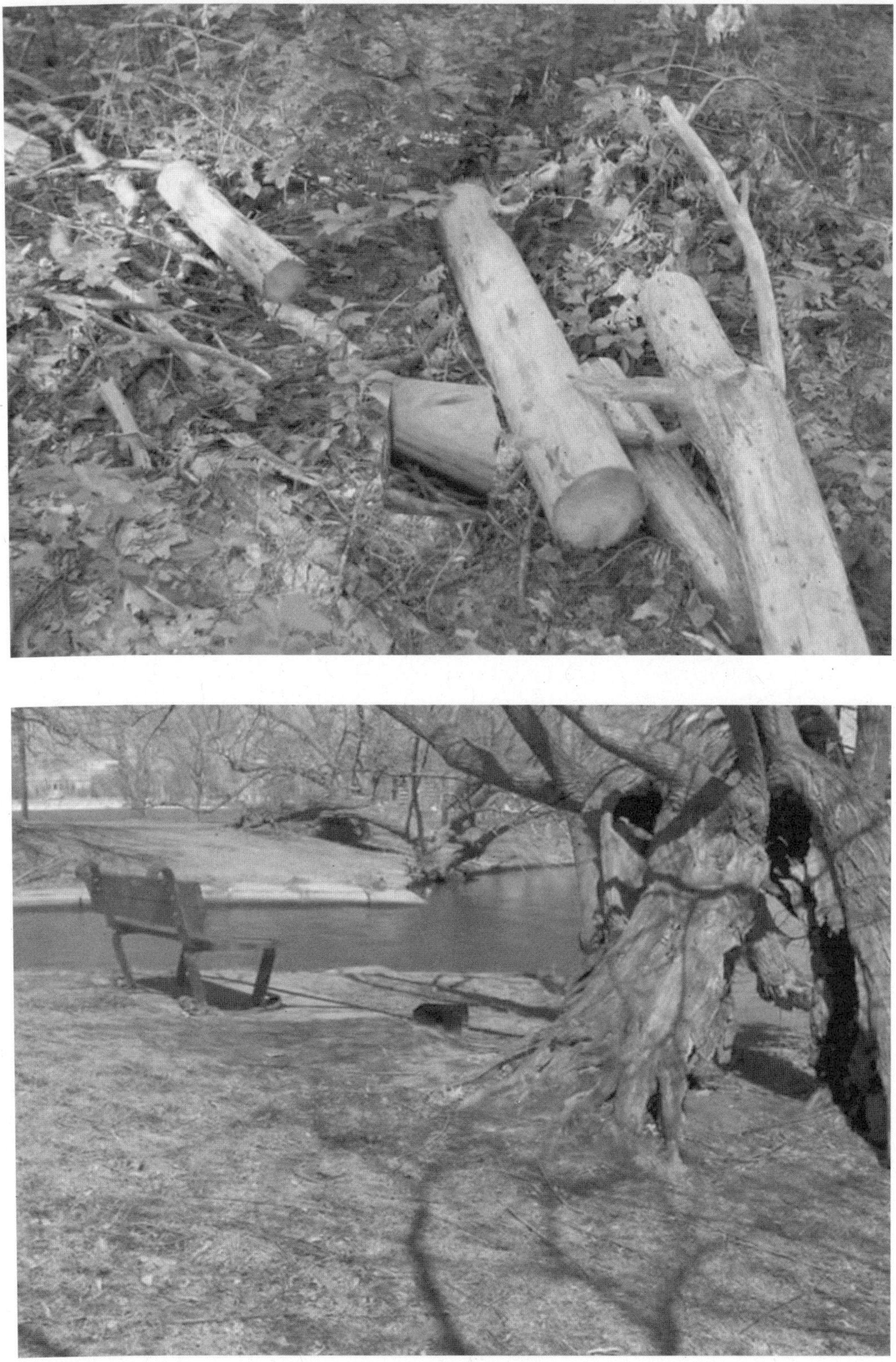

 Andrew Owens et al.,
Camouflaging an Object from Many Viewpoints, 2014
(pp.071–074)

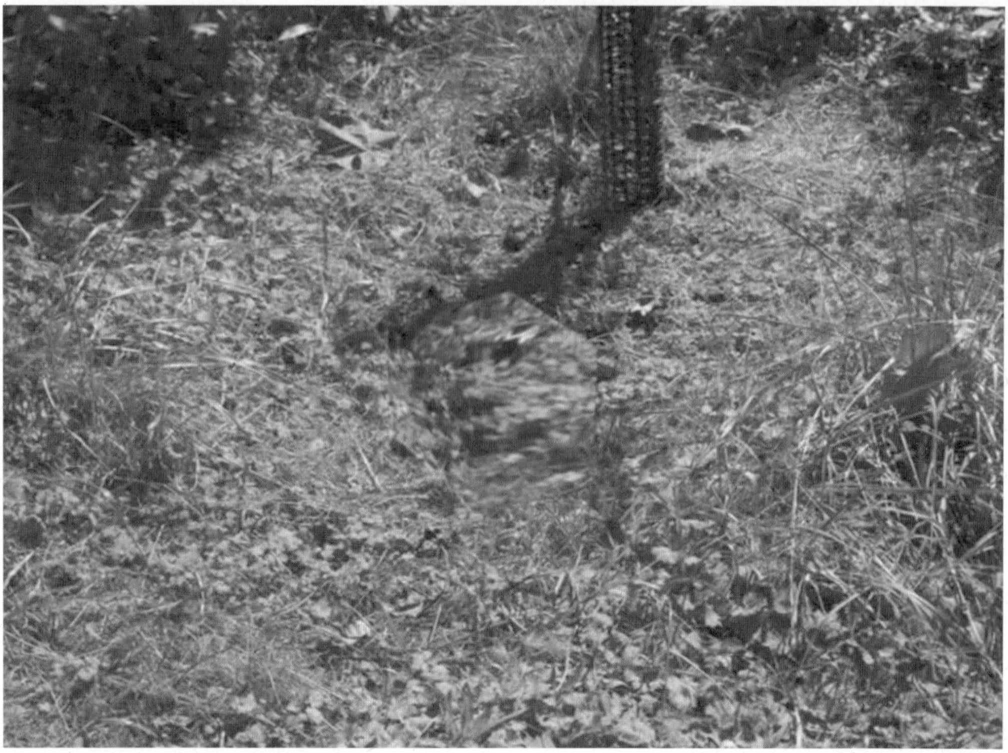

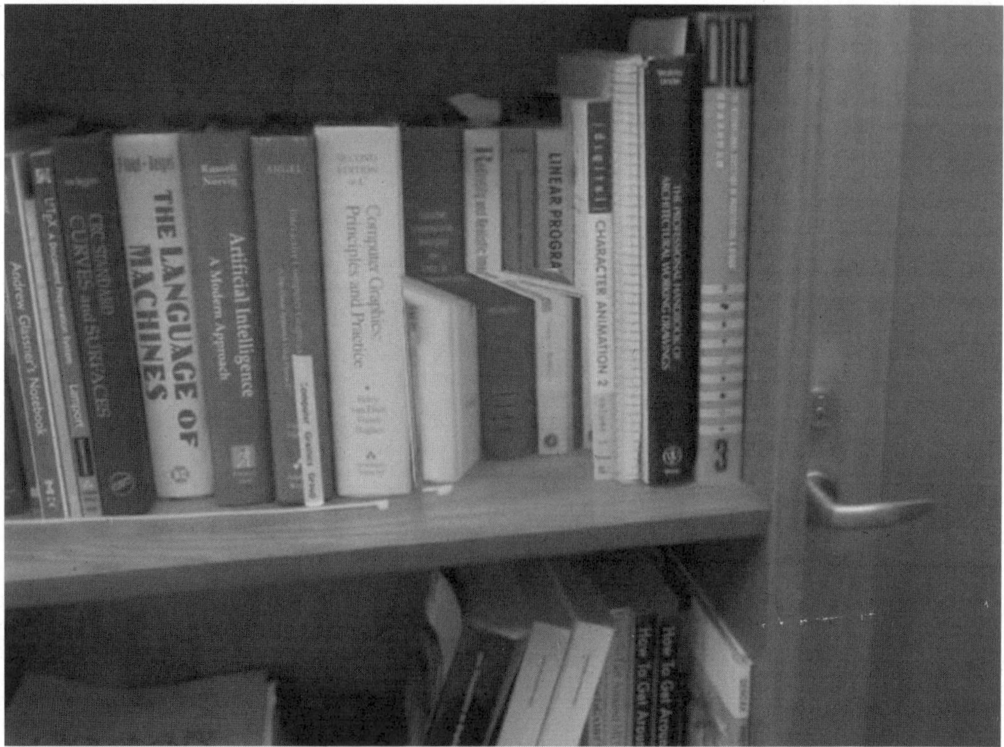

Andrew Owens et al.,
Camouflaging an Object from Many Viewpoints, 2014
(pp.071–074)